PCs For Teachers,™ 2nd Edition

Open a window

Use one of these methods to launch an application:

- ✔ Double-click the application's icon.
- ✔ Click the application's icon and then press Enter.
- ✔ Choose Start⇨Programs; then click the application's name.
- ✔ Choose Start⇨Documents; then click the document that you want to open.

Close a window

Use one of these methods to close a window:

- ✔ Double-click the Application Control icon.
- ✔ Click the Application Control icon (it appears at the left end of the application title bar) and then choose Close.
- ✔ Press Alt+F4.
- ✔ Choose File⇨Exit.

Move a window

Position the mouse pointer on the window's title bar; then click and drag the window to a different location.

Size a window

Position the mouse pointer on a window border until you see a two-headed arrow; then click and drag the border until the window is the desired size.

Web wonders

Visit these exciting places on the World Wide Web:

    http://www.travlang.com/
    languages/
    http://forum.swarthmore.edu/
    http://www.hmco.com/hmco/
    school/index.html
    http://web66.coled.umn.edu/
    http://www.sdserv.org/
    http://sln.fi.edu/tfi/
    hotlists/museums.html
    http://marvel.loc.gov/
    homepage/lchp.html
    http://www.yahooligans.com
    http://www.zen.org/~brendan/
    kids.html
    http://www.microsoft.com/

Keyboard shortcuts

These shortcuts are common to most Windows 95 programs: Microsoft Works 4.0, Microsoft Word, WordPerfect for Windows, Lotus 1-2-3 for Windows, Excel, PowerPoint, Freelance Graphics, Quattro Pro for Windows, and others.

Keystroke	Function	Keystroke	Function
Ctrl+A	Select All	Ctrl+O	Open Document
Ctrl+B	Bold	Ctrl+P	Print
Ctrl+C	Copy	Ctrl+R	Right Align
Ctrl+E	Center Align	Ctrl+S	Save Document
Ctrl+F	Find	Ctrl+U	Underline
Ctrl+G	Go To	Ctrl+V	Paste
Ctrl+H	Replace	Ctrl+W	Close Document
Ctrl+I	Italicize	Ctrl+X	Cut
Ctrl+J	Justify Align	Ctrl+Y	Repeat Action
Ctrl+L	Left Align	Ctrl+Z	Undo Action
Ctrl+N	New Document		

...For Dummies: #1 Computer Book Series for Beginners

PCs For Teachers,™ 2nd Edition

Cheat Sheet

Common Windows 95 elements

Close button

Maximize button

Program icon

Minimize button

Title bar   Menu bar   Toolbar

My Computer

File   Edit   View   Help

My Computer

- 3½ Floppy (A:)
- Big (C:)
- (D:)
- Control Panel
- Printers
- Dial-Up Networking

Program window

6 object(s)

Status bar   Window borders

IDG BOOKS WORLDWIDE

Common toolbar elements

These toolbar buttons are common for all modules of Microsoft Works. Many of the buttons are also used in most Windows 95 programs.

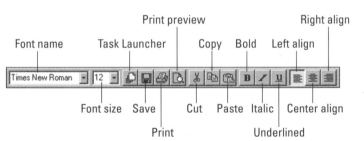

Font name   Task Launcher   Print preview   Copy   Bold   Left align   Right align

Times New Roman   12

Font size   Save   Cut   Paste   Italic   Center align

Print   Underlined

Access open windows

Use one of these methods to access another open application:

- ✔ Press Alt+Tab until the desired open application appears.
- ✔ Press Alt+Esc until the desired open application appears.

Access menu commands

Use one of these techniques to access menu commands:

- ✔ Click the menu name and then click the command.
- ✔ Press Alt+ the underlined letter of the menu name; then press the underlined letter of the menu command.

...For Dummies: #1 Computer Book Series for Beginners

PCs
FOR
TEACHERS™
2ND EDITION

PCs FOR TEACHERS™
2ND EDITION

by Pamela R. Toliver & Carol Y. Kellogg

IDG Books Worldwide, Inc.
An International Data Group Company

Foster City, CA ♦ Chicago, IL ♦ Indianapolis, IN ♦ Southlake, TX

PCs For Teachers™, 2nd Edition

Published by
IDG Books Worldwide, Inc.
An International Data Group Company
919 E. Hillsdale Blvd.
Suite 400
Foster City, CA 94404
http://www.idgbooks.com (IDG Books Worldwide Web site)
http://www.dummies.com (Dummies Press Web site)

Library of Congress Catalog Card No.: 97-72420

ISBN: 0-7645-0240-9

Printed in the United States of America

10 9 8 7 6 5 4 3 2 1

2B/QV/QW/ZX/IN

Distributed in the United States by IDG Books Worldwide, Inc.

Distributed by Macmillan Canada for Canada; by Transworld Publishers Limited in the United Kingdom; by IDG Norge Books for Norway; by IDG Sweden Books for Sweden; by Woodslane Pty. Ltd. for Australia; by Woodslane Enterprises Ltd. for New Zealand; by Longman Singapore Publishers Ltd. for Singapore, Malaysia, Thailand, and Indonesia; by Simron Pty. Ltd. for South Africa; by Toppan Company Ltd. for Japan; by Distribuidora Cuspide for Argentina; by Livraria Cultura for Brazil; by Ediciencia S.A. for Ecuador; by Addison-Wesley Publishing Company for Korea; by Ediciones ZETA S.C.R. Ltda. for Peru; by WS Computer Publishing Corporation, Inc., for the Philippines; by Unalis Corporation for Taiwan; by Contemporanea de Ediciones for Venezuela; by Computer Book & Magazine Store for Puerto Rico; by Express Computer Distributors for the Caribbean and West Indies. Authorized Sales Agent: Anthony Rudkin Associates for the Middle East and North Africa.

For general information on IDG Books Worldwide's books in the U.S., please call our Consumer Customer Service department at 800-762-2974. For reseller information, including discounts and premium sales, please call our Reseller Customer Service department at 800-434-3422.

For information on where to purchase IDG Books Worldwide's books outside the U.S., please contact our International Sales department at 415-655-3200 or fax 415-655-3295.

For information on foreign language translations, please contact our Foreign & Subsidiary Rights department at 415-655-3021 or fax 415-655-3281.

For sales inquiries and special prices for bulk quantities, please contact our Sales department at 415-655-3200 or write to the address above.

For information on using IDG Books Worldwide's books in the classroom or for ordering examination copies, please contact our Educational Sales department at 800-434-2086 or fax 817-251-8174.

For press review copies, author interviews, or other publicity information, please contact our Public Relations department at 415-655-3000 or fax 415-655-3299.

For authorization to photocopy items for corporate, personal, or educational use, please contact Copyright Clearance Center, 222 Rosewood Drive, Danvers, MA 01923, or fax 508-750-4470.

About the Authors

Pam Toliver has more than 15 years of teaching experience in the business education classroom. She purchased her first computer for a high school classroom in 1979 when most people had only just begun to hear about computers.

Since then, she's experienced the trauma of working in the "unfriendly" environment of PCs, been thrown into a classroom full of dummies (computers without storage devices, not the students), and struggled to introduce students to software concepts, sometimes without the benefit of a computer, books, or software. And she learned, through necessity, how to develop teaching materials and exercises designed to strengthen student productivity while making sure that students had fun doing the exercises.

Pam spent years staying only a day or two ahead of her students, learning both the technology and techniques required to make software packages work the way they're supposed to work. She has groped her way through seminar and workshop presentations for students ranging from third-graders through "non-traditional" college-age students (you and me) and has published course materials, textbooks, and reference guides for a number of different publishers and training firms. The topics? Anything from "What is a PC?" to "Advanced Spreadsheet Macros" — in other words, they cover the gamut of computer education. Does she still keep just a day ahead of her students? Of course — just not so frequently now.

Pam has a bachelor's degree in business education from Southern Illinois University, Carbondale, and a master's degree in vocational education with emphasis in industrial technical/business education from Louisiana State University, Baton Rouge. She divides her professional time among her favorite activities: writing, learning new software, and teaching software applications. Her greatest challenge is finding time to do it all. (Sound familiar?)

Carol Kellogg is an English teacher at Plainfield High School, Plainfield, Indiana, where she has taught since the late 1970s. Education has provided her with joys and frustrations — from awards as an outstanding teacher to reading research paper rough drafts on Mother's Day.

Constantly on the lookout for new approaches to teaching, Carol became attracted to computers when she taught a Business Communications class in which the students' only tools were pens and some paper. Reluctant learners, the students became frustrated by having to type their assignments (and their corrections) using the old typewriter method. Computers changed all that. These same students could quickly (and happily) edit their mistakes with just a few keystrokes. The results were proud students and better products.

Since then, Carol has engaged her students in technology, but always as it *supports* the curriculum — she is first an English teacher devoted to improving the curriculum. While claiming to be a non-expert in technology, she nevertheless regularly presents information about her school's "Technology Across the Curriculum" program at various conferences, and teaches at Plainfield High School's summer institute of technology cosponsored by the Indiana Department of Education.

ABOUT IDG BOOKS WORLDWIDE

Welcome to the world of IDG Books Worldwide.

IDG Books Worldwide, Inc., is a subsidiary of International Data Group, the world's largest publisher of computer-related information and the leading global provider of information services on information technology. IDG was founded more than 25 years ago and now employs more than 8,500 people worldwide. IDG publishes more than 275 computer publications in over 75 countries (see listing below). More than 60 million people read one or more IDG publications each month.

Launched in 1990, IDG Books Worldwide is today the #1 publisher of best-selling computer books in the United States. We are proud to have received eight awards from the Computer Press Association in recognition of editorial excellence and three from *Computer Currents*' First Annual Readers' Choice Awards. Our best-selling *...For Dummies*® series has more than 30 million copies in print with translations in 30 languages. IDG Books Worldwide, through a joint venture with IDG's Hi-Tech Beijing, became the first U.S. publisher to publish a computer book in the People's Republic of China. In record time, IDG Books Worldwide has become the first choice for millions of readers around the world who want to learn how to better manage their businesses.

Our mission is simple: Every one of our books is designed to bring extra value and skill-building instructions to the reader. Our books are written by experts who understand and care about our readers. The knowledge base of our editorial staff comes from years of experience in publishing, education, and journalism — experience we use to produce books for the '90s. In short, we care about books, so we attract the best people. We devote special attention to details such as audience, interior design, use of icons, and illustrations. And because we use an efficient process of authoring, editing, and desktop publishing our books electronically, we can spend more time ensuring superior content and spend less time on the technicalities of making books.

You can count on our commitment to deliver high-quality books at competitive prices on topics you want to read about. At IDG Books Worldwide, we continue in the IDG tradition of delivering quality for more than 25 years. You'll find no better book on a subject than one from IDG Books Worldwide.

John Kilcullen
CEO
IDG Books Worldwide, Inc.

Steven Berkowitz
President and Publisher
IDG Books Worldwide, Inc.

Eighth Annual
Computer Press
Awards ≥1992

Ninth Annual
Computer Press
Awards ≥1993

Tenth Annual
Computer Press
Awards ≥1994

Eleventh Annual
Computer Press
Awards ≥1995

IDG Books Worldwide, Inc., is a subsidiary of International Data Group, the world's largest publisher of computer-related information and the leading global provider of information services on information technology. International Data Group publishes over 275 computer publications in over 75 countries. Sixty million people read one or more International Data Group publications each month. International Data Group's publications include: **ARGENTINA:** Buyer's Guide, Computerworld Argentina, PC World Argentina; **AUSTRALIA:** Australian Macworld, Australian PC World, Australian Reseller News, Computerworld, IT Casebook, Network World, Publish, Webmaster; **AUSTRIA:** Computerwelt Osterreich, Networks Austria, PC Tip Austria; **BANGLADESH:** PC World Bangladesh; **BELARUS:** PC World Belarus; **BELGIUM:** Data News; **BRAZIL:** Annuário de Informática, Computerworld, Connections, Macworld, PC Player, PC World, Publish, Reseller News, Supergamepower; **BULGARIA:** Computerworld Bulgaria, Network World Bulgaria, PC & MacWorld Bulgaria; **CANADA:** CIO Canada, Client/Server World, ComputerWorld Canada, InfoWorld Canada, NetworkWorld Canada, WebWorld; **CHILE:** Computerworld Chile, PC World Chile; **COLOMBIA:** Computerworld Colombia, PC World Colombia; **COSTA RICA:** PC World Centro America; **THE CZECH AND SLOVAK REPUBLICS:** Computerworld Czechoslovakia, Macworld Czech Republic, PC World Czechoslovakia; **DENMARK:** Communications World Danmark, Computerworld Danmark, Macworld Danmark, PC World Danmark, Techworld Denmark; **DOMINICAN REPUBLIC:** PC World Republica Dominicana; **ECUADOR:** PC World Ecuador; **EGYPT:** Computerworld Middle East, PC World Middle East; **EL SALVADOR:** PC World Centro America; **FINLAND:** MikroPC, Tietoverkko, Tietoviikko; **FRANCE:** Distributique, Hebdo, Info PC, Le Monde Informatique, Macworld, Reseaux & Telecoms, WebMaster France; **GERMANY:** Computer Partner, Computerwoche, Computerwoche Extra, Computerwoche FOCUS, Global Online, Macwelt, PC Welt; **GREECE:** Amiga Computing, GamePro Greece, Multimedia World; **GUATEMALA:** PC World Centro America; **HONDURAS:** PC World Centro America; **HONG KONG:** Computerworld Hong Kong, PC World Hong Kong, Publish in Asia; **HUNGARY:** ABCD CD-ROM, Computerworld Szamitastechnika, Internetto online Magazine, PC World Hungary, PC-X Magazin Hungary; **ICELAND:** Tolvuheimur PC World Island; **INDIA:** Information Communications World, Information Systems Computerworld, PC World India, Publish in Asia; **INDONESIA:** InfoKomputer PC World, Komputek Computerworld, Publish in Asia; **IRELAND:** ComputerScope, PC Live!; **ISRAEL:** Macworld Israel, People & Computers/Computerworld; **ITALY:** Computerworld Italia, Macworld Italia, Networking Italia, PC World Italia; **JAPAN:** DTP World, Macworld Japan, Nikkei Personal Computing, OS/2 World Japan, SunWorld Japan, Windows NT World, Windows World Japan; **KENYA:** PC World East African; **KOREA:** Hi-Tech Information, Macworld Korea, PC World Korea; **MACEDONIA:** PC World Macedonia; **MALAYSIA:** Computerworld Malaysia, PC World Malaysia, Publish in Asia; **MALTA:** PC World Malta; **MEXICO:** Computerworld Mexico, PC World Mexico; **MYANMAR:** PC World Myanmar; **NETHERLANDS:** Computer! Totaal, LAN Internetworking Magazine, LAN World Buyers Guide, Macworld Netherlands, Net, WebWereld; **NEW ZEALAND:** Absolute Beginners Guide and Plain & Simple Series, Computer Buyer, Computer Industry Directory, Computerworld New Zealand, MTB, Network World, PC World New Zealand; **NICARAGUA:** PC World Centro America; **NORWAY:** Computerworld Norge, CW Rapport, Datamagasinet, Financial Rapport, Kursguide Norge, Macworld Norge, Multimediaworld Norge, PC World Ekspress Norge, PC World Nettverk, PC World Norge, PC World ProduktGuide Norge; **PAKISTAN:** Computerworld Pakistan; **PANAMA:** PC World Panama; **PEOPLE'S REPUBLIC OF CHINA:** China Computer Users, China Computerworld, China InfoWorld, China Telecom World Weekly, Computer & Communication, Electronic Design China, Electronics Today, Electronics Weekly, Game Software, PC World China, Popular Computer Week, Software Weekly, Software World, Telecom World; **PERU:** Computerworld Peru, PC World Profesional Peru, PC World SoHo Peru; **PHILIPPINES:** Click!, Computerworld Philippines, PC World Philippines, Publish in Asia; **POLAND:** Computerworld Poland, Computerworld Special Report Poland, Cyber, Macworld Poland, Networld Poland, PC World Komputer; **PORTUGAL:** Cerebro/PC World, Computerworld/Correio Informático, Dealer World Portugal, Mac*In/PC*In Portugal, Multimedia World; **PUERTO RICO:** PC World Puerto Rico; **ROMANIA:** Computerworld Romania, PC World Romania, Telecom Romania; **RUSSIA:** Computerworld Russia, Mir PK, Publish, Seti; **SINGAPORE:** Computerworld Singapore, PC World Singapore, Publish in Asia; **SLOVENIA:** Monitor; **SOUTH AFRICA:** Computing SA, Network World SA, Software World SA; **SPAIN:** Communicaciones World España, Computerworld España, Dealer World España, Macworld España, PC World España; **SRI LANKA:** Infolink PC World; **SWEDEN:** CAP&Design, Computer Sweden, Corporate Computing Sweden, Internetworld Sweden, it.branschen, Macworld Sweden, MaxiData Sweden, MikroDatorn, Nätverk & Kommunikation, PC World Sweden, PCAktiv, Windows World Sweden; **SWITZERLAND:** Computerworld Schweiz, Macworld Schweiz, PCtip; **TAIWAN:** Computerworld Taiwan, Macworld Taiwan, NEW ViSiON/Publish, PC World Taiwan, Windows World Taiwan; **THAILAND:** Publish in Asia, Thai Computerworld; **TURKEY:** Computerworld Turkiye, Macworld Turkiye, Network World Turkiye, PC World Turkiye; **UKRAINE:** Computerworld Kiev, Multimedia World Ukraine, PC World Ukraine; **UNITED KINGDOM:** Acorn User UK, Amiga Action UK, Amiga Computing UK, Apple Talk UK, Computing, Macworld, Parents and Computers UK, PC Advisor, PC Home, PSX Pro, The WEB; **UNITED STATES:** Cable in the Classroom, CIO Magazine, Computerworld, DOS World, Federal Computer Week, GamePro Magazine, InfoWorld, I-Way, Macworld, Network World, PC Games, PC World, Publish, Video Event, THE WEB Magazine, and WebMaster; online webzines: JavaWorld, NetscapeWorld, and SunWorld Online; **URUGUAY:** InfoWorld Uruguay; **VENEZUELA:** Computerworld Venezuela, PC World Venezuela; and **VIETNAM:** PC World Vietnam. 3/24/97

Dedication

To my son, David — Congratulations on your college graduation! May the road rise to meet you and the wind nudge you gently toward home. May the sun shine warmly upon your face wherever you travel. Never forget to look behind you and remember everything that *life* has taught you.

Pam

To my three favorite girls, the bookends of my life: Bessie, Allison, and Marla. You support, motivate, and enrich me. I treasure you always.

Carol

Authors' Acknowledgments

From Pam Toliver:

I feel like an Academy Award winner — unprepared at the podium and trying to remember all the people I'm supposed to thank and not leave anyone out. Here goes . . .

For John — my husband and best friend — my sounding board, my support — thanks for being there.

For my friends who listened, thank you — it can't always have been easy.

For teachers around the world — without you there would be no need for this book — thanks for your dedication and inspiration — and for making learning fun.

For children of every age — thank you for demanding to learn — especially about computers.

Working with those terrific IDG people in Indianapolis was like coming home. I grew up just across the border in Illinois — and they made me feel so welcome. Special thanks to Diane Steele for believing in my ability to complete this work; to Mary Bednarek and Mike Kelly for making sure I did.

Special thanks to Nancy DelFavero, the Project Editor. I really do know my project wasn't the only one you had.

To Joyce Pepple and Heather Dismore, thanks for showing me how to share the wares and for making sure we did everything right — on the CD-ROM, anyway.

To Kathy Simpson, the copy editor, bless you for muddling through those vast reams and always having a keen eye. For Martha Johnson — technical editor — some may question the soundness of our minds but not the accuracy of the book — thanks, and I'll see you same time, same place, next year!

Thanks, too, to Barb Coulter Terry — who continues to believe in me. Without you this project would never have been.

And last, but certainly not least, to Carol Kellogg, my co-author and sounding board and support — you picked up where I left off, filled in all the blanks, and cleaned up my mess. We complemented each other well. Drop by for that glass of champagne! Cheers!

From Carol Kellogg:

To Karl, for being Karl so well; to my dad, my sons-in-law, and my grandson for adding a wonderful dimension to life.

To Diane Steele and Mary Bednarek, thanks for the chance to revise this writing project. For a short while I shared with my students the pressure of meeting deadlines — whew!

To all the people at IDG Books Worldwide who helped bring this book to print. What a job you do!

To Jackie Carrigan, my friend and motivator in the world of technology. Thanks for taking me along with you.

To all my colleagues at PHS who have been part of my growth and to the students over the years who have inspired me to improve and be innovative.

To Pam Toliver, who agreed not only to take me on again as a sidekick but to teach me the intricacies of templates, attachments, Microsoft Network — all the essentials to make our book move from computer to computer and become reality. Do you think we could zip up a bottle of champagne and e-mail it? Let's try!

Publisher's Acknowledgments

We're proud of this book; please send us your comments about it by using the IDG Books Worldwide Registration Card at the back of the book or by e-mailing us at feedback/dummies@idgbooks.com. Some of the people who helped bring this book to market include the following:

Acquisitions, Development, and Editorial

Project Editor: Nancy DelFavero

Acquisitions Editor: Michael Kelly, Quality Control Manager

Product Development Director: Mary Bednarek

Media Development Manager: Joyce Pepple

Associate Permissions Editor: Heather H. Dismore

Copy Editor: Kathy Simpson

Technical Editor: Martha Johnson

Editorial Manager: Mary C. Corder

Editorial Assistants: Chris H. Collins, Steven H. Hayes, Darren Meiss

Production

Project Coordinator: Regina Snyder

Layout and Graphics: Linda M. Boyer, J. Tyler Connor, Dominique DeFelice, Angela F. Hunckler, Brent Savage

Proofreaders: Betty Kish, Carrie Voorhis, Ethel Winslow, Joel K. Draper, Rachel Garvey, Robert Springer, Karen York

Indexer: Liz Cunningham

Special Help

Kevin Spencer, Associate Technical Editor, and Access Technology, Inc.
Stephanie Koutek, Proof Editor
Constance Carlisle, Copy Editor
Diana R. Conover, Copy Editor
Gwenette Gaddis, Copy Editor
Patricia Yuu Pan, Copy Editor
Tina Sims, Copy Editor

General and Administrative

IDG Books Worldwide, Inc.: John Kilcullen, CEO; Steven Berkowitz, President and Publisher

IDG Books Technology Publishing: Brenda McLaughlin, Senior Vice President and Group Publisher

Dummies Technology Press and Dummies Editorial: Diane Graves Steele, Vice President and Associate Publisher; Judith A. Taylor, Brand Manager; Kristin A. Cocks, Editorial Director

Dummies Trade Press: Kathleen A. Welton, Vice President and Publisher; Stacy S. Collins, Brand Manager

IDG Books Production for Dummies Press: Beth Jenkins, Production Director; Cindy L. Phipps, Supervisor of Project Coordination, Production Proofreading, and Indexing; Kathie S. Schutte, Supervisor of Page Layout; Shelley Lea, Supervisor of Graphics and Design; Debbie J. Gates, Production Systems Specialist; Tony Augsburger, Supervisor of Reprints and Bluelines; Leslie Popplewell, Media Archive Coordinator

Dummies Packaging and Book Design: Patti Sandez, Packaging Specialist; Lance Kayser, Packaging Assistant; Kavish + Kavish, Cover Design

◆

The publisher would like to give special thanks to Patrick J. McGovern, without whom this book would not have been possible.

◆

Contents at a Glance

Introduction 1

Part I: Teacher In-Service 7

Chapter 1: What's a PC, and What Does It Do? 9
Chapter 2: Peeking through Windows — 95 19
Chapter 3: Getting Start — ed 35
Chapter 4: 95-Style Windows Accessories 55
Chapter 5: Breaking through Windows: The 3.x Family 75
Chapter 6: Getting the Fax about Printers 87

Part II: Microsoft Works — For Teachers 101

Chapter 7: Microsoft Works 4.0: A Primer 103
Chapter 8: Documenting Words: Using the Works Word Processor 117
Chapter 9: Celling You on Spreadsheets 141
Chapter 10: Profiling a Database 159
Chapter 11: Publish It and Present It! 179

Part III: Communicating with the Outside World 199

Chapter 12: Connecting to the Net 201
Chapter 13: Going Online with Microsoft Network 211
Chapter 14: Surfing the Net 227

Part IV: The Softer Side of Computers: Software 239

Chapter 15: Software Musts for Educators 241
Chapter 16: The Multimedia Explosion: CD-ROM 251
Chapter 17: Multimedia Fun in Windows 95 263

Part V: Lagniappe (Lan-Yap) — Something Extra for Nothing 271

Chapter 18: Teaching with Any Number of Computers (Including None) 273
Chapter 19: Foolproof Ways to Finance Your Computer Needs 283
Chapter 20: Stuff You Can "Hardly" Live Without 289
Chapter 21: Help and Helpful Resources 303

Appendix A: Techno Terms Translation 311

Appendix B: About the CD 321

Index 333

IDG Books Worldwide, Inc., End-User License Agreement 353

Installation Instructions 357

IDG Books Worldwide Registration Card .... Back of Book

Cartoons at a Glance

By Rich Tennant • Fax: 508-546-7747 • E-mail: the5wave@tiac.net

page 7

page 239

page 101

page 199

page 271

Table of Contents

Introduction *1*

Why Should You Believe Us? 1
Behavioral Objectives 2
Our Lesson Plan 2
    Part I: Teacher In-Service 3
    Part II: Microsoft Works — For Teachers 3
    Part III: Communicating with the Outside World 3
    Part IV: The Softer Side of Computers: Software 3
    Part V: Lagniappe (Lan-Yap): Something Extra for Nothing 4
Watch for Icons — They're Special Characters 4
Feedback 5

Part I: Teacher In-Service *7*

Chapter 1: What's a PC, and What Does It Do? 9

What Is a PC? 9
Hardware (You Know, the Equipment) 10
Going Soft with Software 13
Powering Up and Down 15
    Turning on the system 15
    What happens after you turn on the system? 16
    Turning off the system 17

Chapter 2: Peeking through Windows — 95 19

A Neat and Orderly Windows 95 Desktop 19
Making Tracks with Your Mouse 22
    Holding the mouse properly 23
    Using the mouse (wisely, of course) 23
Opening and Closing Windows 26
    Opening windows, launching programs 26
    Manipulating windows 28
    Closing windows 28
Ordering from the Menus 29
Carrying on a Dialogue — with a Box! 31
Taking a Shortcut 32

Chapter 3: Getting *Start* — ed **35**

Getting Past Go: Basics of Using the Start Menu 35
　　Displaying the Start menu 36
　　Making menu choices 37
Launching Programs 38
Opening Documents 41
Controlling Settings 42
　　Designing your window is merely child's play 42
　　Creating a peekaboo taskbar 46
Finding Things 48
Crying for Help 50
Running Around: The Run Feature 52
Shutting Down 53

Chapter 4: 95-Style Windows Accessories **55**

My Computer: My Pride and Joy 55
　　Peeking inside a folder or drive 57
　　Exploring some more 58
　　Claiming your own space: creating folders 59
Tooling Along with Windows 95 Accessories 60
　　Tallying scores with Calculator 60
　　Working with words — in a pad 62
　　Arranging accessories on-screen 63
Cutting, Copying, and Pasting 65
　　Clipping stuff on the Clipboard 65
　　Selecting text 66
　　Clipping, snapping, and pasting text 67
Using Undo: Your Very Best Friend 68
Closing Applications and Answering Questions 69
Recycling: A Fickle Person's Friend 70
Customizing the Desktop: Creating Shortcuts 71
　　Locating program files 71
　　Creating a shortcut 72

Chapter 5: Breaking through Windows: The 3.*x* Family **75**

Ten Distinctive Features of Windows 3.*x* 76
Ten Features That Survived the Transition to Windows 95 76
What Does Windows Look Like? 78
Working with Windows 79
Using File Manager 81
　　Opening File Manager 81
　　Using toolbars 82
　　Navigating File Manager 83
　　Creating folders 83
Using Windows 3.*x* Accessories 84
Closing Applications 85

Chapter 6: Getting the Fax about Printers 87

   Printers 101 87
      Dot-matrix: a slow, low-cost, low-quality printer 88
      Inkjet: a faster, low-cost, higher-quality printer 89
      Laser: a fast, higher-cost, high-quality printer 90
   Playing with Little Lord Font 91
      Enhancing your character image 93
      Sizing up your fonts 93
      Installing new fonts 94
   Putting Print on Paper 95
      Connecting the printer 95
      Getting the printer and computer on speaking terms 96
      Ready, set, print! 97
   Letting Your Fax Take Charge 98

Part II: Microsoft Works — For Teachers **101**

Chapter 7: Microsoft Works 4.0: A Primer 103

   Selecting the Right Works 103
   Separating Works Modules from Modes 104
      Putting Works into action 107
      Thumbing through the pages of Task Launcher 107
   Training Works: The Common Elements 109
      Tooling the toolbars 109
      Punching navigation buttons 110
      Looking for an Open(ing) dialog box 110
      Saving and then Saving As 112
   Making a Template Decision 114
      Choosing a template 114
      Working with wizards 115

**Chapter 8: Documenting Words: Using
the Works Word Processor** 117

   Taking the First Steps toward Creating Your Document 117
      Calling up the Word Processor 118
      Dissecting the Word Processor screen 119
   Putting Pen to Paper: Typing 121
      Pressing on and Enter 121
      Saving a space at the end of sentences 121
      Correcting errors 122
      Dressing characters to the nines 124
   Setting Up the Document 126
      Rulings and the ruler: setting tabs and indents 126
      Lining up those paragraphs 128

Saving, Saving, Saving 130
    When should you save? 131
    How to save 131
    Close it up! 131
    Get it back! 132
Applying Your Skills 133
    Challenge 1: Designing a letterhead template 133
    Challenge 2: Saving a letterhead as a template 137
    Challenge 3: Customizing test templates 138

Chapter 9: Celling You on Spreadsheets **141**
Spreadsheets: An Overview 141
Scratching out Your First Spreadsheet 142
    Navigating the sheet 144
    A grade book spreadsheet 145
    Formulating the sheet 148
    Laying out the spreadsheet 151
    Go ahead — drench it in dressing! 153
Applying Your Skills 154
    Challenge 1: Customizing the grade-book template 154
    Challenge 2: What lesson-plan template? 155

Chapter 10: Profiling a Database **159**
Database Ground Rules 159
Plotting the Database Playing Field 160
    Defining your fields 161
    Saving your database creation 162
    Viewing data differently 163
Putting Data in the Field 164
    Adding records to your database List View 165
    Adding records in Form View 165
Changing the Database Landscape 166
    Moving fields in a form 166
    Sizing fields in a form 168
    Renaming fields 169
    Adding and removing fields 169
Picking and Choosing Database Players 170
    Finding records 170
    Redisplaying records 171
Applying Your Skills 171
    Challenge 1: Merging data into a letter 172
    Challenge 2: Profiles to portfolios 175

Chapter 11: Publish It and Present It! **179**
Using Perky Presentation Programs 179
Desktop Publishing: A Proliferation of Programs 182
Web Weavers: Web Page Authoring Tools 183

Playing with More Works Pets 184
Saying it with pictures 184
Creating words of art with WordArt 187
Adopting Fresh Ideas 188
For teachers 188
For students 189
Applying Your Skills 190
Challenge 1: Creating a simple presentation 190
Challenge 2: Publishing your work.......................... 194
Challenge 3: Reaching out to the World Wide Web 196

Part III: Communicating with the Outside World 199

Chapter 12: Connecting to the Net 201

Oh, Dem Modems! 201
The ins and outs of buying a modem 201
It's baud, not Maud 202
Modeming the fax 203
Talking to a modem: the soft stuff 204
Locating your modem 204
Online Services: New Ways to Reach Out and Touch Someone 205
Routes to the Net: online services 205
Routes through the Net: browsers 206
How to Divvy Up Online Time 208
Setting limits 208
Controlling online time 208

Chapter 13: Going Online with Microsoft Network 211

E-Mail: An Overview 211
Getting Set Up — and Liking It 212
Naming yourself 213
Passing the word 213
Connecting close to home 214
Accounting matters 215
Plunging Directly Online 216
Sign on, please 216
Hi, good morning, welcome 217
Communicating across Party Lines 218
Reading your mail 219
Creating and sending your first message 221

Chapter 14: Surfing the Net 227

The Internet: Facts to Know 227
Defining the Net 228
Setting up a Net niche 228
Untangling.Internet.strings 228

An Educator's Wonderland 230
    Special education — for teachers only 230
    Internet special features: forums, bulletin
       boards, and newsgroups 232
    Downing loaded stuff 232
Protecting Everyone from Online Danger 233
Student Fun 235
Learning to Spot Good Sites 236
Informing Others of Online Rules 236

Part IV: The Softer Side of Computers: Software 239

Chapter 15: Software Musts for Educators 241

Software-Buying Tips 241
Getting a Taste of What's Out There 242
    Drill and practice 243
    Productivity software 244
    Multimedia software 245
    Simulation software 246
    Management programs 246
Teacher-Approved Computer Resources 248

Chapter 16: The Multimedia Explosion: CD-ROM 251

Hard Stuff for Getting Into Multimedia 251
Advantages of CD-ROMs 252
Multimedia Focus of the CD-ROM 253
    Where have all the card files gone? 253
    Online reference sources 254
    Survival requirements for all students 254
Reference Works 255
    Encyclopedias and general reference 256
    Dictionaries and atlases 257
    Productivity and creativity for all ages 258
Directed Studies 258
    Good titles for lower to middle grade levels 259
    Good titles for middle and upper grade levels 260
Getting Material off the CD-ROM 262

Chapter 17: Multimedia Fun in Windows 95 263

Sounding Off with Music, Noise, and Narration 263
    Playing music softly 264
    Recording your voice: music for your students 266
Viewing Vibrant Videos 267

Looking at videos — simply looking 268
Capturing videos on-site 269
Showing Off 270

Part V: Lagniappe (Lan-Yap) — Something Extra for Nothing 271

Chapter 18: Teaching with Any Number of Computers (Including None) 273
Ten Tips for Nada Computer 273
Tips for the Classroom Lone Ranger 275
Ten Tips for Going to the Lab 279

Chapter 19: Foolproof Ways to Finance Your Computer Needs 283
Research Past Fund-Raising Successes 283
Advertise to the Masses 284
Throw a Party 284
Solicit Grants 284
Take in Strays 285
Hold a Tag Day 286
Start Adoption Procedures 286
Sell Computer Time 287
Pick a Plan Your Students Can Handle 287
Work with a Practical Schedule 287
Keep Up with Current Legislation 288

Chapter 20: Stuff You Can "Hardly" Live Without 289
Ten Pieces of Hardware to Make Life Easier 290
LCD panels 290
Scanners 290
Touch screens 291
OCR devices 292
Zip drives and all that Jazz 292
Laptops 293
Video paraphernalia 293
Microphones and speakers 295
PCMCIA cards 295
Projection systems 296
Ten Tips for Upgrading Hand-Me-Downs 296
Add memory 296
Install a bigger hard drive 297
Add a CD-ROM drive 297
Change floppy-disk drives 297

Get a color printer 297
Change the motherboard 298
Add a modem 298
Get a new monitor 298
Update to Windows 95 298
Sound things out with a new sound card 298
Feeding Your Computer Supplies Habit 299
Computer paper 299
Colored paper 299
Designer transparencies 299
CD-ROMs with clip art and photo images 300
Disks 300
Printer cartridges 300
Erasable ink markers 300
Marker-board erasers 301
Miscellaneous paper supplies 301
Cleaning kits 301

Chapter 21: Help and Helpful Resources **303**

Ten Troubleshooting Tips 303
The computer doesn't work 303
The monitor is blank 304
I have a Nonsystem Disk or Disk error 304
The keyboard froze up 304
I have an Out of Memory error 305
I lost my document — it just disappeared! 305
I deleted my file from the disk 305
Access to my file is denied 306
My printer gives me squiggles 306
My mouse is dead 307
Ten Tips That Are Just Plain Good to Know 307
You are in charge 308
Insert one disk at a time 308
Restart using a "warm" boot 308
Use your escape hatch 308
Clean the keyboard with a damp cloth 308
You don't have to upgrade your software 308
Saving and backing up your files is important 309
Floppy disks are sensitive 309
You don't have to know everything 310
If your computer's sick, leave the kitchen sink at home 310

Appendix A: Techno Terms Translation *311*

Appendix B: About the CD *321*

Index *333*

IDG Books Worldwide, Inc., End-User
License Agreement *353*

Installation Instructions *357*

IDG Books Worldwide Registration Card .... *Back of Book*

Introduction

*I*t's hard to believe that a year has passed since Carol and I wrote the first edition of *PCs For Teachers*. When we were approached about doing this second edition, our immediate thought was, "How can it possibly be time to update the book?"

But then we realized that many exciting advancements have occurred in computer technology (and in its impact on education) during the past year:

- ✔ Increased speed on the Information Superhighway
- ✔ New ways to get connected and new places to visit
- ✔ New companies producing fantastic educational software
- ✔ New Windows and shelf software (the kind you can buy at the store) to make your life easier . . . and on, and on, and on

Carol and I are still the same positive people we were a year ago, still endeavoring to bring the world to the bright young (and not-so-young) faces we see every day. We're still sometimes overwhelmed by the task of keeping on top of technological advances.

The more we learn, the more we realize what there is yet to know! By sharing what we've learned with you, we pass on the baton. There's *still* so much that we have to tell you.

Why Should You Believe Us?

We are teachers. It's as simple as that — we are teachers with a combination of more than 35 years of classroom experience, a thorough understanding of student behavior (we've seen it all, well, almost), and so many stories to tell that "You won't believe what *Johnny* did today . . . " is part of our everyday vocabulary. Are Carol and I experts on computers? Nah! But we're very knowledgeable about how to get the most from them — especially in ways that *you'll* need to use them.

We pooled our resources again for this second edition. Carol graded Pam's work, and Pam checked Carol's work. We bled all over the manuscript and then turned it over to someone else to double-check our work (and they bled some, too). We searched for fantastic software to pack into the CD-ROM and solicited donations from teachers to come up with the activities that you'll find at the end of some of the chapters. In fact, we worked so closely on this book that you'll see us referred to as "I" throughout.

Behavioral Objectives

If you are a beginner, this book is for you. If you are already on speaking terms with computers and have played around with them a bit, this book is for you. If you are a super-duper computer whiz who designs your own software, you'll also find some things in this book that you can use — and identify ways to help your students understand you!

We hope that you won't run screaming from the room at any time while you work your way through the information that we've packed into the chapters (at least not as a result of anything that we say!). Here's what we hope you *will* be able to do after absorbing the information provided in this book:

- ✔ Identify common computer terms
- ✔ Use the computer to accomplish the tasks that *you* have to do every day
- ✔ Use the computer to dress up your lesson plans
- ✔ Build student computer activities into your curriculum
- ✔ Learn to connect to and explore the Internet
- ✔ Identify computer equipment and programs that are designed to make your life easier

Sounds simple, doesn't it? We hope so. We've spent months trying to narrow down the subject matter; we just have so much to share with you!

Our Lesson Plan

This book is divided into five parts, each of which focuses on a particular topic. We know how teachers operate, you see, so we've made each part independent of the others. That way, you can use this book as a reference manual or work your way through an entire part from start to finish.

Part I: Teacher In-Service

We start with a basic overview of PCs, tell you what equipment you *need* to begin your exploration, and simply show you how to turn the computer on and off. We introduce you to computer terms so that you can start talking intelligently with your students and your fellow teachers, and also show you how to do Windows (95 style). We describe some of the features of the Windows 95 operating system, take a look back at the Windows 3.*x* family, and give you the "fax" about printing.

Part II: Microsoft Works — For Teachers

We chose Microsoft Works 4.0 for Windows 95 as your guide to getting some work done, because it often comes installed on classroom computers and is a great program for learning the basics of several software applications at the same time. The primer introduces Works basics, and each chapter in this part acquaints you with a different program module. You find out how to produce lesson plans, grade books, student files, and presentations. We show you how to design publications and create Web pages.

Part III: Communicating with the Outside World

This fun part can keep you "talking" for days. You find out what you need to connect to the Internet, how to schedule online time, and how to use some of the innovative programs that are designed specifically to make your voyage through cyberspace easier. We share some do's and don'ts for communicating, show you how to protect your students from online monsters, and discuss some ways that you can connect to the Internet free.

Part IV: The Softer Side of Computers: Software

You'll find the software jungle to be *amazing* — literally! We give you some tips for identifying the software that you really need and how to buy that software (or get it free). We also list software programs that other teachers recommend. We introduce you to the glamour of CD-ROM and multimedia, and show you how to get the most out of the multimedia features of Windows 95.

Part V: Lagniappe (Lan-Yap): Something Extra for Nothing

When all else is said and done, there's still much more that we want to tell you. The lagniappe part allows us to pack in everything else we think you ought to know, stuff you want to know, or things we want to tell you into lists (ten of this and seven of that).

These lists are designed to give you just the basics, Ma'am — just the facts. You'll find ten tips for making the most of your one-computer classroom, ten tips for going to the lab, ten tips for raising funds for computers and supplies, ten pieces of hardware (well, almost ten) designed just for teachers, ten tips for upgrading your hand-me-down computers, and ten great shareware programs you may want to download from the Internet.

The glossary in Appendix A is updated from the glossary in the first *PCs For Teachers* book. Appendix B tells you about what's on the CD that comes with this book and how to get the information from the CD-ROM onto your computer.

Watch for Icons — They're Special Characters

Throughout this book, we've marked things that we think are important (or just kind of cute). Consider the following icons to be your special guides:

Teacher Approved — Tried-and-true items, activities, and features that other teachers have found to be particularly useful.

Techno Terms — New or technical words identified somewhere in paragraphs guarded by this cute little character.

Heads Up — Important stuff! It's time to quit daydreaming, sit up, and pay attention.

Try This — Steps for accomplishing a task. You get to *do* something other than just sit and listen . . . and do it on the computer, too!

On the CD — Software programs, shareware programs, files, and other stuff that you'll find on the CD-ROM that comes with this book. Check this stuff out.

 Warning — Things to watch for and avoid. Read these paragraphs before you try something that you shouldn't.

Feedback

Okay, take a deep breath. Pull your shoulders to your ears and hold them for a second. Shake all over to relax before you plunge ahead. Then pick a spot or topic in the book and look at it. When you look up, you may be amazed by how much time has passed.

After you've had time to thumb through this book, we'd like to know what you think. Do you need to know more about certain topics? Have you found programs that we should mention? Have you discovered techniques that are worth including in the next edition of this book? Let us know — and also tell us how you like what we included in the book. We're teachers, so we know that there's always room for improvement.

Send feedback to:

IDG Books Worldwide, Inc.
7260 Shadeland Station, Suite 100
Indianapolis, IN 46256

Or e-mail your comments to IDG Books at feedback@idgbooks.com. You can also check out IDG's Web page at http://www.idgbooks.com.

Part I
Teacher In-Service

The 5th Wave   By Rich Tennant

"WELL! IT LOOKS LIKE SOMEONE FOUND THE `LION'S ROAR' ON THE
SOUND CONTROL PANEL."

In this part . . .

*I*n a recent USA Today article, I read that "Teaching Is Hot!" Although at first I feared that the article would describe how teachers are once again in the "hot seat," I was relieved to discover that the purpose of the article was to recognize teaching as a profession that's attracting new fans — and that many people in other professions are going back to school to become teachers. Teacher satisfaction is on the rise. A commonly cited reason behind teaching's new popularity is the desire of these professionals to enter a service profession.

Well, we've known for years that teachers teach because they want to serve humankind! It's nice to know that we're off the hot seat and into something hot. Now it's time to start heating up those computers and getting on the PC trail. In this first part, you pick up some basics that will help you put your computer to use, as well as some techy terms that you need to know. You also learn a new way to do Windows, explore some of the helpers that come with Windows 95, and get the "fax" about printing.

What you can learn in this part is designed to keep you off the hot seat!

Chapter 1

What's a PC, and What Does It Do?

● ●

In This Chapter

▶ Reviewing computer-techie terms and definitions

▶ Identifying PC components (the equipment)

▶ Reviewing software (the instructions)

▶ Turning on the computer

▶ Turning off the computer

● ●

*E*very teacher remembers the first year of teaching because it is marked by so many other firsts: the first student who entered your classroom, your first-period class, your first recess duty, your first bulletin board, your first discipline challenge, and so on. Now it's time for another first: your first classroom computer . . . and we certainly want to make *this* first more enjoyable than your first discipline challenge!

Did you know what to do with that first computer? Have you used the computer yet, or is it still sitting there on the desk, looking lonely and forlorn? If your answer to either of these questions is no, you've come to the right chapter. It's time to get that computer up and running!

What Is a PC?

The term *PC* is an acronym for *personal computer*. A PC is sometimes referred to as an *IBM PC* (the personal computer developed by International Business Machines Corporation), a *clone*, or a *compatible*. Clones and compatibles look and act like IBM PCs, but they are not made by IBM, so they can't carry the IBM trademark. You'll often find the name of the company that made or built the PC emblazoned on the front of the computer, just as you find the name of the company that made your car emblazoned on a strategic location near the front end or bumper.

Although you can tell people who ask that what you have is an IBM compatible, more often than not, they really want to know what kind of *processor* you have — and that gets a bit more sticky if you don't know. Telling people that you have a clone may make them think that you've confused your PC with a sheep. (Okay, you can groan now!).

The following list presents some terms to get you going. You'll find more information about each piece of equipment in the following section. Every PC system needs four basic pieces of equipment:

- **Input device:** a unit that helps you get data (the facts, just the facts) into the computer.
- **Processor:** a device that processes the data. A process can be anything that changes the data or performs an action, such as adding, subtracting, or putting letters on a page.
- **Output device:** a unit that allows you to get processed data from the computer.
- **Storage device:** a unit that stores the data and information until you need it again.

Hardware (You Know, the Equipment)

They say that a picture is worth a thousand words, but sometimes the things that you see in a picture need some explanation. Check out Figure 1-1 to locate each computer part.

Okay, you know what the pieces of equipment look like; now what do they do? Table 1-1 provides a little insight into the purpose of each piece of hardware.

Table 1-1	What Each Piece of Hardware Does
Hardware	*Function*
Monitor	Displays text and graphics, usually in color.
CD-ROM drive	Holds CD-ROM program discs and audio CD discs.
Floppy disk drive	Holds disks that you can put in and take out. These disks are used to store files.

Hardware	Function
Keyboard	Enables you to type data and text and to create files. Keyboards these days have four pads: the standard keypad, which contains alphabetic keys and resembles a typewriter keyboard; the numeric keypad, which appears at the right end of the keyboard and resembles a 10-key adding-machine keypad; function keys, which appear at the top of the keyboard or at the left end of the keyboard (or in both places) and are identified by an *F* followed by a number; and the special keys keypad, which appears between the standard keypad and the numeric keypad. The keys on the special keys keypad vary depending on the company that made the keyboard and how old the keyboard is. Each key on this keypad is labeled so you can locate the arrow keys and other navigation keys.
Mouse	Enables you to point at and select stuff on-screen.
Printer	Puts your text, graphics, and data on paper.
System unit	Holds the processor, memory, and power supply that make your computer work, and provides outlets where you can plug in disk drives and attachments.
Hard disk	Fits inside the computer and stays there to hold your programs.

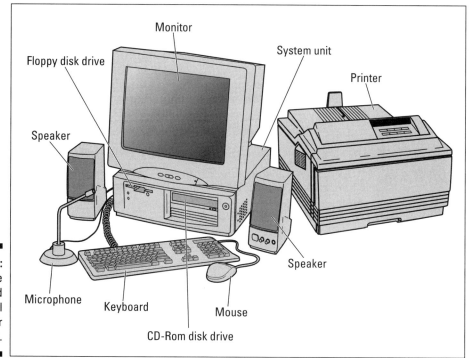

Figure 1-1:
The remodeled personal computer system.

How do these pieces of equipment fit into the scheme of required PC components? Here's the scoop:

- Input devices: keyboard and mouse
- Processor: housed in the system unit
- Output devices: monitor and printer
- Storage devices: disk drives (CD-ROM and floppy)

Identifying the devices and showing how they fit into the scheme of the system is fine, but what if your computer doesn't look like the one in Figure 1-1? Here's a hardware supplement cut down to size:

- The system unit's case houses the workings of the computer, including the electronics needed to get the computer running. *Intel Inside* often appears on this case (yes, just as you see on TV) to identify the company that made the processor. The system unit is sometimes referred to as the *console* and can appear as a tower (as shown in Figure 1-1) or in a case that rests horizontally on the desktop.

- Processors come in a variety of types and speeds; you want to get a fast one to meet the needs of today's fantastic programs. The most common processors today are 486 and Pentium processors.

- Most monitors these days are color monitors. If you don't have a color monitor, insist on one; you need it to get the most from the programs that you'll want to run.

- The CD-ROM drive has become essential since the advent of bigger, better, more powerful programs that incorporate multimedia techniques designed to entertain as well as educate. You can get a CD-ROM drive that attaches to the outside of the computer so that you can move it from computer to computer when you need to.

- You still need the floppy drive to store your work and the work of your students. The $3^1/_2$-inch floppy drive is the size that you need for most disks; the $5^1/_4$-inch disks are no longer being made.

- Disk drives have names. Floppy disk drives are usually named A and B, hard disks are normally C, and CD-ROM drives are usually D. Drive names are followed by a colon (:) to tell the computer that you're talking about a *place* (the drive).

Becoming attached to your attachments

Confused by what you see hanging out on your computer? Relax! You simply have different attachments — and that's good! Look up some of these cute little characters in a computer catalog or check out Chapter 20 — it has pictures of some of this equipment:

✔ A trackball — looks like an upside-down mouse, except the ball is much bigger

✔ A koala pad — imagine a drawing tablet made digital

✔ A scanner — a hand-held scanner resembles a hand vacuum; a flat-bed scanner looks like a small copy machine

✔ A microphone

✔ A camera — the most common type is in the shape of a ball and resembles how I always thought "Big Brother" would look

✔ Speakers

Going Soft with Software

Now that you're through the "hard" stuff, you can focus on the soft stuff: computer software. *Software* refers to the programs or instructions that tell the computer what to do. I know, you thought that *you* would be able to tell the computer what to do — and you can, up to a point. After the stuff that you type gets into the processor in English or some other language, the computer has to decode that stuff so that it understands what you want it to do. Software programs help the computer decode your messages.

Software comes in two basic varieties:

✔ **Operating system.** Operating-system software, which comes with your machine, starts the computer and tells it what to do. This software should already be loaded on your machine when you get the computer; if it isn't, ask someone to install it before you take the computer home. Then ask for the system disks so that you'll have them in an emergency — and don't pay extra just because you asked for the disks! Trying to use a computer without an operating system is like trying to teach without students.

PCs use the DOS operating system, which stands for *disk operating system,* or the Windows 95 operating system. You'll find DOS operating-system software on some of the older computers as well as on computers running Windows 3.*x.* Windows 95 is the operating system that is shipped with new computers.

✔ **Applications.** Application software is designed to help you accomplish something useful, such as creating lesson plans, tracking your budget, keeping student grades, and drawing designs. You learn more about specific types of applications software in Parts II and IV.

Ticky-tacky techno technicalities

Do you have a taste for the bizarre terms that you often hear computer whizzes bandying about, but avoid joining a conversation for fear of embarrassing yourself? Here are a few techie-type terms to help you out:

✔ **RAM** refers to *random access memory*, which allows the computer to access the information that you call for. Compare locating songs on an audiocassette tape with finding songs on an audio CD. You have to fast-forward through a tape to get to the song that you want to hear, whereas on a CD, you can skip directly to the song. RAM is more like locating songs on a CD; the computer goes directly to the information that you want.

RAM gradually fills with instructions for the programs that you tell the computer to load; then it adds the data that you type each time you start your computer. When you turn off the computer, RAM empties. Therefore, RAM is considered to be temporary memory (sort of like the way your students cram information into their brains just before a test and then forget it all the next day!).

✔ **ROM** stands for *read-only memory*. Read-only memory is built into the machine at the factory so that the computer knows what to do when you turn it on. ROM is permanent; it doesn't go away when you turn off the computer.

✔ **Bit** stands for *binary digit*, the itty-bitty smallest unit of computer data. Bits are so small, it takes eight of them to create a *byte*.

✔ A **byte** is made up of eight bits and is the amount of memory that each character (r, x, 4, tab, and so on) takes up in RAM.

✔ A **kilobyte** is approximately 1,000 bytes. (Get it? *Kilo* means 1,000.)

✔ A **megabyte** is about 1 million bytes. (Do you see a trend here?)

✔ A **gigabyte** is approximately 1 billion bytes (or 1,000 megabytes).

✔ **Megahertz** (mega *what*?) is the speed of the computer. Get a fast machine (120 MHz and up) if you plan to get on the Information Superhighway! Speeds on newer computers range anywhere from 66 to 200 MHz, but you need a Pentium processor to run the faster speeds of 120 MHz or more.

People who are in the know always want to know your megabytes of RAM, your megabytes or gigabytes of hard disk space, and the megahertz of your processor. They rarely want to know your ROM, however (and if they do, just make something up; they won't know the difference!).

Both types of software are stored on disks (CD-ROMs and floppy disks), which you can insert and remove from the disk drives in your computer. The most popular format for storing large programs from the major software developers (Microsoft, Lotus, Corel, and so on) is the CD-ROM, because it can store large, powerful programs on one disc. Installing programs from one CD-ROM is much easier than inserting and removing more than 30 floppy disks of the 3¹/₂-inch variety. In addition, developers can pack neat, fun stuff on CD-ROMs to take up the extra space. (Teachers *love* getting something free!)

I always said that the first two words my children could read were "Free Inside!"

Powering Up and Down

Powering up your computer merely refers to turning on the system. *Powering down,* of course, means turning off the system.

Turning on the system

Depending on the type of computer system that you have, its age, and its case design, turning on the computer can be a challenge. You not only have to worry about the main power switch (on the system unit), but you also have to locate the switch to turn on the monitor. Follow these easy steps to get started:

1. **Locate the monitor switch and turn the monitor on.**

   The monitor switch usually is a button on the front of the monitor, with a light indicator beside the button. A steady light appears when the monitor and computer are both on; the light sometimes flashes when the monitor is on but the computer is off.

2. **Locate the switch on the system unit and flip it, push it, or rock it to turn on the computer.**

If pressing and releasing the on/off button or switch seems to do nothing, you may need to hold the on/off button in until the computer beeps at you. Some manufacturers of newer computers added this safety device to prevent novice users from accidentally turning off their computers and losing valuable data.

If you have a computer system that requires an engineering degree just to get it up and running, you may want to explore alternative setups. Here are some tips for making your computer pieces fit together:

- ✔ Check to see whether your monitor can be plugged into the system unit. If it can, you can leave the monitor switch on and power up both components by turning on the system unit.

- ✔ Plug all your equipment into a power strip so that you can get all pieces up and running by flicking the master switch.

What happens after you turn on the system?

A couple of things can happen after you turn on the system, depending on how your computer is set up. When you turn it on, the computer goes through the standard boot (startup) procedure, and a lot of technical information pops up on-screen followed by more info that scrolls on and off the screen quickly. When the computer settles down, your screen changes, and here's wherein the differences lie.

Computers that are three to five years old may have Windows 3.*x* installed. If you have Windows 3.*x,* you'll want to review Chapter 5, which gives you the basics of working with the first release of Windows.

If your computer system is more than five years old, you'll see DOS in all its old glory — the lonely C:/> on a black screen — and you'll know it's time to launch your campaign for a new computer. Otherwise, you'll miss out on some of the best stuff on the CD-ROM that comes with this book.

Most new computers (those manufactured or bought within the past two years) come with the Windows 95 operating system, which runs automatically when you turn on the computer. When a computer running Windows 95 settles down, the screen changes colors and displays several little pictures. Your screen probably looks different from the one shown in Figure 1-2 because the programs that you have on your computer most likely are different from those that I have on mine.

You learn more about the features of the Windows desktop in Chapter 2. Then you can learn how to use some of the tools that come with Windows 95 in Chapter 3 and Chapter 4.

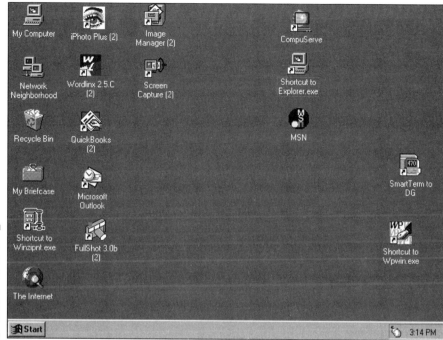

Figure 1-2:
The
Windows 95
desktop,
neat and
orderly!

If you don't see the Windows 95 desktop, you may have a previous release of Windows on your computer. If you see a Program Manager window similar to the one shown in the figures in Chapter 5, you can skip Chapters 2–4 for now and get to work with Chapter 5. When you have time, don't forget to go through Chapters 2–4 to see what's new and improved in Windows 95.

Turning off the system

Close your eyes for a moment, and imagine your classroom with sparkling-clean windows that you have to touch to find out whether they are open or closed. Then imagine how much elbow grease went into getting those windows squeaky-clean!

Working with Windows 95 gives you the flip side of "doing windows." Windows 95 cleans up all by itself — *if* you power down your computer properly. If you're ready to quit work now, follow these steps (if you want to continue exploring and working with other chapters, you can come back to this procedure later):

1. **Press and hold down the Alt key on the keyboard; then press and release the F4 key.**

   You see the window shown in Figure 1-3.

The black dot identifies the active choice.

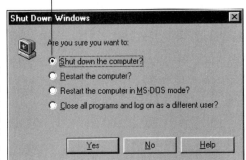

Figure 1-3:
Shutting
down is just
a click
away.

2. **Ensure that the words Shut Down the Computer have a dashed border and that a black dot appears in the adjacent option button.**

   If the black dot appears beside a different choice in the list, press the Alt key and then press and release the S key.

3. **Press Enter.**

   Windows tucks everything neatly away so that it can find what you need the next time you work on the system. Eventually, a message tells you that it's OK to turn off your computer.

4. **Flip all the switches and press all the buttons that you used to turn on you computer to power it down.**

Oh, gee, just when you were beginning to have fun, the bell rang! It's okay to stay after school and play some more if you want to; the teacher won't mind!

Chapter 2
Peeking through Windows — 95

· ·

In This Chapter

▶ Identifying features of the Windows 95 desktop

▶ Using the mouse

▶ Opening and closing windows

▶ Reading menus

▶ Manipulating windows

▶ Using the taskbar

▶ Defining keyboard shortcuts

· ·

*Y*ou saw the Windows 95 commercials, and you may have wondered what all the fuss was about. You heard the hype (and probably ignored it) for a while. You may even have wandered through the stores, saying that you weren't interested, yet you stopped to see the demonstrations. Then you bought a new computer, and Windows 95 was installed on the computer when it arrived. You were delighted!

But then you began to wonder what in the world you were going to do with the program, where you should start, and how to find the stuff that you knew was buried somewhere in the computer.

This chapter provides essential information about Windows 95 and introduces some of the basic techniques for getting around. If you have Windows 3.*x,* feel free to take a peek at this chapter on Windows 95 before jumping on over to Chapter 5. You, too, just might get hooked!

A Neat and Orderly Windows 95 Desktop

If you reviewed Chapter 1, you had a peek at the Windows 95 desktop. Although the desktop pictured in Chapter 1 looked good, it really was quite cluttered. When you power up a computer that's running Windows 95 for the first time, you most likely will see a much cleaner display, more like the one shown in Figure 2-1.

Icons   Desktop

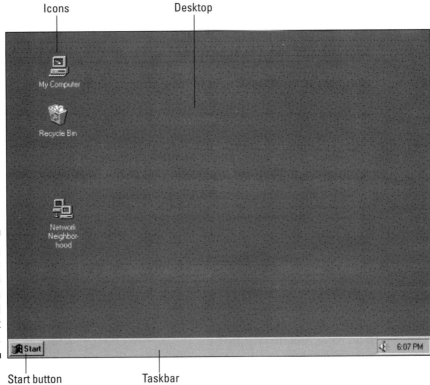

Figure 2-1:
The
Windows 95
desktop is
clean until
you start
cluttering it.

Start button   Taskbar

TECHNO TERMS

Sticky and gooey windows

The first time I heard the word *gooey* mentioned in computerese, I thought, "Uh, oh, things are fixin' to get a bit sticky."

Questions started rolling around in my head. Just what is *gooey*? How is *gooey* going to affect me? Is *gooey* going to help me, or is it something else that will complicate my life even more?

Actually, *gooey* is simply the pronunciation of the acronym *GUI*, which stands for *Graphical User Interface*. Oh, wonderful — more words that you don't know! Breaking this GUI apart (and maybe putting it to music, Maestro?) may help:

✔ *G* is for *graphical* (which, of course, means picture).

✔ *U* is for *user* (you).

✔ *I* is for *interface* — the new word. In computerese, interface means to bridge the gap between the computer operating system (Windows 95) and something else. In this case, the something else is, again, you.

With both Windows and Windows 95, GUI pads the space between you and the workings behind the window that keep the computer up and going. All that's left is for you to learn to be manipulative — with your windows, anyway.

Some of the features that you should note about the Windows 95 desktop
include:

- ✔ **The taskbar:** Displays system information and running programs

- ✔ **The Start button:** Appears at the left end of the taskbar and displays a
  menu that organizes system features into groups

- ✔ **Icons:** Appear on the desktop and represent programs that come with
  Windows 95

- ✔ **The desktop:** The screen (all of it)

It's relatively uncomplicated, this Windows 95 desktop. The three icons
described in the following list provide different ways to get a look at what's
inside your computer system:

- ✔ **My Computer** displays a list of all the programs and files contained on
  all drives attached to your computer (not mine).

- ✔ The **Recycle Bin** holds the stuff that you delete from the hard disk, so
  that you can get it back if you need it. You control when the Recycle Bin
  is emptied (and of course, Murphy's Law says that you won't need a file
  that you've deleted until you empty the Recycle Bin!).

- ✔ The **Network Neighborhood** icon appears when your computer is
  networked with another computer or several other computers. By
  using the Network Neighborhood, you can actually connect to other
  computers on the network and open files from the other computers'
  hard disks! If you don't see the Network Neighborhood icon, your
  computer most likely isn't networked.

You may see other icons on your desktop in addition to the three icons
shown in Figure 2-1:

- ✔ You can use **My Briefcase** to "check out" files from the hard disk, take
  the files home to work on them, and then "check in" the files to update
  them on the hard disk.

- ✔ The **Internet** icon appears when you have a way to connect to the
  Internet from your computer.

- ✔ The **MSN** (The Microsoft Network) installation icon is automatically
  installed on machines that contain a modem. You can use the installation icon and the Windows 95 CD-ROM to get up and running on the
  Microsoft Network. See Chapter 13 for more information about using
  Microsoft Network.

The nitty-gritty on networks

Are you connected to a network? Connecting to a network should not be confused with getting connected to the World Wide Web or Internet; we're talking about physically connecting here.

Networked computers have an extra cable attached to their system units; this cable connects those computers to other computers. All it takes to create a network is two computers.

For example, I have a network set up in my home office that connects my two computers. Using my network, I can be on one computer and actually work from the hard disk of the other computer. I can double-click my Network Neighborhood icon to see a list of the computers connected to my network, then I can click the name of my other computer (yes, just like children, you can name your computers!), and locate files on the other hard disk. If I need to, I can copy those files from the other computer to the hard disk or a disk in the floppy drive of the computer that I'm using.

Networks can, of course, expand across the miles to link schools within a district, can be held strictly within the confines of a building to keep teachers in touch with one another, or can link computers in one department of a school. By using special networking software, you can set up an inter- or intra-school e-mail system, enable teachers to access the school computer from their home computers, and set up any number of additional features.

You don't have to allow access to your hard disk when you create a network; I wanted that feature because I never know where I've put files. But networking a classroom full of computers makes accessing program files easier and saves the disk space that installing programs on each hard drive would use.

Maybe it's time that you investigated and got to work on your network! Check it out with your school's technology coordinator; a network may already be an option for you. If not, you might put a bug in the coordinator's ear.

Making Tracks with Your Mouse

If you plan to use Windows 95, you need a little helper: your mouse.

Your mouse helps you open, move, or close windows and programs. If you've already got this little character (your mouse) under control and made it your best friend, feel free to skip the first part of this section and move on to "Opening windows, launching programs" later in the chapter.

The following sections provide tips that I share with students who are meeting the mouse for the first time.

If you're a lefty (like me), you may want to operate the mouse with your left hand. Refer to the Windows 95 manual to find out how to change the mouse buttons so that you can use your left hand. I use my right hand with my mouse, and that works pretty well, too. From now on, I refer to the right-handed mouse, so you lefties will have to reverse the directions (something that most of us are used to doing, anyway!).

Holding the mouse properly

Pick up your mouse and look it over. Notice the ball on the bottom? The ball rolls on the mouse pad so that the arrow (called the *mouse pointer*) on-screen goes where you want it to, but the ball needs guidance. That's where you come in. Here are some tips for making the mouse easier to manipulate:

✔ As you hold the mouse, can you feel its back against your palm? The mouse cord should extend from the space between your index finger and your middle finger. If you try to move the mouse by using just your fingers (one on either side of the mouse), you'll lose control, and the mouse won't go where you want it to go. So, keep the mouse palmed in a light and steady grip.

✔ Place the mouse back on the mouse pad, but don't lose your grip. A relaxed grip won't hurt the mouse, but squeezing it will! Now, roll the mouse around on the pad. Get a good feeling?

✔ Before you start pointing, make sure that your index finger rests on the left mouse button (if you're using your right hand to move the mouse) and that your middle finger is on the right mouse button. Using two fingers, one for each button, makes it easier to keep your place on the buttons so that you know which button you're clicking without looking.

Using the mouse (wisely, of course)

Got a grip on the mouse? Great! You'll need a good grip as you take off on your first exploration of Windows 95 desktop features. The following drill gives you an overview of some of the things that happen when you apply your mouse skills (pointing, clicking, dragging, and right-clicking):

1. **Place the mouse on the mouse pad and grip it properly; then relax.**

2. **Roll the mouse across the mouse pad and watch the mouse pointer on-screen.**

   Notice how the arrow (the current mouse pointer shape) moves in the direction in which you roll the mouse?

3. **When your mouse reaches the edge of the pad, pick up the mouse and place it on the opposite edge of the pad; then continue rolling.**

   For the mouse pointer to move, the mouse's roller ball has to be in contact with some surface. That's why when you pick up the mouse, the arrow doesn't move.

Mouseology!

As you become acquainted with your mouse, you need to know some basic mouse terms and how most people use them. Here are some tips to get you started:

- ✔ **Point.** Roll the mouse across the mouse pad (the rubber mat you place beside the computer to hold the mouse) or desk (if you don't have a mouse pad) until the arrow on-screen points to an icon or area of the screen.

- ✔ **Click.** To select something on-screen, click and release the primary mouse button (the left one for right-handed users and the right one for left-handed users who have changed their mouse setup) quickly and lightly. Avoid *maaaaashing* the button or holding it down — and please don't beat the poor mouse to death; a dead mouse makes a useless helper. On the desktop, whatever you're pointing to when you click appears highlighted to show that it's selected.

- ✔ **Double-click.** To activate something on-screen, click and release the primary mouse button twice in rapid succession.

This technique is a tough one to master, but if you keep your hand relaxed, hold your tongue between your teeth just right, and hold the mouse still, you should master it quickly. Double-clicking goes something like click, click rather than click . . . pause . . . click. Double-clicking stuff on the desktop activates the program that is represented by the icon you double-click.

- ✔ **Drag.** To move or size something on-screen, hold down the mouse button while you move the mouse across the pad. Remember that a light touch helps preserve your mouse. Dragging icons on the desktop moves them to new locations; dragging a window's border changes the window's size.

- ✔ **Right-click.** To display special menus, click and release the right mouse button (if you've changed the mouse setup so that it's left-handed, use the left mouse button and call it left-clicking) lightly and quickly. When you right-click, you see a menu of commands related to the icon or area of the screen that you are pointing to.

4. **Now move the mouse so that the mouse pointer points to the taskbar at the bottom of the screen.**

5. **Point to the time display at the right end of the taskbar.**

Day and date

Time display

6. **Roll the mouse so that the mouse pointer points to the My Computer icon.**

7. **Click (press and release without *maaaaashing*) the left mouse button.**

   The icon appears shadowed, and the icon name is highlighted in a darker color.

8. **Hold down the left mouse button to pick up the My Computer icon and drag the icon (roll the mouse on the pad while you continue to hold down the mouse button) to the right side of your screen.**

   Did the icon move to the other side of your desktop? If you accidentally drop the icon (release the mouse button before you want to) before you get it positioned precisely where you want it, just pick it up and continue dragging it to the desired position.

9. **Point to a blank spot on the desktop and right-click (press and release the right mouse button).**

   The shortcut menu displayed in Figure 2-2 pops down.

10. **Point to the My Computer icon and right-click to display the shortcut menu shown in Figure 2-3.**

Figure 2-2:
Click on a
blank spot
on the
desktop for
this menu.

Figure 2-3:
Shortcut
menu.

11. **Point to the taskbar and right-click.**

    The taskbar shortcut menu shown in Figure 2-4 pops up.

If you're still having trouble, you may want to get better acquainted with your mouse. When you start calling it by its first name, you know that you're well acquainted! But if it starts answering you, it's time for a break.

Figure 2-4:
Taskbar
shortcut
menu.

Opening and Closing Windows

When it comes to opening and closing windows in Windows 95, you can use several techniques. The technique that you choose depends on how skilled you are with the mouse and how comfortable you are with the keyboard.

Opening windows, launching programs

Most of the icons that you see on the Windows 95 desktop represent software programs that are designed to accomplish specific tasks. As a result, when you open a window by clicking icons on the Windows 95 desktop, nine times out of ten, you are actually launching a program — getting it up and running so that you can use it. Here are other techniques that you can use to open a window:

- Press an arrow key on the keyboard until the icon that represents the program that you want to open is highlighted; then press Enter.

- Point to the icon on the desktop, click to select the icon, and then press Enter.

- Point to the icon on the desktop and double-click (click twice in rapid succession).

- Point to the icon on the desktop, right-click, and then click Open in the shortcut menu.

For practice, open the My Computer window by using one of the techniques described in the preceding list. Notice the basic window features identified in Figure 2-5.

What does each of these features do? Here's some help:

- The **title bar** identifies the program/window name.

- The **program icon** appears at the left end of the title bar and is the same icon that you see on the desktop.

- The **Minimize button** enables you to reduce the window to a button on the taskbar (to get the window out of the way, yet leave the program running).

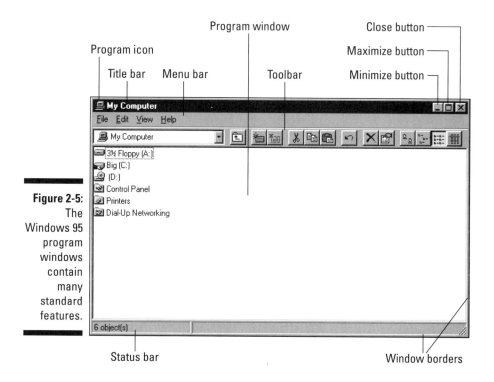

Program window

Close button

Program icon

Maximize button

Title bar   Menu bar   Toolbar   Minimize button

Figure 2-5:
The
Windows 95
program
windows
contain
many
standard
features.

My Computer

File   Edit   View   Help

My Computer

3½ Floppy (A:)
Big (C:)
(D:)
Control Panel
Printers
Dial-Up Networking

6 object(s)

Status bar   Window borders

✓ The **Maximize button** enables you to make the window fill the screen.

✓ The **Close button** closes the program and window with a single click.

✓ The **window border** is like a frame; it outlines the window. You can drag the border to change the size of the window.

✓ The **status bar** contains information about what's happenin' with the program.

✓ The **menu bar** groups program commands by type. If you see a menu bar, you know that you're looking at a program window.

✓ The **toolbar** provides single-step shortcut buttons for issuing the most common menu commands. If you don't see the toolbar, that's okay — someone closed it. To display the toolbar, point to the View menu and click. Then point to Toolbars and click.

✓ The **program window** displays lists of folders, documents, and additional program icons or provides work space, depending on the type of program that you launch. If the folders and other icons in your window appear different from those in the window shown in Figure 2-5, a different button view is active. To change the display, select a different icon size from the Toolbars area of the View menu or check into Chapter 4 for more details.

Manipulating windows

Although manipulating windows may be somewhat less satisfying than manipulating the questions that you ask your students (you know, so that the answer is a dead giveaway), I think that you'll find manipulating windows to be easier to master. Here are some techniques to try:

- ✔ To move a window, point to the window's title bar (make sure that you're pointing to an area of the title bar that doesn't contain buttons) and hold down the left mouse button as you drag the mouse across the pad.

- ✔ To size a window, position the mouse pointer on the window border until you see a two-headed mouse pointer; then drag the border.

  To make sizing the window easier, make sure that you point to the correct border. Drag a side border left or right to change the window's width; drag a top or bottom border up or down to change the window's height; drag a corner left, right, up, or down to change the height and width of the window at the same time.

- ✔ To minimize a window, click the Minimize button at the right end of the window's title bar. The window name appears in the taskbar.

- ✔ To restore a minimized window, click the window button in the taskbar.

- ✔ To maximize a window, click the Maximize button in the title bar. Some changes occur in the maximized window, as shown in Figure 2-6.

- ✔ To restore a maximized window, click the Restore button in the title bar. That button took the place of the Maximize button, as shown in Figure 2-6.

Before moving on to another fun task, practice some of the techniques outlined in this section to get the feel of working with different window features.

Closing windows

Closing windows is simple, but again, you have several choices:

- ✔ Hold down the Alt key on the keyboard while you press and release the F4 key at the top of the keyboard. Be careful here; the F4 key is one key, not F and then 4.

- ✔ Point to the Close button at the right end of the title bar and click the left mouse button.

- ✔ Point to the program icon at the left end of the title bar and double-click.

Complete toolbar   Restore button

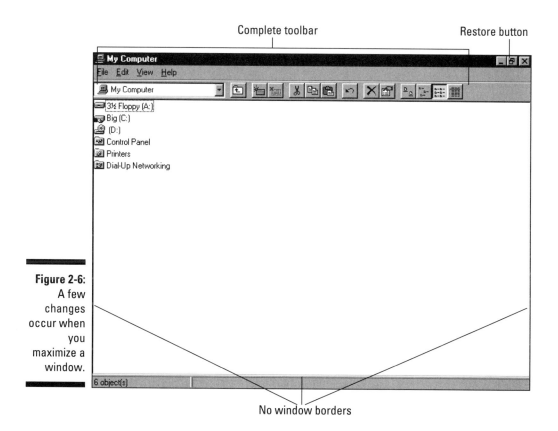

Figure 2-6:
A few
changes
occur when
you
maximize a
window.

No window borders

  ✔ Point to the program icon at the left end of the title bar, click to display
    the program menu, and then click the Close command.

  ✔ Point to the File menu and click; then point to Close and click. (Some-
    times, the command in the File menu is Exit instead of Close.)

Close the My Computer window by using one of the techniques identified in
the preceding list. Then reopen the window by using an opening technique
different from the one that you used earlier. When you're done, try using a
different closing technique, too. Give all the techniques a try to see which
one works best for you.

Ordering from the Menus

You may have noticed a difference in the way that commands appear in the
File menu if you used the File⇨Close technique to close an open window.
Programs that are designed to run with Windows 95 (and other Windows
programs, as you see in Chapter 5) follow a structured plan for displaying
menu items, as shown in Figure 2-7.

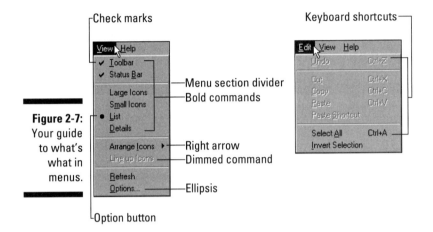

Figure 2-7:
Your guide
to what's
what in
menus.

Table 2-1 describes these menu features.

Table 2-1	Your Guide to Menu Features
Feature	*What It Means*
Check mark	The feature is active (or displayed). Several features can be active at the same time if they are all marked with a check mark.
Option button	The feature is active (but only one feature at a time in a group can be active).
Dimmed command	The command is not available.
Bold command	The command is ready for you to use.
Right arrow	The command has a secondary menu (sometimes called a *submenu*).
Underlined letter	The letter is a *hot key,* which means that you can select the command by pressing the keyboard key for the underlined letter.
Ellipsis	Choosing the command opens a dialog box in which you get to make some additional choices.
Menu section divider	Commands between dividers are somehow related.

By now, you may have guessed that Windows 95 offers options for most actions — and that displaying and choosing menu commands follows the multiple-option pattern. Here are some ways to display menus and choose commands:

  ✔ Point to the menu bar and click to display the menu; then point to the menu command that you want to choose and click it.

✔ While holding down the Alt key on the keyboard, press and release the underlined character of the menu item that you want to display (the F in File or the V in View, for example); then press the underlined character of the command that you want to choose (without the Alt key).

The underlined characters in menu names and commands are often called *hot keys* or *mnemonic characters*. Use the term *hot keys* with your students; that term is easier to remember. When you want to impress a coworker, though, use the term *mnemonic characters,* and wait for someone to ask you what you're talking about!

Carrying on a Dialogue — with a Box!

Dialog boxes, which enable you to carry on a dialogue with the computer, provide you with a way to tell the program and computer what you want them to do. By using a dialog box, you can select features that you want to activate, choose program options, enter values, type responses, and choose options from lists. Dialog boxes contain many common features, as shown in Figure 2-8.

Drop-down arrow   Spin buttons

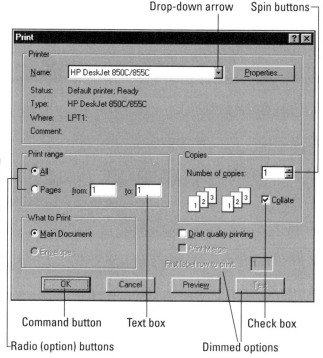

Figure 2-8:
Using a
dialog box
is quick and
easy — and
a dialog box
doesn't talk
back!

Command button   Text box   Check box

Radio (option) buttons   Dimmed options

Sorting through so many features seems almost overwhelming, doesn't it? Well, Table 2-2 provides some guidance to help you sort out these dialog-box features.

Table 2-2	Your Guide to Dialog-Box Features
Feature	*What It Means*
Drop-down arrow	A list of options is available; simply click the arrow to see your choices.
Radio button	Only one option in the group can be active at a time, and you must choose one option. These buttons are sometimes called *option buttons*.
Text box	You can type values or text in the box, depending on the nature of the text box and the entry that makes sense. (You know what I mean; some of your students probably have answered a "What" question with "Yes" before.)
Check box	You can click a check box to add or remove a check mark, which indicates that an item is active. More than one option in a group of check boxes can be active at the same time.
Spin button	You can increase or decrease the value (spin the value up or down) in the value box by clicking the up- or down-arrow button. These buttons are also known as *nudge* buttons.
Command button	You can perform an action or open another dialog box by clicking a command button; an ellipsis identifies buttons that open dialog boxes.
Dimmed option	The option is not available.

Taking a Shortcut

I once had a principal who said that if a shorter way to accomplish a task existed, I would find it. When it came to finding out about keyboard shortcuts, however, I was bowled over by a Mac user, and I had to learn to do Windows before I could use these shortcuts.

The term *keyboard shortcuts* refers to combinations of keys that are designed to perform specific commands. Each Windows program comes with certain built-in shortcuts, which are standard across all Windows programs. As a result, when you learn a keyboard shortcut in one Windows application, you can use the same keyboard shortcut in a different application and get the same result.

How will you identify keyboard shortcuts? That's easy — they're the keys that appear to be added together, such as Ctrl+S or Alt+F as shown back in Figure 2-7. To use keyboard shortcuts, simply press and hold the first key down while you quickly press and release the second key.

Look for a guide to these keyboard shortcuts on the Cheat Sheet that appears inside the front cover of this book.

Chapter 3
Getting *Start* — ed

In This Chapter

▶ Accessing the Start menu

▶ Starting programs

▶ Opening documents

▶ Working with settings

▶ Finding folders and files

▶ Looking through Help

▶ Using the Run dialog box

▶ Shutting down

"Go directly to jail — do not pass Go — do not collect $200." This famous statement from Milton Bradley's Monopoly game is a symbol of a straightforward, no-nonsense approach to giving directions.

Although other catchy phrases pass through our minds each day, I can't help but think that Microsoft used the Monopoly directive as an example of determining a direct, foolproof (well, almost) way to show novice users where to *go* after Windows 95 is up and running. If you consider the challenge of developing a course of study that is intuitive for people of all ages, all backgrounds, and all capability levels who live all over the world, you see what a task Microsoft faced. Yet for Microsoft, the answer to the dilemma appears to have been simple: the Start button.

Getting Past Go: Basics of Using the Start Menu

When you start a computer on which Windows 95 is installed, the Windows 95 desktop displays automatically, and the Start button appears at the left end of the Taskbar. If you aren't certain what the things that you see on your Windows 95 desktop represent, see Chapter 2, where I give you details about what you see on your Windows 95 screen.

Displaying the Start menu

Choose one of these techniques to display the Start menu:

✔ Point to the Start button and click.

✔ Press and release the Tab key (a dashed border appears around *Start* on the Start key); then press Enter.

✔ Hold down the Ctrl key; then press and release the Esc key.

✔ Press and release the special Start key that's available on many new keyboards — it's the key that's marked by the same Windows flag you see on the Start button.

Use one of the preceding techniques to display the Start menu on your computer; then compare it with the Start menu shown in Figure 3-1.

Special features ─

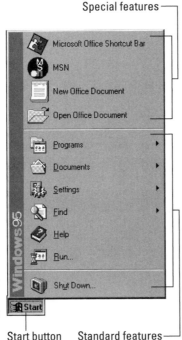

Figure 3-1:
The Start menu gets you past Go!

Start button   Standard features ─

The Start menu displayed in Figure 3-1 contains features (sometimes called *commands* or *items;* I prefer the term *features*) that are standard to all Windows 95 Start menus. Just as each of your students is unique in some way, however, each Start menu may contain a few features that are unique to your computer, depending on what programs you have on your hard disk. If you don't see anything in your Start menu above Programs, that's okay — it simply means that none of the programs on your computer put an icon on the main Start menu. In fact, the Start menu shown in Figure 3-1 was taken from one of my computers and is different from the Start menu you'll see in other figures in this chapter.

As you can see in the figure, I have Microsoft Office on this computer — see the Shortcut Bar, New Office Document, and Open Office Document icons at the top of the menu? I also have Microsoft Network; that's the MSN icon that you see in the figure.

Making menu choices

Making choices from the Start menu is easy. You even have a choice of techniques for making choices:

- ✔ Point to the menu feature; you don't need to click.
- ✔ Press the hot key (the underlined letter) for the menu feature that you want to access.

Point to one of the menu features and notice how the feature "lights up." The highlighting tells you which menu item you're pointing to (just in case you're still fine-tuning your pointing skills).

Some of the features display right arrows along the right edge of the menu. Arrows indicate the presence of a *submenu* (sometimes called a *cascading menu*). When you point to a feature that has an arrow, another menu appears. Figure 3-2 shows you what happens when you point to the Settings feature.

The Settings submenu contains standard features; I've never seen any other items listed in this submenu. The Programs and Documents submenus, however, vary from machine to machine, depending on what programs are installed on the computer and what documents were created with the programs. The Programs feature is covered in the "Launching Programs" section, later in this chapter; the Documents feature is explained in the "Opening Documents" section of this chapter.

Other Start menu features, such as Shut Down and Run, display an ellipsis after the feature name. Ellipses indicate that selecting the feature opens a dialog box in which you get to answer more questions, issue commands, and make additional selections.

As you continue your exploration of the Start menu, you run into lots of new things: programs, icons, dialog boxes, and so on. The standard features that you see in this menu are described in the following sections of this chapter.

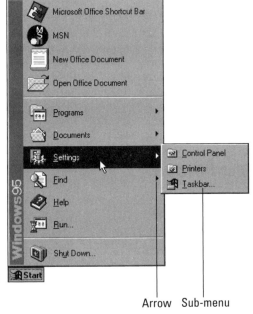

Figure 3-2:
When you point to the Settings feature, subsettings display in a submenu.

Arrow   Sub-menu

Launching Programs

In computerese, *launching* refers to getting a program up and running, just as christening a new ship means naming a ship just before putting it in the water (or something like that!). Actually, launching programs from the Windows 95 Start menu is much easier and requires a great deal less preparation than launching a ship, and you'll feel a great deal of satisfaction when you get your first program up and running.

You can launch some programs directly from the Programs submenu of the Start menu; other programs are grouped and must be launched from the group submenu. To launch programs, follow these simple steps:

1. **Display the Start menu.**

   Use one of the techniques described in "Getting Past Go: Basics of Using the Start Menu" earlier in this chapter to display the Start menu.

2. **Point to Programs.**

   A submenu of programs available on your computer appears. Your list most likely looks much different from the menu shown in Figure 3-3. Only programs installed on your computer appear in the Programs submenu. The most observant among you will realize that the Start menu shown here is different from the menu shown in graphics earlier in this chapter — I switched computers because the Programs

Group icons   Additional submenus

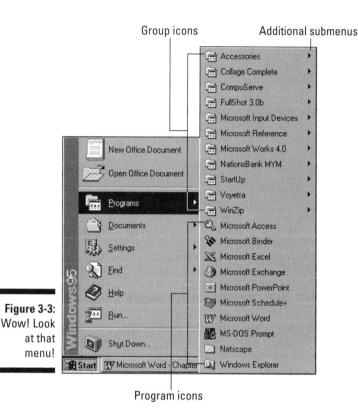

Figure 3-3:
Wow! Look
at that
menu!

Program icons

submenu on that other computer filled the entire screen! This Programs
submenu is much more manageable (and tells me it's time to clean
some programs off the other computer!).

**3. Drag the mouse to the right, and point to the program that you want
to launch.**

If you drag the mouse pointer off the word Programs in the Start menu
before moving the pointer to the submenu, you may accidentally lose
the submenu. If this happens, simply point to Programs again to
redisplay your submenu.

For practice, launch the Windows Explorer program. Your window
won't match the one pictured in Figure 3-4 exactly; again, the display
depends on what programs and pieces of hardware you have.

**4. Display the Start menu again, point to Programs, and then point to a
group icon to display a submenu of programs contained in the group.**

For practice, point to the Accessories group to display the submenu.
Figure 3-5 shows the Accessories submenu on one of my computers. If
your Accessories match mine, you get a gold star! If your submenu is
different, that's okay; we have different programs installed on our
computers.

Figure 3-4:
Ah! Your
first
successful
launch may
make you
feel like
"Exploring"!

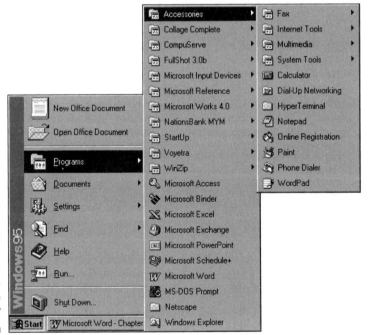

Figure 3-5:
Neat new
programs —
and *more*
groups!

Can you believe that *more groups* are listed in the Accessories submenu, which means *another* submenu? This could go on all day! What's neat about the arrangement of submenus is the way they sometimes pop out at you from a different side. For example, when there's not enough room to display a submenu on the right side of another submenu, Windows simply displays the next submenu on the left side of the other submenu (and you're probably wanting to call a substitute teacher right about now). Just watch for these surprises and smile.

5. **From the Accessories submenu, choose the program that you want to launch, or select an Accessories group and then choose a program from the sub-submenu.**

Launch additional programs until you think that you've got the hang of it; this is self-paced learning. Notice that some programs take longer to appear than others do. In general, the more powerful programs take longer because they contain more instructions that the computer has to load into RAM. (For some information on RAM, check out Chapter 1.) Just be patient and allow the computer to do its work.

When you finish practicing, close the programs that you have open by clicking the Close button (the *X* button at the right end of the title bar).

Opening Documents

The Documents feature in the Start menu displays a submenu of the last 15 documents opened on the computer. The icon next to a document identifies the program that was used to create the document.

Hanging out with your groups

If you're a Windows user from the old school (the Windows 3.*x* family), you may think that your Program Manager has deserted you. Well, in a way, it has.

Here are some tips to get you oriented:

✔ Think of the Start menu as being a sort of minimized Program Manager that you can display with a single click. (Remember the first time you tried to double-click?)

✔ Group icons in Windows 3.*x* contain program icons, and you find your groups in Windows 95 in the Programs submenu; they even look almost the same.

✔ Group icons in the Programs submenu are identified by an arrow on the right side of the submenu. Point to the group to display your program icons.

For those of you who never really got the hang of double-clicking, the new single-click method for launching programs is sure to delight you. It's designed to make you computer comfy in record time.

Choosing a document from the Documents submenu automatically launches the application and opens the document at the same time. To open a document from the Documents submenu, follow these steps:

1. **Display the Start menu and point to <u>D</u>ocuments.**

   Your Documents submenu may be empty if you haven't used your computer to open files or used programs on the computer to create files. And, of course, your documents will be different from mine (unless you copied!).

2. **Click a document in the submenu to select it.**

   The program that was used to create the document launches and displays the document. Pretty slick, huh?

Controlling Settings

The Settings feature in the Start menu displays options that enable you to set your computer up to work the way that you want it to work. Think of Settings as a way of getting your classroom ready for a new class. Table 3-1 describes the features in the Settings submenu.

Table 3-1	Your Guide to Settings Features
Feature	*Function*
Control Panel	Enables you to change settings for your monitor, mouse, keyboard, and other hardware attached to your computer. Control Panel also includes options for adding and removing hardware and software, as well as for changing the system date and time for your computer.
Printers	Enables you to tell the computer what kind of printer you have, so that it can install the correct printer instructions. (For more information about printers and printing, check out Chapter 6.)
Taskbar	Enables you to choose options that control the way that your taskbar appears and to add programs to or remove programs from the Start menu Programs submenu.

Designing your window is merely child's play

Don't worry — I'm not going to tell you which control settings to change. I'm simply going to give you an idea about *how* to change some of the settings. Think of this stuff as child's play because getting your window design set up is kinda fun.

My RAM runneth over

If you've ever seen a child pour his or her first glass of milk, you may remember holding your breath as the milk approached the top of the glass. *Someone* would have to mop the countertop and floor when the glass overflowed.

As you launch more programs, RAM fills up. But unlike a glass that overflows when it gets full, RAM tells you when it just can't take any more (information, that is). When you see a message that there is not enough memory to run the program, click the OK button in the message window to tell the computer that you read the message.

Close the programs you aren't using to free some RAM. Then try relaunching the program.

Isn't it nice to be able to throw away the mop?

To access any of the Control Panel features, you need to open the Control Panel. Follow these easy steps:

1. **Display the Start menu and point to Settings.**

   Control Panel appears at the top of the list of Settings.

2. **Choose Control Panel.**

   The Control Panel that you see resembles the one shown in Figure 3-6. Depending on the hardware that you have installed on your computer, you may see different icons.

Figure 3-6:
Look, but don't touch — changing stuff that you don't know about is dangerous!

Naming files: Acronyms or hieroglyphics?

In the old days, filenames could contain only one to eight alphanumeric characters followed by a period and three more characters. (This file-naming scheme was often referred to as the *8.3 rule.*)

Coming up with descriptive filenames seriously challenged users' creative talents! With the advent of Windows 95, however, file naming is much looser; you can use up to 255 characters to name your files. You still have to follow these rules, though:

✔ Filenames can contain a mixture of alphabetic and numeric characters and a few symbols.

✔ Most Windows 95 applications automatically add a period at the end of the filename and then attach three program-specific letters (that together are called an *extension*). Adding program extensions associates the file with the correct program, so that when you launch the file from the Documents submenu, the correct program starts.

✔ Each filename must be unique; no identical twins are allowed in the same folder.

✔ When you copy a file to a floppy disk, Windows 95 automatically clips the filename and formats according to the old 8.3 rule. A tilde (~) appears in place of the left-out characters.

Just because you *can* name files more descriptively now doesn't mean that you *have* to use long filenames. Long filenames can make the computer run slower, so feel free to revert to the old 8.3 format. The key is to make filenames meaningful so you can find them later.

A good rule of thumb: If you don't know what a feature is or what it does, leave it alone! Get some help from a computer guru before messing with features, options, buttons, and bows!

3. **Double-click the icon that represents the feature that you want to explore.**

   Just for fun, double-click the Display icon to open the Display Properties dialog box. Using the tabbed pages of the dialog box shown in Figure 3-7, you can set up a screen saver, change the background color of your desktop, or wallpaper your monitor (figuratively, of course) by changing the design that appears behind icons on the Windows 95 desktop.

   Use the scroll bars to display additional wallpaper and pattern listings, choose the effect that you want, and watch the display change so that you can preview the effect. When you find a pattern and/or wallpaper that you want to use, leave the selections highlighted.

Page tabs   Scroll bars

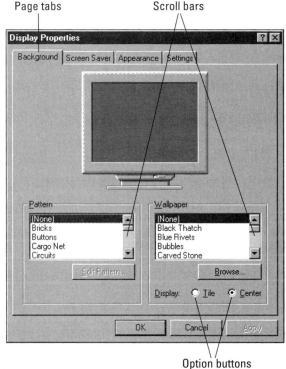

Figure 3-7:
A multiple-
page dialog
box groups
features
and options
by type.

Option buttons

4. Click a page tab for the feature that you want to display.

For practice, click the Screen Saver page tab. (*Screen savers* help preserve your monitor by displaying constantly moving objects on-screen.) The drop-down list identified in Figure 3-8 enables you to see a list of additional screen savers installed on your computer. Choose one and view the results.

You also need to tell the computer how long to wait before kicking in the screen saver. The wait time represents the time of inactivity on your computer, as in "If no one types or moves the mouse for *x* number of minutes, it's OK to start the screen saver." The *spin buttons* (the upward and downward pointing arrows beside the Wait value box) allow you to set the time.

5. Click OK.

If you want to change the color scheme of your desktop, feel free to explore the options in the Appearance page of the Display Properties dialog box. To change the resolution of your monitor, play with the settings in the Settings page.

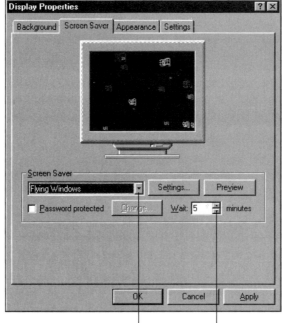

Figure 3-8:
Flying
windows?
Not like the
*Flying
Dutchman,*
is it?

Drop-down list arrow   Spin buttons

If things get into a bit of a mess, just press Esc on the keyboard or click the Cancel button in the dialog box to discard your changes. You may not want to show your students these settings. Imagine the mess that you'll end up with if all your students decide to customize the screen to meet their individual preferences! I can imagine flying fists, rather than flying windows, as students try to resolve or (shudder) compromise, can't you? On the other hand, some of your students already know — or will quickly find out — about these possibilities. You can relax, knowing that by pressing a couple of keys, you can get everything back to normal (on the computer screen, that is!).

The window that opens when you choose a feature from the Control Panel window contains different options depending on the feature that you choose. You may see a multiple-page dialog box (dialog boxes don't have menus or toolbars, remember?) with page tabs that group options, buttons, option boxes, check boxes, and so on. Choosing other features opens other windows that have additional features.

Creating a peekaboo taskbar

The taskbar that appears at the bottom of your desktop takes up screen real estate, and when you *really* start using your computer to get some work done, that screen real estate becomes more valuable. The problem is that the taskbar is important — it holds the Start button, right?

Reclaiming your screen real estate is quite simple if you follow these steps:

1. **Display the Start menu and choose Settings.**

2. **Choose Taskbar.**

   The Taskbar Properties dialog box, shown in Figure 3-9, opens. Notice that you have two pages of options to set.

Page tabs   Preview area

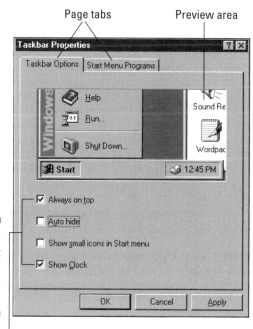

Figure 3-9:
Check out
these
taskbar
options!

Options

As you select and deselect options, active settings appear in the preview area of the dialog box. Check marks indicate active settings. You can mark a check box or remove the mark by clicking the box (using the same technique to turn an option on and off is referred to as *toggling*).

3. **Choose the options that you want to apply.**

   Just for practice, check each of the options and preview them. Then apply the Auto hide option, the Always on top option, and the Show Clock option.

4. **Click the Apply button.**

5. Click the OK button to close the dialog box.

Do you see the taskbar at the bottom of your screen? If you choose the Auto Hide option in Step 3, you won't see the taskbar until you move your mouse to the bottom of the screen; then it pops up. (See why I called it peekaboo?) Cool, huh?

Finding Things

One of the neatest club activities that my FBLA (Future Business Leaders of America) chapter sponsored was a treasure hunt — on the computer. A treasure hunt is a great way to get students acquainted with a hard-disk file structure or with the software programs installed on their computer. The activity also saves you the hassle of finding an available copier and pumping out lots of copies of review sheets. Simply type the document, save it in some remote folder on your computer, and time students to see who can find the sheet in the shortest amount of time. Then have each student open the document and print it.

The Find feature in the Start menu is your tool for searching for more than just files on your computer. You can use Find to locate a specific computer attached to your network (if you have a network) as well as information on the Microsoft Network. All you have to do is tell the computer what you want to find and where to look. Here's how:

1. Display the Start menu and choose Find.

The submenu shown in Figure 3-10 displays options that tell the computer what to find and where to look.

Figure 3-10:
Finding sends you on a treasure hunt.

2. Choose the option that identifies what you want to find.

For practice, choose Files or Folders. The window displayed in Figure 3-11 opens.

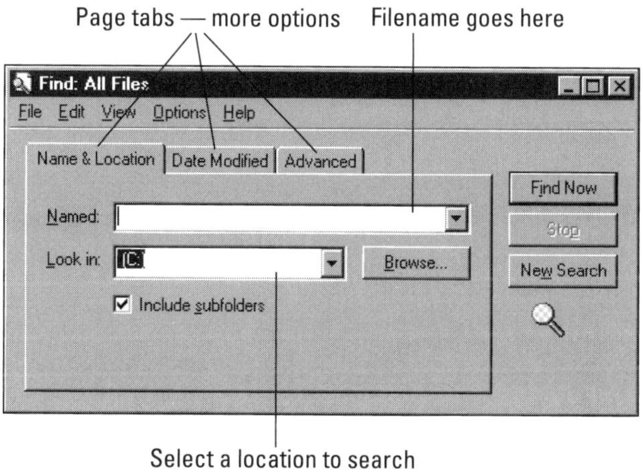

Page tabs — more options   Filename goes here

Figure 3-11:
The Find: All
Files
window —
search for
anything,
anywhere
(well,
almost!).

> **Find: All Files**
> File   Edit   View   Options   Help
>
> Name & Location | Date Modified | Advanced
>
> Named:
> Look in: [C]   ☑ Include subfolders
>
> Find Now
> Stop
> New Search
> Browse...

Select a location to search

3. Type a file name in the Named text box.

For practice, type **calculator** in the Named text box.

4. Click the drop-down list arrow next to the Look in text box and choose the drive or folder you want to search.

For practice, choose the C drive to tell the computer to look through-out the hard disk for the file you're trying to locate. If [C:/] is already displayed in the text box, you can skip this step.

5. Click the check box next to Include subfolders.

Unless it's been changed, there should already be a check mark in the check box, but it doesn't hurt to make sure that there is one.

6. Click the Find Now button to start the search.

When you start the search, the Find: Files *named whatever* window expands to display a list area at the bottom to hold the names of files with the filenames you specify. The time it takes the computer to locate your files depends, of course, on how big your hard disk is and how fast your computer works. If you're searching for *calculator,* for example, you should see results listed in the space at the bottom of the window in just a few seconds.

Wild and woolly wildcards

As your list of files grows, the chances that you'll remember the precise name of every single file that you save diminish. So there are *wildcards*.

Wildcards enable you to locate a file even if you know only part of its filename.

Unfortunately, deuces aren't wild on the computer; the asterisk (*) is. Here's how this computer wildcard works:

✔ If you know that the filename ends with the word school but aren't certain how the filename starts, enter ***school** in the Find window Named text box.

✔ If you know that the word *school* is the first word in the filename but can't recall the rest of the filename, enter **school*** in the Named text box.

✔ If you know that the filename contains the word *school* somewhere, you can enter ***school*** in the Named text box; your computer looks for all filenames that contain *school,* regardless of what text precedes or follows *school.*

If all else fails, jump up and down and shout and scream — it'll make you feel better to get a little wild yourself!

The selection you make from the Find submenu determines what Find window opens. The information you need to supply to find a computer on your network or something on the Microsoft Network will vary. Chapters 13 and 14 explore ways to locate great finds on the Microsoft Network. Be sure to check them out. And if you're trying to find a computer attached to your network, you'll need to know the computer's name so that you can enter the name in the Named text box.

Crying for Help

Imagine a classroom in which a teacher could multiply physically as many times as necessary, so that each child in the classroom received one-on-one instruction. Don't laugh — after Dolly, the cloned sheep, such actions may one day be possible! Because I'm only one person (for the time being), I can't sit beside you and guide you through your Windows 95 adventure. Windows 95, on the other hand, stays right there with you, to guide, direct, and answer your questions; all you have to do is cry "Help!"

The structure of the Help feature of Windows 95 is the same as the structure of Help in many Windows products. Learning the basics in this section can help you when you start working with different applications. Windows Help stores basic information about topics of interest and features of your computer, as well as basic steps for accomplishing many tasks.

To use Help, you must first open the Help dialog box. Here's how:

1. Display the Start menu and choose <u>H</u>elp.

The Help Topics: Windows Help dialog box opens (see Figure 3-12).

Help topics

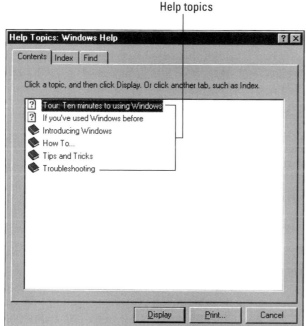

Figure 3-12:
You can cry
for Help by
using any of
three tabs.
(Contents
tab is
shown.)

2. Click the page tab for the type of help that you want to use.

Each page tab displays different options:

* The Help Contents page of the dialog box displays "books" (see the icons?) containing topics that you might find in a table of contents.

* The Help Index is an alphabetical list with all related help topics listed in groups.

* The Help Find page displays an alphabetical list of words you can use to search for help.

3. Type the topic that you want to review in the text box at the top of the Help page, or click the book icon in the Contents page that relates to your topic.

4. Choose the topic that you want to review and click <u>D</u>isplay.

The help topic that you choose appears in a window of its own. You can review the information and use the navigation buttons and features built into Help to work your way around and access additional Help topics.

Here are some things to watch for in the Help window:

- Small square buttons mixed in with steps start demos that show you how to accomplish some tasks and that perform other tasks for you.

- Buttons in the Help window toolbar take you back to the Help Topics window, return you to the preceding Help window, or display Options that enable you to print and play with the Help window.

- Green words with dotted underlining are vocabulary words; click one of these words to see a definition.

- Tips for using some of the features appear after the steps for accomplishing a task.

- Related Topics listed at the bottom of the window allow you to move directly to other Help windows when you need to investigate a topic further.

Running Around: The Run Feature

Although it may seem that the Run feature in the Start menu has you running all over your computer, the Run feature actually provides the following:

- An alternative approach to launching a program (provided that you know where to look for the commands that you need to launch the program)

- A feature that helps you install new programs on your computer

Because it's easier to launch a program from the Programs submenu, you'll rarely use the Run feature to launch programs. You will, however, use Run to install software (unless, of course, you have someone who performs this task for you).

When you choose Run from the Start menu, the Run dialog box opens (see Figure 3-13). In the Open text box, type the name of the disk drive that contains the new program disk; then click Browse to see what's on the new program disk.

Figure 3-13:
Run
programs
or install
software by
using the
Run dialog
box.

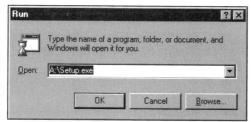

New programs usually have some type of setup program (named Setup.exe, of all things) or install program (yup, it's named Install.exe) that sets up the program on your computer. This is no small feat — it has to tell Windows 95 all about the program that you're installing so that Windows can make notes in special files contained in your System folder and so that the program runs correctly. If you tried to add these notes yourself, installing one measly little program might take you all day — and then there'd be no guarantee that it would work right!

Depending on the complexity, power, and size of the program that you're installing, setting up a new program can take just a few seconds or as much as an hour. If installing a new program takes longer than an hour, check the manual that comes with the program to see how long installing the software should take. The old "if all else fails, read the manual" approach may provide some hints that speed the installation process.

Shutting Down

Okay, it's down to the last feature — shutting down. Steps for shutting down the computer are addressed in Chapter 1 where you can become acquainted with your computer. After you develop your mouse and computer skills, you can use the mouse to display the Start menu and shut down the computer. Here's how:

1. Display the Start menu, and choose Sh<u>u</u>t Down.

The Shut Down Windows dialog box appears.

2. Choose the <u>S</u>hut Down the Computer? option.

3. Choose <u>Y</u>es.

When the bright orange message telling you that it's okay to turn off your computer appears, press the buttons, throw the switches, and don't forget to close the door on your way out.

Chapter 4

95-Style Windows Accessories

. . . .

In This Chapter

▶ Using My Computer

▶ Creating folders

▶ Using Windows 95 accessories

▶ Using the Recycle Bin

▶ Cutting, copying, and pasting

▶ Using Undo

▶ Creating shortcuts

. . . .

*H*ave you spent any time exploring Windows yet? If you have, congratulations! You've probably discovered ways to find out what's on your computer and may have even discovered some of the accessories that come with Windows 95. In this chapter, I show you how to find your way around My Computer (your computer, really — the icon is named My Computer), how to use some of the Windows 95 accessories, and how to get the most out of recycling. You have fun copying and pasting (visions of kindergarten may be flying through your mind!) and begin arranging your desktop with stuff that you'll need.

My Computer: My Pride and Joy

What I'm about to tell you may come after the fact — the fact being that you may have already been poking around and exploring some of the things that you see on the desktop. (Okay, now, 'fess up — how many of you have already been double-clicking? I'm the first to confess; I would have been double-clicking quite madly, trying to see everything all at once.)

If you read Chapter 2, you discovered that you can get a pretty good overview of your computer by looking at My Computer.

Whether you've already been exploring or have waited patiently until your teacher instructed you to do so, you should find these steps to be enlightening:

1. Click the My Computer icon on the Windows 95 desktop.

See how the icon turns blue and appears to be shadowed? It's holding its breath until you say "Go!"

2. Press Enter.

Those of you who are expert double-clickers will be delighted to know that you can open the window by double-clicking instead of pressing Enter. Whichever window-opening approach you use, the My Computer window displayed in Figure 4-1 appears.

My Computer menu   My Computer toolbar

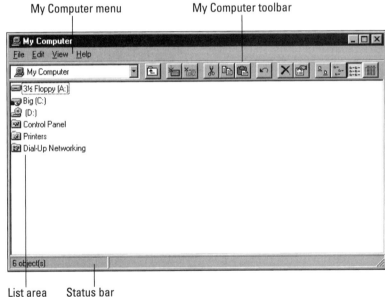

Figure 4-1:
Lots of neat
stuff shows
up in
the My
Computer
window.

List area   Status bar

If you don't see a toolbar, you can display it by choosing the View menu and selecting Toolbar. If the icons are larger than those shown in Figure 4-1, that's okay — you have a different view displayed. Change the display by choosing a different view from the View menu.

Peeking inside a folder or drive

You can consider the My Computer window to be a file room, because it serves as your access to other file cabinets (disk drives) and certain hardware equipment as well. To see what's in a different folder or stored on a disk in a disk drive, use one of the following techniques to open the folder or disk drive:

- ✔ Double-click the icon in the List area of the My Computer window.

- ✔ Click the drop-down list arrow at the right end of the Open folder/drive text box (when you point to the toolbar text box, a message box — called a *ToolTip* — appears that contains the instruction Go to a different folder) to display the list. Then select the folder or disk drive that you want to open.

When you select a folder or a disk drive, the My Computer window displays important details about the folder or drive. When you open a folder or disk drive, a list of folder or disk contents appears in the list area of the My Computer window. The folder name or disk drive name appears in the text box on the toolbar.

Try selecting and then opening one of the folders or one of the drives that's attached to your computer. To look at a folder's contents or display what's on a disk drive, follow these steps:

1. **Point to the folder or drive that you want to open, and click.**

   For practice, click the C drive.

2. **Look at the status bar to identify disk capacity.**

   The status bar identifies how much disk space is used by the files in the open folder/drive.

3. **Double-click the folder or disk drive, or press Enter, to open it.**

   Wow! If you opened the hard disk (C), exploring everything that you see listed in the My Computer window could take all day. You can continue using the double-click procedure (or clicking and pressing Enter) to open and look in additional folders. When your head starts spinning, take a break; all those folders will still be there tomorrow.

Some people prefer to think of the relationship of disk drives to main folders to subfolders to files as they think of grandparents to parents to children to grandchildren and so on. You can make this comparison as long as you don't try to marry off any files!

Exploring some more

Although the My Computer window makes accessing and opening folders on your computer or disks easy, some people prefer to explore two windows at the same time. When you want to display a list of folders on one side of the window and the list of files and subfolders contained in the open folder on the other side of the window, you may want to call on Windows Explorer.

To launch Windows Explorer, follow these steps:

1. Choose Start⇨Programs.

A list of programs installed on your computer appears.

2. Click Windows Explorer.

The window shown in Figure 4-2 appears and displays the contents of a folder on the C drive. Notice that the Exploring window is divided into two sections (one on the left and one on the right) that are referred to as panes (get it — window panes?).

Notice a couple of things about the Exploring window shown in Figure 4-2:

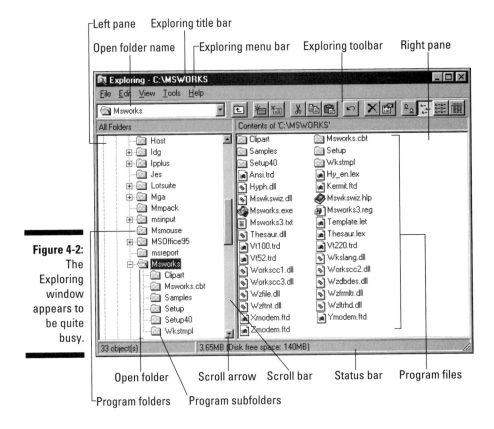

Figure 4-2:
The
Exploring
window
appears to
be quite
busy.

✔ The program and data-file folders appear in the left pane of the window.

✔ Folders containing subfolders are identified by a plus sign (+) to the left of the folder name in the left pane. Subfolders appear in the right pane before individual files.

✔ Subfolders within a main folder appear below the main folder in the left pane after you click the plus sign (+) that appears by the folder. Files that are contained in the open folder appear in the right pane along with subfolder names.

✔ The active folder is highlighted in the left pane, and the folder name appears beside the disk-drive name in the window title bar.

✔ The status bar tells you how many files appear in the right pane, how much hard disk space these files use, and how much space on the hard disk is free.

To learn more about navigation, exploring, and changing the view of Windows Explorer, pick up a copy of *Windows 95 For Teachers* by Michelle Robinette (IDG Books Worldwide, Inc.). It's packed with great tips for exploring further.

Claiming your own space: creating folders

Although you probably think that you have enough folders on your hard disk, you may have noticed that you have no special place that's all your own. What you need is a folder with your name on it where you can store your files. Eventually, you can stuff your files right into that folder so quickly that you'll never give it a second thought. Then you can create a complex filing system to separate your files by grade level, class period, subject matter, handouts, tests . . . you get the picture. This may be easier than New Year's resolutions!

You can use both the Exploring window and the My Computer window — whichever you like better — to create folders. Launch the program that you want to use and open the C drive. (If you don't know how to launch My Computer, refer to "My Computer: My Pride and Joy," earlier in this chapter. If you don't know how to launch Windows Explorer, refer to "Exploring some more," also earlier in this chapter.)

When you're ready to start, follow these easy steps:

1. **Click the C-drive icon in the Exploring window, or double-click the C icon in the My Computer window.**

   You want your folder to be a main folder on the hard disk for now, so you need to be sure that the C drive is open. If a different folder is open when you create a new folder, the new folder becomes a subfolder of the open folder, and finding your folder is a greater challenge.

2. **Choose File⇨New⇨Folder.**

   A new folder appears at the bottom of the My Computer window or at the bottom of the file list in the right pane of the Exploring window.

   The folder name will be highlighted, so typing your new folder name automatically replaces the generic text New Folder.

3. **Type your first name.**

4. **Press Enter.**

   Hurrah! You finally see your name in lights (well, pixels, really, but that's a whole different discussion). Clap your hands and say, "Yes!" (and try to do it the way that the students do, with the hand motion and everything).

Tooling Along with Windows 95 Accessories

When you think of accessories, do you picture belts, scarves, socks, and ties, or do you think Calculator, Clock, and the like? What comes to mind depends on your focus, of course. Well, I'd like your attention, please. I want to talk about computer accessories — not the ones that you find in your closet at home. You'll love the way that Windows 95 groups your accessories. You guessed it; they all appear in the Programs Accessories group.

To see what Accessories are installed on your computer, it's time to get started. Follow these steps:

1. **Choose Start⇨Programs.**

   Your Accessories group appears at the tip-top of the Programs list.

2. **Point to the Accessories group.**

   A submenu of Accessories similar to the one shown in Figure 4-3 appears.

Depending on the equipment that is attached to your system, your accessories may differ from mine. You may have more accessories; then again, you may have fewer. Certain accessories are standard, and each accessory is a program. When you want to start an accessory, all you do is point to the accessory and click; the program starts right up.

Tallying scores with Calculator

The Calculator is one of the simplest and handiest applications. Need to tally lunch money? Need to average grades? Need to figure out whether your paycheck is accurate? Simply get this fellow up and running, and these calculations are a snap. To start the application, choose Calculator from the Accessories submenu. The Calculator pad shown in Figure 4-4 opens.

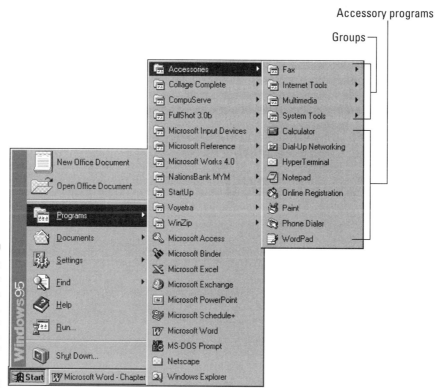

Accessory programs

Groups

Figure 4-3:
You not only have Accessories, but you also have groups of Accessories!

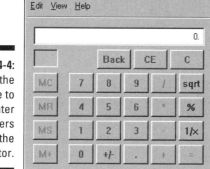

Figure 4-4:
Use the mouse to enter numbers into the Calculator.

What's really cool about the Calculator is that it allows you to use different approaches to get the calculated results that you want:

- ✔ Click the number buttons and function buttons.
- ✔ Press the numbers and function keys on the keyboard.

Because you already know how to use a calculator (I know that you've had to average grades!), operating one on the PC is relatively intuitive. Try both of the techniques described in the preceding list to see whether your Calculator program is working correctly (you know — giving you the right answers), and when you get comfy with its operation, move on to the next accessory. Seems sort of like an open classroom, doesn't it?

For now, leave the Calculator open on-screen.

Working with words — in a pad

The WordPad that comes with Windows 95 provides a simple, easy-to-use word processor. The WordPad's icon portrays the word processor as being a little stenotype notebook with the spiral binder at the top. To start the application, choose WordPad from the Accessories submenu. The WordPad opens (see Figure 4-5).

You can find out more about word processing in Part II of this book, but for now, keep these things in mind:

- ✔ The vertical bar winking at you in the top-left corner of the screen is the *insertion point,* which marks the place where characters that you type appear.

- ✔ The mouse pointer changes shape as you point to different places on-screen. The strange-looking mouse pointer shown in Figure 4-5, techni-cally called the *I-beam* (I say that it looks more like a dog bone), appears often as you work with Windows applications. The I-beam makes fitting and positioning the insertion point between two charac-ters easier.

- ✔ The ruler contains a scale that measures the typing line — not the width of the page. By default, WordPad leaves 1.25 inches for left and right margins.

- ✔ You can click a toolbar button to accomplish multiple-step tasks.

For practice, type your name (or some other equally inane text) in the WordPad window, just to get the hang of processing words. Then, if you want to practice arranging accessories on-screen, leave WordPad running, and check out the following section.

Typing point   Standard toolbar   Formatting toolbar   Ruler

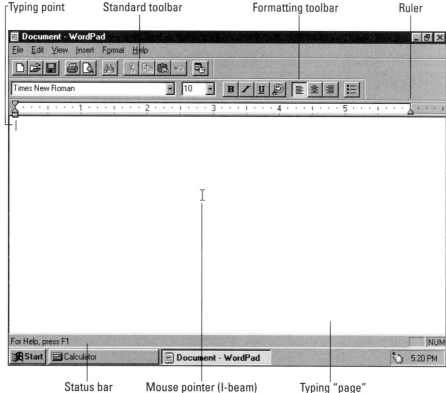

Figure 4-5:
You can
type notes
to parents
in the
WordPad
window.

Status bar   Mouse pointer (I-beam)   Typing "page"

Arranging accessories on-screen

One neat little Windows 95 trick that I discovered quite by accident is how to arrange two windows on-screen so that you can see both simultaneously, as shown in Figure 4-6. Arranging Calculator and WordPad side by side makes averaging grades on the Calculator while you're typing a note to a parent much more efficient. When you start copying and pasting in the next section, you see how this arrangement can be even more beneficial.

To get the screen that you see in Figure 4-6, try this:

1. **Close any other programs that you have running, leaving only WordPad and Calculator open.**

   Closing other programs reduces the number of programs that have to share the screen. (If you aren't certain how to close programs, see Chapter 2.)

Just thumbing around

You can "thumb through" open windows by using this key combination:

✔ While you hold down the Alt key, press and release the Tab key. When you see the program that you want, release the Alt key.

Or, for more key combo action, try this other method to run through open windows.

✔ Press Alt+Esc repeatedly until the program that you want appears in the middle of your screen.

2. **Point to a blank area of the *taskbar* (the bar that runs along the bottom of the window) and right-click.**

The shortcut menu displays taskbar options and helps you manage the screen. If you don't see the same shortcut menu, you may be pointing to a button or to the desktop. Try pointing to a blank area of the taskbar and right-clicking again.

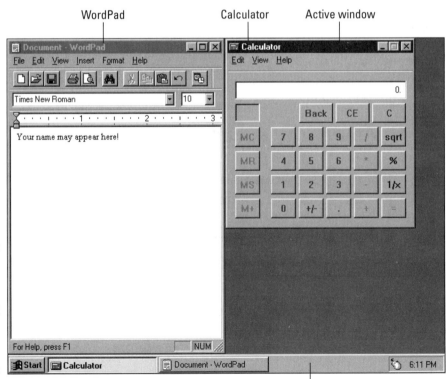

WordPad   Calculator   Active window

Figure 4-6:
See whether you can get your screen to look like mine.

Task bar

3. Choose Tile <u>V</u>ertically.

Voilà! The screen splits (tiles) vertically and divvies up the screen space among all open programs. Can you guess how these programs would appear if you had chosen Tile <u>H</u>orizontally? You got it — one program would appear at the top of the screen and the other would appear at the bottom of the screen. Of course, if you have more programs open, the amount of space each program is entitled to is significantly reduced.

Cutting, Copying, and Pasting

Everyone has to go back to elementary school to understand cutting, copying, and pasting. I'm not trying to insult your intelligence; I'm merely trying to differentiate between two basic techniques so that you understand what happens when you choose one technique over the other. The difference between cutting and copying? Back to basics for a quick review:

- ✔ Cutting removes information (pictures, text, data, formulas, and so on) from its current location, so that you can paste it somewhere else instead.

- ✔ Copying leaves information (pictures, text, data, formulas, and so on) where it is and allows you to paste it somewhere else.

Clipping stuff on the Clipboard

Have you ever coached little kids on a sports team? Remember the wonderful clipboard that you used to keep the roster straight and to keep track of who was doing what (or who's on first)? Normally, you recorded your roster and handed it to the referee, umpire, or other official so that he or she could record it. Sometimes, the official returned your roster; sometimes, the official kept your roster as an "official" paper. Either way, you'd put a clean sheet of paper on your clipboard and continue with the next cause of concern: player performance.

Windows incorporates a similar concept to hold the stuff that you cut or copy. You can launch Clipboard Viewer (a program in the Accessories group) to see what's on the computer Clipboard — but most of the time, you won't need to bother, because opening the Clipboard Viewer is more time-consuming than pasting and undoing are.

A temporary holding area in your computer, the *Clipboard* stores one electronic "piece of paper" at a time (not to be confused with one page of text on a word processor; the Clipboard can store many pages, as long as they are all cut or copied at the same time). Anything that you cut or copy from one program is stored on the Clipboard until you cut or copy something else. The new stuff that you cut or copy replaces whatever was already on the Clipboard. Always be careful, then, that you paste the first material before you cut or copy something else.

Don't confuse cutting and copying with inserting and deleting. Typing text that appears somewhere else is *not* the same as copying, and deleting text is *not* the same as cutting. Deleting does not place stuff on the Clipboard; text must be cut or copied to the Clipboard. If the text is not on the Clipboard, you can't paste it. If you delete it, it's gone; if you cut or copy it, it's in temporary storage, waiting for you to claim it.

Selecting text

To cut or copy text, pictures, formulas, and so on, you first must select the information. WordPad provides a convenient work area for you to practice text-selection techniques. Before exploring these techniques, you must type some text. Go ahead and type something — your name, the name of your school, or whatever you want.

Not everyone prefers to use the same technique to select text and other objects. As a result, you can choose among several text-selection options. The option that you choose depends on how well you and your mouse are getting along. (Have you given it a name yet?) Try each of the following techniques to see which one you like best:

✔ Position the I-beam on the word that you want to select and double-click to highlight the word.

✔ If your insertion point is at the end of the text, hold down the Shift key while you press the Home key to highlight all text from the insertion point to the left margin.

✔ If your insertion point is at the beginning of the line of text, hold down the Shift key and then press End to highlight all text to the end of the line.

✔ To highlight a character at a time, press Shift and then press one of the arrow keys until the text that you want to select is highlighted.

✔ If more than one line of text appears, triple-click (be sure to hold your tongue between your teeth just right to master this technique) to select the complete paragraph.

✔ Position the I-beam just before the first character you want to select, click and drag the I-beam across the text you want to select. When you try this technique for the first time, you'll know why I put it last!

All right — two thumbs up (especially if you're beginning to think that you're *all* thumbs). Now that the text is selected, be careful what key you press — you're in replace mode. Pressing any key on the keyboard automatically removes selected text and replaces it with the character that you type. Even pressing the Enter key removes the selected text. Now, do you think that this caution is going to prevent accidents from happening? Of course — *not*. But magic is on the way. Check out "Using Undo: Your Very Best Friend," later in this chapter.

Clipping, snapping, and pasting text

 Okay, you know the difference between cutting and copying, but the procedure that you use to cut or copy something to the Clipboard is different. Try each of the following two procedures and watch what happens.

To copy something to the Clipboard, follow these steps:

1. **Click the WordPad window anywhere to make it active and type some text.**

   When you type calculations on the computer, use the asterisk (*) to indicate multiplication, the slash (/) to represent division, the caret (^) to raise to a power, and so on.

   For practice, type the calculation $6*8-4/2+9^2$. You need something that you can paste to a different application later.

   If you make a mistake, simply press the Backspace key to remove the error and then type the correct character.

2. **Select the text.**

   Use one of the techniques described in "Selecting text" earlier in this chapter to select your formula.

 3. **Click the toolbar Copy button or choose Edit⇨Copy.**

   You may prefer to use the keyboard shortcut Ctrl+C to perform the Copy command. You see the shortcut listed beside the Copy command in the Edit menu.

Your text stays highlighted when you copy; you may think that nothing happened. To see whether there's anything in the Clipboard, try to paste.

To paste the Clipboard's contents into the document, follow these steps:

1. **Press the End key to move the insertion point to the end of the typed line to remove the highlighting.**

2. **Press Enter to move to a new line.**

3. Click the toolbar Paste button (do you like the little clipboard?) or choose Edit⇨Paste.

Lo and behold, as if by magic, your text appears again. Is the text still on the Clipboard? You bet. Your formula stays in the Clipboard until you cut or copy something else. And did you notice the Ctrl+V shortcut for Paste? It's like an inverted caret — the tip that I give students to help them remember this particular shortcut.

4. Press Enter again, but this time try pressing Ctrl+V.

Your formula appears again.

You can create answer sheets for your tests by using the copy, cut, and paste techniques. I find these techniques to be extremely useful for creating tests that need several blanks for true/false or multiple-choice answers, for instance, or for duplicating instructions from one version of a test to another. (And you thought that cutting, copying, and pasting were such elementary things!) If you want to see what happens when you cut text, type some new text, select it, and click the toolbar Cut button (you guessed it — the Cut button has scissors on it!). Then paste the cut text into the document, just to see that the cut text replaces the copied text in the Clipboard.

What's even neater is that you can paste anything that's in the Clipboard into other Windows applications. All Windows applications share the Clipboard, which means that they also share its information. If you have a formula in your WordPad, try copying it to the Clipboard again. Then launch the Calculator program (if it isn't open), paste the formula into the Calculator, and click the equal sign (=).

Remember that the stuff you copy is held in the Clipboard only until you cut or copy something else.

Using Undo: Your Very Best Friend

Sometimes, you perform an action and then wish that you hadn't — such as your students do when they shout out an answer without being called on. Accidents happen, and when they do, don't panic; you can reverse the action by using a really, really great feature called *Undo*. Undo is so useful that it even has its own keyboard shortcut: Ctrl+Z.

1. Open the WordPad, if it isn't already open, and type some text.

If you already have text displayed in the WordPad page, just use it.

2. Press Ctrl+Z to undo the action.

Your text goes away if you just typed it. If you're using text from a previous activity, whatever you last typed or copied to the page disappears. If your last action before using Undo was cutting text from the page, the text appears again.

The Undo feature is available for most applications; you can sometimes even reverse more than the last action. Right now, if you undo your last action, you are actually undoing your undo, which means that your last action is redone and your text is placed back where you just removed it. (Want that explanation again?)

Test time: See whether you can find the Undo command in one of the WordPad menus.

Closing Applications and Answering Questions

By closing each application before you turn off your machine, you sort of tuck everything back into its designated place. Closing each application helps ensure that everything is where you expect it to be when you need it again. Organizing your computer desktop is much easier than organizing your *real* desk.

To exit (close, land, or whatever you want to call it) an application, use one of these techniques:

- Click the application's Close button.
- Press Alt+F4.
- Click the application icon in the upper left corner of the title bar and then choose Close.
- Double-click the application icon.
- Choose File⇨Exit, if that command is available.

Remember that minimizing an application window does not close the application. Minimizing merely reduces the window to a button in the taskbar but leaves the application running. A running application takes up memory and may limit the other applications that you can launch.

Go ahead and choose a method for closing the Calculator application. Done? Move on to the WordPad, and choose a different method to close it.

What happens when you try to close the WordPad? A message box like the one shown in Figure 4-7 appears.

Figure 4-7:
Message
boxes need
to be
answered.

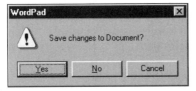

Most applications display a message window similar to Figure 4-7 any time you add information or change information in a document. (The Calculator doesn't allow you to save your formulas, so you do not get a message when you close it.)

Because the text that you typed in the WordPad has no real significance, go ahead and choose No to tell WordPad that you don't want to save your work.

All done?

Recycling: A Fickle Person's Friend

The Recycle Bin displayed on your Windows 95 desktop can become one of your best friends. The Recycle Bin stores all the documents, program files, and folders that you "throw away" (that is, delete), so it's sort of like your trash can (the one that the janitor remembers to empty only when you need to get something out of it first thing in the morning). The Recycle Bin is empty until you throw away your first document or program.

You won't have to worry about the janitor's emptying your Recycle Bin, however, because *you* control when it is emptied. Unlike retrieving a paper that accidentally falls off the desk into the trash can, you can retrieve anything that you accidentally delete from the hard disk — until you dump the trash. The Recycle Bin is recyclable; you can dump the entire contents of the Recycle Bin back onto the hard disk or select individual documents and programs. You probably will find that you don't need to recycle something until *after* you empty the bin, however. (Is that a new Murphy's Law?)

What you may have to worry about is that the Recycle Bin will fill up, taking up valuable hard disk space. I checked my Recycle Bin recently and found that I deleted 682 documents and programs, which totaled 43.8MB of hard-disk space. (Whew — I thought that I was about out of room on my hard disk.) Because I'm sure (ahem) that I won't need these files again, I can empty the Recycle Bin and free extra hard-disk space.

You can open the Recycle Bin by double-clicking on the Recycle Bin icon on the Windows 95 desktop and explore a bit. If you see something you want to retrieve, simply drag the file icon onto the desktop or right click on the file and choose Restore. Choosing Restore sends the file back to the folder it came from. To empty the Recycle Bin, choose File⇨Empty Recycle Bin — and then hold your breath that no one wants something that was in the trash.

Customizing the Desktop: Creating Shortcuts

The keyboard shortcuts I describe in Chapter 2 and list on the Cheat Sheet that came with your book are written by programmers who write Windows programs. Windows 95 offers you the opportunity to create some shortcuts of your own and to place them smack-dab in the middle of your desktop so that you know where to find them.

Locating program files

The challenge of creating shortcuts is locating the program file for the program that you need. A little trial and error may help. But trial and error works, of course, only if your logic agrees with the programmer's logic (and my dad says that my logic doesn't agree with anyone's).

Review the following tips for locating a program file before you begin your search:

- ✔ Program files carry an .exe or .com *extension* (the three characters that follow the period).

- ✔ Program files are often identified by the program icon that appears in the Programs submenu.

- ✔ Accessories and standard Windows programs usually are in your Windows 95 folder.

- ✔ If you're looking for a program file for an application that's not installed with Windows 95, look at the file folders on the C drive carefully, and try to determine which one contains the program that you want. I know, I know — the folder names are significantly abbreviated.

- ✔ Sometimes, applications are grouped under a software-company name, such as MSAps for Microsoft Applications or LotusAps for Lotus Applications.

✔ If you're pretty sure that you're in the correct folder but don't see the program file, look in one of the folders inside the folder. Generally, the program file contains the first couple of letters (or maybe the first letter) of each word in the name by which the program is commonly known. The file may also carry the name of the company that developed the program. Microsoft Works, for example, is in the MSWorks folder and carries the program name MSWorks.exe.

✔ Sometimes displaying the file details helps identify file types. Click the Details button on the Browse, My Computer, or Exploring window toolbar, select a file, and review the file details to determine if it's a program file.

Creating a shortcut

You need to be able to scroll in the following steps, so if you aren't familiar with this technique, refer to Chapter 3. To create a shortcut, open the My Computer window and then complete the following steps:

1. **Double-click the C drive in the My Computer window.**

   A list of all folders on the C drive appears.

2. **Scroll the window until you see the folder that most likely contains the program file; then double-click the folder to open it.**

   For practice, open the folder named Win95, Windows 95, or Windows. You're going to create a shortcut for a program that we all have on our computers.

   Now, if the school guru or the person who set up your system is witty or ornery, he or she may have hidden the Windows 95 stuff in a folder with a different name. If all else fails, ask whoever set up your system where he or she put your Windows files.

3. **Scroll the folder contents again until you see the program filename, or open another folder and search its contents.**

   Look for the little Calculator icon, followed by Calc.exe, if you're following along with the practice activity. If you're creating a shortcut on your own, continue to open folders until you find the file that most likely represents the program that you're trying to find. If you have no idea what the program file looks like, review "Locating program files" earlier in this chapter.

4. **Point to the program name and right-click.**

   The shortcut menu shown in Figure 4-8 appears.

5. **Click Create Shortcut.**

   The window jumps to the end of the file and document list and identifies the shortcut that you just created as Shortcut to Calc.exe.

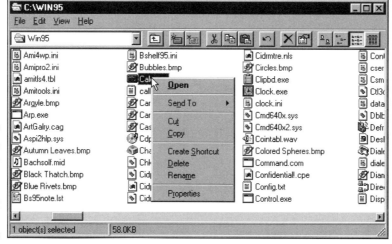

Figure 4-8:
Right-
clicking
displays a
shortcut
menu.

The Calculator icon appears. The arrow in the white box indicates that the icon is a shortcut to the program (see the figure that follows). An arrow appears on each icon that has a shortcut.

The problem now is that the shortcut icon is in the My Computer window, and you want it to be on the desktop. You can use a couple of methods to get the shortcut on the desktop; for right now, try my favorite technique.

6. **Drag the shortcut icon onto the desktop and drop it.**

   When you get the shortcut icon on the desktop, you can position the icon anywhere. To use the shortcut to launch the program, simply double-click the icon right there on the desktop.

You'll want to create additional shortcuts to make accessing your most frequently used applications easier. Before you know it, your desk will be as messy . . . I mean, as colorful . . . as mine!

Chapter 5

Breaking through Windows: The 3.*x* Family

. . . .

In This Chapter

▶ Ten distinctive features of Windows 3.*x*

▶ Ten features that originated in Windows 3.*x*

▶ Identifying Windows' standard screen features

▶ Opening and closing windows

▶ Manipulating windows

▶ Using the File Manager

. . . .

Keeping up with the Microsofts, Lotuses, and WordPerfects is like trying to keep up with the Joneses! It's a fact — not every school upgrades its computers every time something new comes up. That's okay — a school's got to do what a school's got to do (which usually translates into what it has the money for).

I recently had to make a choice about which version of Windows to reinstall on my son's computer. (Someone had messed around with some of the Windows files — someone who didn't know what he was doing!) Because my son doesn't have a CD-ROM drive and the programs he uses most often were designed for the Windows 3.*x* environment, the decision was easy to make. I couldn't afford to purchase a complete new system, and the 6-year-old computer that he's using isn't powerful enough to support a CD-ROM drive. Windows 3.1 went on quite nicely.

If you are finding success by using the hardware and software that you've had since Windows first hit the scene, there's no reason to worry about upgrading — yet. Eventually, you'll want to catch up.

For right now, though, I want to provide an overview of the features that you'll find if you're working in the Windows 3.*x* environment.

Ten Distinctive Features of Windows 3.x

Looking at a different version of Windows is like walking into a different classroom in your school; the environment is totally different, but it's still recognizably a classroom. Before you get too deeply into the nitty-gritty features of the Windows 3.x environment, I thought you might like to see an overview of what you can expect to find. I narrowed the following list down to ten basic differences between Windows 3.x and Windows 95 (no easy task, as you will see):

- ✔ A Program Manager oversees your computer; it hogs the desktop.
- ✔ Groups and programs appear in the Program Manager window instead of in menus.
- ✔ The application or document title is centered in the title bar.
- ✔ The Maximize and Minimize buttons contain arrows.
- ✔ Filenames are limited to the 8.3 format — see Chapter 3 for more detailed information.
- ✔ Windows 3.x has no Recycle Bin.
- ✔ There's no Taskbar.
- ✔ Windows 3.x has no Close button.
- ✔ Windows 3.x requires more double-clicking to get things going.
- ✔ Windows 3.x products are DOS enhancers, not operating systems.

The term *DOS enhancer* means that Windows uses the features available in DOS, but it reformats and organizes the information so that it appears graphically (as pictures) on-screen.

When Windows 3.x first came onto the scene, this graphical environment was much more welcoming and less intimidating than its plain predecessor (the old DOS C:\>, which is commonly referred to as the *C prompt*). Students of all ages and grade levels responded much more readily to this graphical environment than they did to the C prompt. The result? Enhanced learning.

Ten Features That Survived the Transition to Windows 95

The phrase "survival of the fittest" may have been coined to refer to the animal kingdom, but it also describes some of the features that survived the transition from Windows 3.x to Windows 95. Look for these old faithfuls in both environments:

✔ Windows Clipboard, which stores the last item that was cut or copied.

✔ Menus that group features by category and display the same symbols (ellipses, and so on).

✔ Toolbars for easy access to the most frequently used menu commands.

✔ Keyboard shortcut keys to make accomplishing tasks easy for good typists.

✔ Maximize and Minimize buttons.

✔ Accessories that you know and love.

✔ File Manager — but it's operating under a new name, Windows Explorer, in Windows 95 and has changed somewhat. Many people think that My Computer is the File Manager's new name so the differences they see are more extensive. Review Chapter 4 for more details.

✔ Control Panel (for customizing your desktop).

✔ Program icons to identify applications and the documents that they create.

✔ Common file extensions (.doc, .exe, .com, and so on).

✔ Undo (your very best friend).

The Windows family

These versions make up the Windows family:

✔ Windows 3.0 started the migration into the GUI environment and made users greedy for additional capabilities.

✔ Windows 3.1 came next and tried to satisfy the needs of those greedy users. This version did a good job, but then people started connecting all their office computers to enable them to communicate (a process called *networking*).

✔ Windows 3.11, which is also called Windows for Workgroups, came along, offering networking features for small businesses.

But — you guessed it — larger businesses that had bigger networks and more computers needed something more: Expanded capabilities.

Something bigger. More powerful. Prettier pictures. Are users ever satisfied? As a result, programmers (those people who have the unenviable task of trying to satisfy everyone's wants) went back to work and developed two additional products:

✔ Windows NT (New Technology) tried to satisfy larger businesses' networking needs.

But guess what came next? Yep, Microsoft went back to the drawing board to design something even more user-friendly, to make productivity easier for new users.

✔ The result was Windows 95 (and guess what year this release came out?). Explore the features of Windows 95 in Chapters 1 through 4.

What Does Windows Look Like?

Windows 3.*x* contains many of the standard features found in Windows 95. Similar features perform similar functions in both the Windows 3.*x* and Windows 95 environments.

Look at the opening Windows screen shown in Figure 5-1. Recognize any familiar faces?

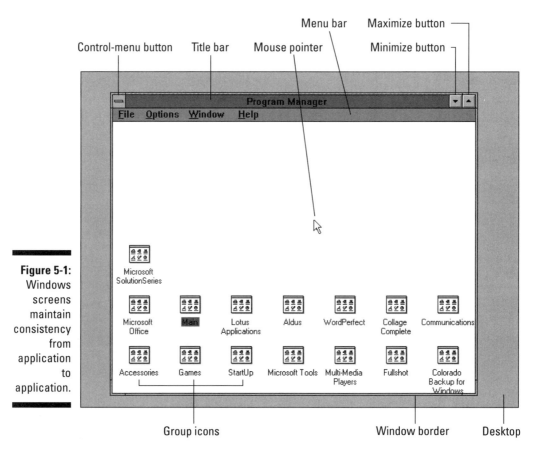

Figure 5-1:
Windows
screens
maintain
consistency
from
application
to
application.

Table 5-1 provides an overview of the features of the Windows 3.1 window.

Table 5-1	Window Features for Windows 3.x
Feature	*What It Does*
Control menu button	Activates a list of things that you can do to control the window. By using this button, you can close, maximize, and minimize the window; switch to other windows; and move the window.
Desktop	Provides working space and a background for your Windows. Compare the desktop with the top of your desk, and visualize each window as being neat and orderly file folders lying on your desk.
Group icons	Store programs and other information in groups, according to the types of programs on your system. Each group appears neatly arranged in the Program Manager window, and you can open the group and get what you want when you want it. You use the Program Manager to manage these groups.
Maximize and Minimize	Provide an easy way to enlarge (maximize) or shrink buttons (minimize) a window. The down arrow minimizes the window so that you can see what's behind it; the up arrow maximizes the window as far as the *workspace* (the entire desktop or screen) allows.
Menu bar	Groups and organizes related commands in categories. Each item in a menu is called a *command* because it tells, or commands, the computer to do something.
Mouse pointer	Points to icons, menus, and other features so that you can select them.
Title bar	Contains an application (program) name, group name, or document name.
Window borders	Allow you to size the window by dragging a border.

Working with Windows

When you're ready to start opening and closing windows, you may think that windows are more like doors; you often have to open several windows to find the window that you want. If you're on speaking terms with your mouse, you'll find opening windows to be a good way to hone your double-clicking skills. (For an overview of mouse techniques, refer to Chapter 2.)

Try opening a window, minimizing it, and then restoring it. Follow these easy steps:

1. **Double-click the Main group icon.**

   The Main window shown in Figure 5-2 opens within the Program Manager window. The Main window contains icons that open more windows. The Main window is simply a holding place for a group of related program icons (thus, the name *group window*).

Control-menu button   Program icon   Title bar   Minimize/Maximize button

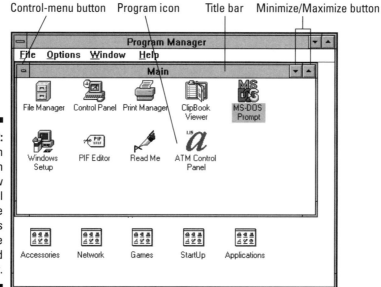

Figure 5-2:
The open
Main
window
shows all
the
programs
that are
grouped
together.

2. **Point to the Minimize button (the down arrow) at the right end of the Main title bar.**

   Be careful. Two Minimize buttons — one for the Program Manager window and one for the Main window — are on-screen. If you click the wrong Minimize button, the whole system may appear to go nuts.

3. **Click the Minimize button.**

   The Main window closes, but the Program Manager window is still on-screen.

If you clicked the wrong Minimize button in Step 3, you may see a blank screen — I mean a *totally* blank screen, except for a small icon in the screen's bottom-left corner. You've actually minimized the Program Manager window (see the words *Program Manager* below the icon?) and cleared the screen. Never fear; you aren't the first to make this mistake. Simply double-click the Program Manager icon to get the Program Manager window back.

Launching a program

Launching programs in Windows 3.*x* is somewhat different from launching programs in Windows 95. You can, however, use several alternative techniques to launch an application in Windows 3.*x*.

To launch an application, use one of the following techniques:

✔ Double-click the application icon (you have to open the group that contains the icon first, of course).

✔ Click the application icon, and press Enter on the keyboard.

✔ Use the arrow keys to highlight the application name, and press Enter.

If you want to practice using some additional window features, try opening another group window and then maximizing it. You see the group window fill the Program Manager window. Maximize the Program Manager to see how you can blot out the rest of your desktop. Don't you wish that blocking out the top of the desk in your classroom was that easy?

Using File Manager

The File Manager from the Windows 3.*x* environment changed its name when it moved to Windows 95 in which, as you may recall, it goes by the name Windows Explorer. The File Manager window shown in Figure 5-3 may give you a sense of déjà vu.

File Manager is your tool for locating things on your computer and for viewing the structure of folders and subfolders, down to the lowliest document. File Manager also can help you perform housekeeping tasks, such as setting up a new folder to hold your work, reorganizing and rearranging things on your hard disk, and removing unwanted files and folders.

Opening File Manager

Okay, it's time to get this File Manager up and running. Ready? Follow these steps:

1. **Double-click the Main group icon in the Program Manager.**

2. **Double-click the File Manager icon.**

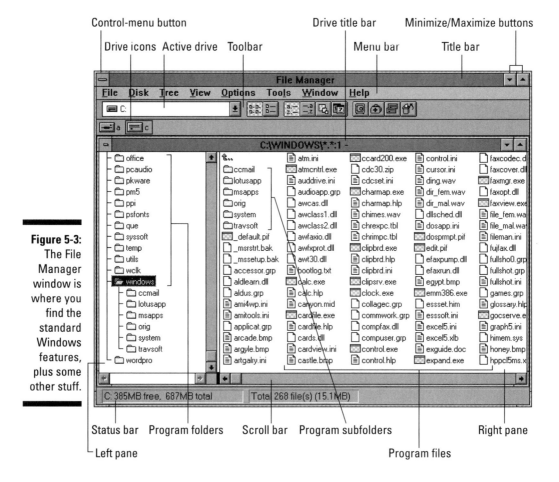

Control-menu button

Drive icons Active drive Toolbar

Drive title bar Minimize/Maximize buttons

Menu bar Title bar

Figure 5-3:
The File
Manager
window is
where you
find the
standard
Windows
features,
plus some
other stuff.

Status bar Program folders Scroll bar Program subfolders Right pane

Left pane Program files

The File Manager window automatically opens in the maximize mode
(unless someone else has been poking around on your computer and
changed its appearance). Does your File Manager look exactly like the
one shown in Figure 5-3? I doubt that it does; the chances are slim that
you have exactly the same programs installed in exactly the same
folders.

Using toolbars

Notice a couple of things about the File Manager window shown in Figure 5-3:

- The program and data-file folders appear on the left side of the window
  in the figure.
- Subfolders within a main folder appear on the right side of the screen,
  along with files that are contained in the folder.

✔ The active folder is highlighted in the left pane, and the folder name appears beside the disk-drive name in the drive title bar.

✔ The status bar tells you how big the hard disk is, how much of the hard disk is free, and how many files appear in the right pane.

Most Windows 3.*x* applications contain the same types of toolbars that you see in Windows 95 applications. Notes called ToolTips or ScreenTips identify the purpose of each button in the toolbar. To display the tip, point to a toolbar button and pause; the tip appears automatically.

Navigating File Manager

The folders on your hard disk may be too numerous to list in the left pane of the File Manager window. To display additional folders, use the scroll bar that appears between the two panes. Here are a few tips that you will find handy while working with your File Manager:

✔ Double-click a folder to open it. An open folder looks as though its mouth is hanging open.

✔ The list of files and folders that appears in the right pane changes as you open different folders.

✔ The list of folders on your hard disk is called the *disk tree* because it so closely resembles a family tree. Change the appearance of the tree by choosing options from the View menu; then stick with the design that you like best.

Creating folders

Although you probably think that you have enough folders on your hard disk, if you think about all the paper folders that you use in the course of a class year, you'll know that at some time, you're going to need another folder. When you do, the File Manager can help you create the folder.

To create a new folder, follow these steps:

1. **Open the folder in which you want to the new folder to appear.**

   Scroll to the top of the left pane of File Manager, and click the C-drive icon for practice. That way, your folder appears among other folders on your hard disk, where it's easier to find.

2. **Choose File⇨Create Directory.**

The Create Directory dialog box appears (see Figure 5-4). A *dialog box* requires a response (a dialogue, if you will) before the box disappears from the screen. The dialog box has buttons that you can click to take an action, as well as spaces in which you can type information.

3. Type the folder name in the Name text box.

4. Press Enter or click OK.

Notice that the OK button has a dark border, which means that the button is active. You can *activate* an active button (make it carry out its action) by pressing Enter.

Figure 5-4:
Be creative with your folder names when you enter them into this dialog box.

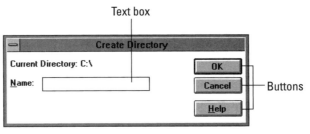

Go ahead and create folders for all your students, if you have time. That way, the folders will be ready and waiting when the students need them.

Using Windows 3.x Accessories

Many of the accessories that are available in Windows 95 originated in Windows 3.*x*. You'll find the handy Calculator, the Clock, and a mini word processor called the Notepad (it, too, appears to have changed its name when it moved to Windows 95). You'll find these accessories in the Accessories group in the Program Manager window.

To launch accessories, you first need to open the Accessories group to display the window shown in Figure 5-5. Do your accessories match mine?

Depending on the equipment that is attached to your system, your accessories may differ from mine. When you want to start an accessory, all you do is double-click the accessory icon. You can, of course, use one of the alternative approaches to launching windows mentioned in the "Launching a program" sidebar earlier in this chapter.

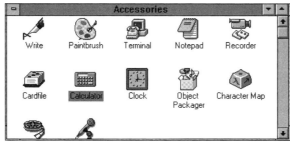

Figure 5-5:
Your
Accessories
group may
differ from
mine.

Launch the Calculator and Notepad programs, and compare them with the Calculator and WordPad programs discussed in Chapter 4. Here's what you'll find:

✔ The Calculator program operates the same way in Windows 3.*x* that it does in Windows 95. You can use the mouse to click the numbers and functions in the Calculator window that works like a little hand-held calculator. You can also type values by using the number keys on your keyboard. Use the +, –, *, and / keys to create formulas.

✔ The Notepad is slightly less sophisticated than the WordPad, which was beefed up for the move to Windows 95. The basic typing and editing functions remain the same, however. You can still select text and cut or copy it to the Clipboard, but you have to use the menus; Notepad doesn't have a toolbar. Thank goodness you can still paste; you can use Notepad to create those answer sheets!

Feel free to investigate additional accessories to determine how you can use them.

Closing Applications

By closing each application before you turn off your machine, you sort of tuck everything back into its designated place. Closing each application helps ensure that everything is where you expect it to be when you need it again. Who wants to come back the next day to a messy desktop?

To exit (close, land, or whatever you want to call it) an application (yes, even File Manager), use one of these techniques:

✔ Press Alt+F4.

✔ Click the application's Control menu button and then choose <u>C</u>lose.

✔ Double-click the application's Control menu button.

✔ Choose <u>F</u>ile⇨E<u>x</u>it, if available.

Go ahead and choose a method for closing the programs that you have open. Be adventuresome; choose a different technique for each open program.

All done? Not quite. You also need to close Program Manager and exit Windows. Use whatever method you prefer for closing windows to close the Program Manager. The system asks whether you're sure that you want to quit. I'm sure that you really don't want to, but humor me; go ahead and answer OK.

When you close Windows, you see the elusive C prompt — something that you don't see in Windows 95 — and that's your signal to power down your computer. Recess!

Chapter 6

Getting the Fax about Printers

· ·

In This Chapter

▶ Identifying types of printers

▶ Setting up printers

▶ Friendly fonts

▶ Printing to printers and fax machines

· ·

*1*n the olden days, whenever you wanted to type anything, you rolled a piece of plain typing paper into the typewriter and typed away. When you needed to make changes, you typed your work again . . . and again . . . and again. You probably even tried to cram as much information as possible into every page of your review sheet to avoid running so many different dittos. (Remember those lovely purple days?)

Well, just as graduating from the ditto machine to a copy machine of some type simplified your life, moving from the typewriter to the computer enhances the appearance of your printed words. And you can throw away the erasers, the razor blades, and the correction fluid (on second thought, better keep a bottle of it handy for emergencies) when you use a printer.

This chapter isn't designed to tell you everything about printers, fax machines, fonts, or even printing. But you can discover the basics — what you *really* need to know so that you can talk intelligently about what you have and use it to get your job done.

If you need more information than this book gives you, don't hesitate to check out *PCs For Dummies* (IDG Books Worldwide, Inc.). Dan Gookin gives you more than just the bare bones. And if all else fails, you can read the manual and other materials that came with your printer.

Printers 101

The *printer* is the piece of hardware that actually holds the paper and rolls it into the printer automatically. That's pretty basic. But printers come in all sizes, shapes, configurations, types, and prices. You may have a printer already assigned to you by your school's technology coordinator. If not, you may get to buy one on your own — with guidance, of course, from the person who's in change of heavy equipment.

How do you know which printer to buy? You most likely choose the printer that you (or your school) can afford. Always keep in the back of your mind, though, what types of items you want to print.

This chapter explores three basic types of printers used with PCs:

- ✔ Dot-matrix printers
- ✔ Inkjet printers
- ✔ Laser printers

The following sections describe the characteristics and costs of each type of printer.

Dot-matrix: a slow, low-cost, low-quality printer

Dot-matrix printers print by firing pins out of the print head so that the pins strike the ribbon, which in turn strikes the paper. The series of dots (get it? *dot*-matrix) that appears on the paper actually forms the characters. Imagine how many times the pins flash in and out just to print one page.

Putting a bunch of dots together to form characters sometimes results in odd-looking character formation. As a result, some later dot-matrix printers have an NLQ mode. *NLQ* stands for *near letter quality*. When this mode is active, the printer double-strikes (the pins work overtime) each character, with the second dot placed in the space between two original dots. Thus, the dots are closer together, and the characters look more normal.

Here's more information about dot-matrix printers:

- ✔ The dot-matrix printer is the least expensive type of printer.
- ✔ The printer uses a ribbon, which marks it as a low-maintenance item. Ribbons last almost forever and cost very little.
- ✔ Dot-matrix printers are noisy because the pin hits the ribbon, which in turn hits the paper.
- ✔ Dot-matrix printers are slow (and I mean *slow!*).
- ✔ You can use low-cost paper in a dot-matrix printer without affecting print quality.
- ✔ You can get a good dot-matrix printer for less than $200 (or a used one for much less).

Driving Miss Printer

Dot-matrix printers were state-of-the-art equipment for many years, because they were the only type of printer that most schools could afford. As a result, you may find a dot-matrix printer in the storage closet of your school. You may even have one attached to your computer, and if you're running Windows 3.*x*, your dot-matrix printer is likely still working.

If you've moved on to the Windows 95 environment, however, you may find that your dot-matrix printer is a challenge to get running again. Why? Because of the driver.

To get a printer on speaking terms with your computer, you need a driver. Most of the

drivers needed to run dot-matrix printers were discarded in Windows 95 because of the infiltration of inkjet printers (described in the following section). As a result, you may have to contact the company that made your printer to see whether it has a driver (a set of instructions) that can handle the sophisticated engine (Windows 95).

Better yet, check out the company's Internet address to see whether the company posted the driver (placed a copy of the file on the Internet) that you need. Downloading a driver from a Web site is infinitely less time-consuming than requesting it by mail.

Dot-matrix printers provide a giant leap forward for teachers who are still using the old typewriter — no more sloppy corrections, strikethroughs, and typeovers!

Inkjet: a faster, low-cost, higher-quality printer

Inkjet printers, which print by spraying a fine mist of ink onto the page, once were considered to be unreliable and extremely messy; they often malfunctioned, and ink was often known to spit out at you — making messy dresses a routine part of the owner's day. That situation has changed, however. Inkjet printers are among the most reliable and popular printers today.

Some of the qualities you'll find with inkjet printers include:

- ✔ Inkjet printers provide a clean, clear image on the page.
- ✔ Thanks to their popularity, inkjet printers are available from a wide variety of manufacturers.
- ✔ Prices vary according to the options, but most inkjet printers that print using only black ink cost less than $200.

✔ Color inkjet printers, which are among the most popular printers, cost less than $300 or more than $500, depending on the number of colors that they print.

✔ Inkjet printers are more costly to maintain than dot-matrix printers are because of the cost of ink cartridges ($29 to $49 each, depending on color and size). These ink cartridge costs are continually dropping so watch for them to go down in price.

✔ Inkjet printers come in a variety of speeds. The faster they print, the more they cost.

✔ Many manufacturers of inkjet printers added settings that allow you to lower the print quality to increase speed.

✔ Higher-quality paper is recommended for inkjet printers. Remember, ink runs when it gets wet, and printing on porous paper results in less-than-crisp copy.

If you're in charge of the school newsletter, or if you commonly send out flyers, a color inkjet printer can help you jazz up your pages. Color grabs attention and can really be impressive. Take a closer look at the flyers that you see, and consider which of them hold your attention.

Laser: a fast, higher-cost, high-quality printer

Laser printers offer the highest-quality printouts faster than inkjet printers do. These printers use *toner* (black powder) and actually seal the toner onto your page by using a laser beam. Laser printers usually cost more than other printers do.

Here's the scoop on laser printers:

✔ Laser printers cost anywhere from $300 to more than $3,000 for color laser printers. (I have a $350 Brother laser that works beautifully, and our high-school media center uses several of these printers for student printouts of reference material.)

✔ Toner cartridges average between $30 and $75, depending on the type of printer that you have.

✔ Laser printers are quiet.

✔ Laser printers print much faster than other printers do. High-volume laser printers can print as many as 15 pages a minute. By comparison, less-expensive laser printers designed for personal use average seven pages a minute.

In addition, laser printers provide the following advantages:

✔ Laser printers produce clean, sharp text in a variety of sizes, shapes, styles, and angles. Many text types, called *fonts*, are built-in and are available automatically. (If you want to print in a language such as Japanese, you need to purchase a special set of instructions.)

✔ You don't have to worry about the ink running if the page gets wet.

✔ Larger laser printers can hold numerous paper trays to handle different sizes of paper and envelopes. You don't have to get up and change paper when you want to print on something other than standard-size paper.

✔ The cost of maintaining a laser printer is relatively small, because the toner is used quite sparingly. You can print more pages with one toner cartridge than you can with an ink cartridge. As a result, you don't have to replace toner cartridges as frequently as you do ink cartridges.

✔ You can print on lower-quality, more absorbent paper without affecting the quality of the printout. Again, cheaper paper means lower cost.

Playing with Little Lord Font

Fonts are wonderful. Fonts are marvelous. Fonts are fun. Fonts change the shapes of the characters that you type and help dress up your document. *Everyone* loves elaborate little curly-letter styles, and you've probably heard positive feedback from students and parents alike when they receive correspondence from teachers who have varied the appearance of their messages.

But please, please, *please,* don't go font crazy! Remember the adage "Less is more" — and working with fonts tests this adage to the limit.

You can change the style of your type face by using a variety of techniques and features:

✔ Font type

✔ Font enhancement

✔ Font size

The fonts that are available on your system depend, to a large degree, on the type of printer that you have. Dot-matrix printers generally have far fewer fonts than inkjet and laser printers do; the pin-pounding-paper approach simply does not provide the technology to form lots of character twists.

Figure 6-1 shows fonts that are common on inkjet and laser printers.

Figure 6-1:
Fonts can
be fun — if
you have
the right
printer.

Times New Roman
Arial
Century Schoolbook
Century Gothic
DESDEMONA

ALGERIAN
Bookshelf Symbol 1
Συμβολ
✲✳■♍♑♒✳■♍♦
Wide Latin
Mistral

Times New Roman, Times, Times NT, or Times by any other name is often the standard font type in most programs. Variations of Times may appear in your newspaper, and this book is printed in a Times-type font. Why? Times is a serif font — and serif fonts soften the character image and make reading easier so that readers' eyes don't get so tired.

Serifs are the little curly ends that you see at the top of the character *a* in the text you are reading and the platform (okay, the line) at the bottom of, for example, the capital *T*. Can you pick out some other serif fonts in Figure 6-1? (Hint: Century Schoolbook and Wide Latin are both serif fonts.) Arial and Century Gothic are both *sans serif* (without curly ends) fonts.

Can you identify all the fonts listed in Figure 6-1? I certainly hope not; if you can, you may be from the planet Ork. Symbol 1, Symbols, and Wingdings, respectively, are the names of the three fonts in the second column.

Font names vary according to the printer that you have attached. Sometimes, you see Helvetica instead of Arial, for example, but the appearance of these fonts is basically the same.

Printing on overhead transparencies

Both inkjet and laser printers can print on overhead transparencies, but you need to be sure that you buy the right type of transparency film.

Get film that's specifically designed for your printer type, or you can really gum up the printer — I mean you could literally melt the transparency sheet inside.

Always handle your transparencies with care. Laser printers seal the image directly onto the film, but because the film is slick, the image can chip off.

Enhancing your character image

 Don't confuse font names with font enhancements. Fonts actually form the characters, whereas enhancements change characters' appearance without changing the fonts themselves. Figure 6-2 shows what happens to text when you apply enhancements to a typical Times font.

Other enhancements may be available, depending on your printer, the fonts that you have installed, and the program that you're using to type your text. In addition, you can change font size to grab attention and create headlines.

Times Plain

Times Bold

Time Italic

Times Superscript above the line

Times Subscript below the line

TIMES SMALL CAPS

TIMES ALL CAPS

Figure 6-2:
Enhance-
ments dress
up your
characters.

Sizing up your fonts

Font size is measured in *points* which represent parts of an inch. An inch has 72 points. As a result, characters sized to 36 points are approximately a half an inch tall. Normal font size for characters is 10 or 12 points. The higher the point size, the larger the characters. Figure 6-3 shows how the Times font appears in different sizes.

Times 12 point

Times 18 point

Times 36 point

Times 72

Figure 6-3:
Size your
text to
create
headlines
that grab
attention!

Changing font size creates an effective pyramid, doesn't it? See how much fun fonts can be? To have even more fun, you can install special font packages onto your system (remember those foreign languages). Font packages usually are available wherever printers and computers are sold; they range in price from $10 (on sale) to $50 to hundreds of dollars, depending on the font and system.

Installing new fonts

If you decide to explore new and different fonts, be sure to read the package so that you know whether the fonts will work with your computer and printer. If the fonts don't work, don't buy them. You need to install any fonts that you buy so that your computer and printer recognize them.

In Windows 95, you install fonts by adding them to the Fonts folder, which is stored in the Control Panel. For more information about opening the Control Panel, refer to Chapter 3. That chapter also contains information about using the Help feature in Windows 95. Use the Help feature to locate information about installing new fonts and follow those instructions when you want to add fonts to your computer.

You'll find some special fonts on the CD-ROM that comes with this book. You may want to install one set of fonts for practice.

Putting Print on Paper

If only there were a way to guarantee perfect printouts every time you put computer to paper! Unfortunately, printing is not *always* that simple. Before your printer starts producing beautiful papers, you may have to get past some roadblocks — and I don't mean your brain.

Connecting the printer

If you're fortunate enough to have a technology coordinator who's in charge of connecting and setting up your printer, great! You can skip this section. If you are hesitant to tackle tasks such as this yourself and have no such person as a technology coordinator, you may want to solicit the help of your school's computer guru. (*Every* school has such a person.) If, on the other hand, you can't wait to become the most knowledgeable person in your school regarding printer matters, don't hesitate to plunge right in. Connecting your printer is not quite so intimidating as you might expect.

Remember all those wires and cables that someone used to connect your monitor and your mouse (and anything else) to your system unit? Well, your printer also needs to be plugged into the system unit.

Most of the time, unless you have an unusual setup, you can use the cord or cable that comes with the printer and successfully connect to the printer port on the back of the system unit. (A *port* works sort of like an electrical outlet but looks different.) Sometimes, the cord doesn't fit. You have to be careful; just because the cord looks as though it will fit doesn't mean that the port you're trying to plug it into is the correct port. The label on the back of the system may actually tell you nothing. (Did you ever try to connect a VCR to the right holes in the back of the TV set?)

Here are some guidelines to help you get your computer and printer attached to each other:

- ✔ Look for outlet labels such as Printer, Monitor, Mouse, and so on. Manufacturers got tired of fixing things after someone tried to plug the cable into the wrong spot (or the wrong cable into the right spot). As a result, outlets on newer systems are identified.

- ✔ Look for something labeled LPT1. (I call this port my laser port, to make it easier to remember that this is the place where I need to plug in my printer cable.) If you have an LPT1, plug your printer into it.

- ✔ Examine the ends of the cord or cable that came with your printer. Do they look exactly alike? If the ends are alike, you can attach one end to the computer and the other end to the printer; it doesn't matter which end goes where.

> ✔ If the ends of the printer cable are different, compare the plugs with the cable ports on both the system unit and the printer to identify which end goes into the printer. The other end goes into the system unit.

If the cord doesn't fit any port on the back of the computer, you need to head down to the local computer store — and please take your cable with you. Tell the employees that you need a connection to attach to the cable so that the cable will plug into your computer. Then grin great big and describe what the outlet on the back of the computer looks like. Explaining what kind of printer you have also helps. Your computer store's employees usually can fix you up for less than $15. (Don't forget to turn in the purchase order so that you can be reimbursed.)

Now, you're not going to get off without reading the manual that comes with your printer; I can't give you instructions for attaching ink cartridges or toner units. So even if you haven't had to consult the manual to plug in the printer, you need to look at it for specific instructions on how to connect all the other stuff.

Getting the printer and computer on speaking terms

When you're over the hurdle of physically connecting the printer to the computer (if you haven't connected your printer yet, see the preceding section), you need to inform your computer that you have a printer. Then you have to put a driver in charge.

Yes — computers use designated drivers, too. Each printer has its own driver to coordinate signals between Windows 95 and other computer programs and the printer. If the wrong driver is in charge, you get gibberish — something that looks like ◆⊠○♌□●◆. Most manufacturers include a disk with their printers that contains the necessary drivers so that you'll have the drivers you need.

Windows 95 comes equipped with Plug-and-Play technology that is designed to recognize hardware that you add to your computer. Although Windows 95 knows when you've attached a printer, it won't know what kind of printer you have. As a result, you have to tell Windows 95 what type of printer you have so that it can add the drivers needed to speak the printer's language.

Most new printers come with printer drivers (instructions to tell the computer how to talk to the printer) on a floppy disk and comprehensive, easy-to-follow instructions to help you get your printer up and running. Follow these instructions carefully and you should be printing up a storm in short order. If you run into problems, check with the school technology coordinator, or someone else who has experience installing a printer, for help. If all else fails, fill your coffee cup and then call the printer manufacturer using the toll-free number provided in the instruction manual — you'll most likely have plenty of time to drain the cup while you wait for a technician to come to the phone.

A Windows 95 wizard presents a series of windows containing questions you need to answer to set up a new printer. You may need to pull out the printer manual before starting the installation.

To start the printer installation process, choose Start⇨Settings⇨Printers and then double-click the Add Printers icon. The Wizard screens are easy to follow.

It's rather exciting to see your printer actually work, and if your printout makes sense, the feeling of satisfaction is even greater. How does *your* printout look?

Ready, set, print!

After you connect your printer, you are finally ready to print. Although the actions may vary slightly within each application (and in some applications, such as the Calculator, you can't print at all), most of the actions are pretty standard. When you print, one of two things may occur:

✔ In some programs, a Print dialog box opens, giving you a chance to check things out before the printer kicks in.

✔ In other programs, the printer starts putting out the hard copy before you can blink your eye.

In general, to start the printing process, follow these steps:

1. Prepare your document (and check it twice).

2. Choose File⇨Print.

Depending on the program you're using, choosing File⇨Print may open a Print dialog box so that you can make additional choices about how you want your document to print, or it may simply tell the printer to start printing. If a dialog box opens, review the information or follow the screen prompts to complete your printing. Usually, following the prompts simply means clicking the OK button to accept the printing defaults.

Your fault, my fault, or defaults

The term *default* means standard, automatic, or the norm. Therefore, a *default* printer is the one that the system tries to find unless you tell it that you want to print to a different printer.

A *default font* is the font that automatically comes up when you start typing unless you tell the system to use a different font.

Computer systems are full of defaults; without them, you would have to answer a lot of questions each time you turned on your system.

Generally, the defaults set in each program have been found to be the most popular settings among computer users (people such as you and me).

Letting Your Fax Take Charge

Although including faxing in a chapter that primarily focuses on printing may seem odd, a reason for the madness does exist. Your fax is a type of printer, so sending a fax from your computer is as simple as printing; all you have to do is select the fax from your list of printers. You can find more information about fax machines in the discussion about modems in Chapter 12.

For now, you just need to learn how to tell your computer to print to the fax, rather than to your printer. Before you fax, you need to know a few things:

- ✔ You need a modem that allows you to send faxes (a fax/modem).
- ✔ After you install the program from the disk that comes with your modem, the fax feature is listed with other printers in the Printers window.
- ✔ You can fax directly from the program that you use to create the document that you want to send.

To tell your fax driver rather than your printer driver to take over, follow these steps:

1. **Complete and save your document.**

2. **Choose File⇨Print to open the Print dialog box.**

   If the program that you're using sends the job directly to the printer without opening the Print dialog box, look for a Printer Setup or Print Setup command in the File menu to open the Print dialog box. Figure 6-4 shows a sample Print dialog box. This dialog box contains a drop-down list from which you can choose the fax machine as your printer.

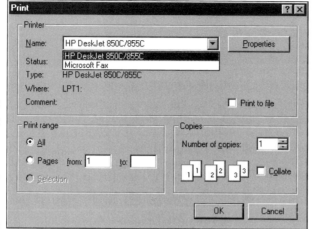

Figure 6-4:
The
WordPad
Print dialog
box is easy
to use and
intuitive.

3. **Click the down arrow beside the Name drop-down list to display the printers (and faxes) installed on your system.**

4. **Click to select the fax driver.**

5. **Choose any additional print options.**

6. **Click OK to print.**

Don't forget to change the printer setting back to your printer after you fax your document. Otherwise, unless you exit the application, each time you choose Print, your documents go to the fax machine instead of the printer. What's worse is that because you won't be getting your printouts, you may think that something is wrong with the printer and issue the same Print command several times before you realize that you have just faxed your annual salary to your sister — five times!

After you turn control over to the fax, you can print by using the procedures outlined in "Ready, set, print!", earlier in this chapter.

Part II
Microsoft Works —
For Teachers

The 5th Wave   By Rich Tennant

"Before I go on to explain more advanced procedures like the 'Zap-Rowdy-Students-who-Don't-Pay-Attention' function, we'll begin with some basics."

In this part . . .

Think back a few years to your first classroom (or, if this is your first year of teaching, try to remember your English class when you were a high school senior). Did you have a chalkboard or maybe even a blackboard? What about an overhead projector — do you remember having one to call your very own? Was there a television set in your classroom, and was the television attached to a VCR? Did you have a computer anywhere — maybe back in the corner, hiding? Did you have plenty of electrical outlets to meet all your technological needs back then? Did you even need more than one outlet?

Now, think about what was expected of you during your early years in the classroom. Did you have clear-cut lesson plans that flowed smoothly from start to finish? Did you accomplish all your objectives each and every day? Did you complete all the material that you had planned to cover? How have the tasks that you performed to meet the administration's expectations changed since those early days in the classroom?

If you compare the physical aspects of a classroom from just a few years ago with your classroom today, you most likely will see remarkable differences. If you compare what your administration expected of you then to what they expect today, the differences are not so noticeable . . . you still have to produce lesson plans; you still have to account for some type of budget; you still prepare tests and review sheets and write out permission slips and notes to parents; and you still average grades. What's different about doing these tasks today versus doing them in the past is the technology that you can use to accomplish them.

Whether technological advances have simplified your life or complicated it depends on your knowledge and skill for putting this new technology to work — for *you!* In this part, you learn to use some of the tools that are designed to simplify your teacher tasks and new ways to implement these tools in your curriculum.

There's no turning back the clock to those early days in the classroom — but, then, why would you want to?

Chapter 7

Microsoft Works 4.0: A Primer

- -

In This Chapter

▶ Differentiating among Works packages

▶ Identifying Microsoft Works 4.0 modules

▶ Previewing the Microsoft Works 4.0 Task Launcher

▶ Locating common elements of Microsoft Works 4.0 modules

▶ Using templates and wizards

- -

*H*ow can I explain Microsoft Works 4.0? I suppose that it would help for you to think of Microsoft Works as being like a department store. When you want shoes, you go to the shoe department. When you want towels, you go to domestics.

With Microsoft Works 4.0, you have a word processing-program, a spreadsheet program, a database program, and a communications program all rolled into one neat little package. You decide what type of task you want to accomplish and then determine which "department" is designed to help you accomplish it. The Task Launcher, a feature built into Works 4.0, keeps you organized and provides alternative routes for you to take to get to the right place.

Selecting the Right Works

You may wonder why I chose Microsoft Works 4.0 when so many Works packages are on the market. The reason is twofold:

✔ Microsoft Works 4.0 is designed to run specifically with Windows 95. As a result, you get the full power of the Windows 95 technology working with the power built into Works.

✔ Microsoft Works 4.0 comes standard and already installed on many of the newest computers that are running Windows 95. As a result, many of you already have Works 4.0.

You may, of course, have an older computer, be running a Windows 3.*x* product, or have a different Works product. Many software companies have developed programs similar to Microsoft Works (you'll see names such as ClarisWorks and WordPerfect Works) to give Microsoft some competition. You'll also see numerous *versions* of these Works packages on the market.

If you don't have a Works package installed on your computer, thumb through the chapters in this part of the book to see whether Microsoft Works 4.0 is the program for you. If you're looking for a program that has different capabilities, check out some of the other products on the market. Many of the Works programs are basically the same; they each have word processing, database, and spreadsheet modules. The way that program features are organized may be different in the Works program you choose, but the way that you put them to work won't vary.

An important consideration is selecting a version of your chosen Works package that is designed specifically for the version of Windows that you're using. Because I'm running Windows 95, I chose Microsoft Works 4.0. If you're running Windows 3.*x,* you can't use Works 4.0, which is designed for the more sophisticated technology available in Windows 95. As a result, you need Microsoft Works 3.0 or another Works package designed for the Windows 3.*x* family. On the other hand, if you already have Microsoft Works 3.0 or some other Works package that is designed for use with Windows 3.*x* products, you can successfully use it with Windows 95 (but your screens will look different from those in this chapter).

Even if you have a Works package that's different from the one that I show you here, you can still use this book; it's full of powerful ideas and basic techniques that you'll find to be useful with any Works program. If you want information specifically about Microsoft Works 3.0, pick up a copy of *Microsoft Works For Teachers*, also from IDG Books Worldwide, Inc. You'll find lots of dynamic instructions for using both Microsoft Works 3.0 and Microsoft Works 4.0!

Separating Works Modules from Modes

Whether you refer to the application tools in Microsoft Works as *modules, modes,* or *components* is irrelevant; what is important is that Works is power-packed with four semi-separate applications, each of which is designed to accomplish a specific task. Each application is part of the whole Works product — not an independent program. I prefer to refer to Works' different components as *modules* (the word-processing module or the database module, for example), so that you know that I'm still referring to Works. (Notice that I've abbreviated the package name, too, so that it's easier to type!)

Are suites the sweeter deal?

When I hear the phrase "new and improved," I often think about software applications. A fresh look at what's happening with software suites only serves to reinforce my thoughts. These new suites have given me a fresh perspective on the *true* meaning of "new and improved."

In software-application terminology, a *suite* is a collection of software programs developed by the same company and designed to work together as a cohesive unit while maintaining their individuality. *Integrated programs* are single programs (such as Microsoft Works) that mesh the capabilities of numerous software applications in one product. You can purchase suite programs separately or as part of the whole suite. You may think of Microsoft Works as being a suite, but when you examine it more closely, you'll discover that you cannot buy or use one module of Works without the other modules. Therefore, Works is *not* a suite.

Purchasing programs as a suite provides several advantages over purchasing each application contained in the suite separately:

✔ The total cost of all the programs in a suite is much lower than the cost of purchasing the programs individually.

✔ Many suites come with a Suite Manager that appears as a toolbar on-screen and makes switching from one application to another more efficient. This manager is packaged only with the suites — not with individual programs.

✔ A master folder stores all the suite's applications, and each program is stored in a separate folder within the master folder. This arrangement enables each application in the suite to share features such as dictionaries (for spell-checking documents). As a result, if you type a document in the word processor and add a word to the dictionary, the word is automatically updated and available the next time that you need it in the suite's spreadsheet application.

✔ Data and information typed in one application of a suite can be copied (often by dragging and dropping) to another application within the suite. The applications speak the same language, as it were.

✔ The programs that make up a suite are often much more sophisticated and powerful than the corresponding modules in integrated programs such as Works.

Works presents four modules right up front. Other features are buried inside the main modules in sort of a layering effect that makes features accessible to only the modules that use them most. Some of the modules that you'll find in Works are:

✔ **Word processor:** a program that helps you create a document, such as a test, a letter to parents, a permission slip, lesson plans, or a newsletter.

✔ **Spreadsheet:** a sheet of paper in a rows-and-columns format that helps you line up numbers, average grades, keep track of attendance, tally lunch money, and monitor your budget.

✔ **Database:** a series of index cards or file folders that you can use to group pieces of information, such as textbook assignments, recipes, or test questions.

✔ **Communications:** a link to your external communications package that allows you to send messages and other documents to your e-mail system.

✔ **Drawing:** a feature inside Works' modules that accesses a version of Microsoft Draw, enabling you to create a picture by using shapes, colors, logos, and other graphics. You can then add these pictures to word processing documents and spreadsheets.

✔ **Charting:** another feature designed to access a version of Microsoft Graph from within a module so that you can plot numeric data graphically.

✔ **WordArt**: accesses the WordArt program so that you can create works of art from the text that you type.

You learn where to find each of these modules and features as you continue to explore Microsoft Works. Enjoy your journey.

Serious stuff

A word about legalities, piracy, and all that stuff: Software is a copyrighted item; therefore, paying attention to your software's rules and regulations is important.

Normally, you can install a program on more than one computer only if you purchase a special license to do so. If your computer came with the software already installed, you aren't supposed to let your friends use the disks; that's illegal. Some software products allow installation on only a specified number of computers at one time to prevent piracy.

But there are legal ways around this regulation. You can purchase what's known as a *lab*

pack — a special agreement between school systems and software developers to permit installation on lab computers for educational use. Network licenses are also available. Check with your school's technology coordinator or the salesperson for the software that you want to use to find out what you can do legally.

Software piracy is a growing problem today. Registering your programs and keeping them safe by abiding by the copyright agreement are important. (By the way, you agree to the copyright agreement when you open the package that contains the disks.)

Putting Works into action

If you are awarded the dubious task of installing Microsoft Works 4.0 on your computer, you discover that one of the decisions that you have to make is whether to place a shortcut to the program on your desktop during setup. If you have a chance, tell the computer YES!!! when you're asked about the shortcut. Shortcuts make launching the program much easier. If Works came installed on your computer, look around your desktop. If you don't see a shortcut anywhere on the desktop, you may want to read Chapter 4 to create a Works shortcut.

To launch Works by using a desktop shortcut, simply double-click the shortcut icon.

You can, of course, launch Microsoft Works 4.0 by using the same procedure you use to launch other programs. Follow these steps:

1. **Choose Start⇨Programs.**

2. **Select the Microsoft Works 4.0 group.**

3. **Click Microsoft Works 4.0.**

The first time you launch Works 4.0, you have the opportunity to view an introduction to the program. Skip the intro by clicking Cancel.

Thumbing through the pages of Task Launcher

When you get Works up and running, the Task Launcher, shown in Figure 7-1, takes control. It might help you to think of the Task Launcher as being a three-subject notebook.

This multiple-page window presents options that enable you to choose the way that you want to work — just the way that you present lessons visually, pictorially, and verbally to account for students' different learning styles. Here's what you'll find in each page of the Task Launcher window:

- ✔ **Task_Wizards.** Select a format for the type of document that you want to create; then answer the wizard's questions regarding document format and style. Fantastic template results are guaranteed!

- ✔ **Existing Documents.** Open a recently saved document from a list.

- ✔ **Works Tools.** Create a new document from scratch by choosing the Works module that you want to use.

Task Launcher page tabs

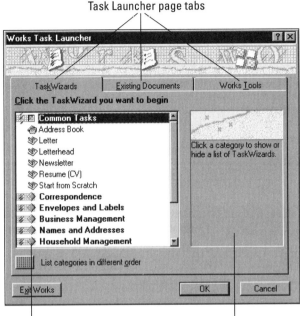

Figure 7-1:
Works is
proud of its
Task
Launcher.

Task buttons

Preview / description box

You'll use each of these Task Launcher pages as you work with different features and perform tasks with Works. If, during your exploration of Works, your Task Launcher disappears, you can call it back; just choose File⇨New, and it pops right up.

TECHNO TERMS

Witty wizards . . . testy templates

Are you intrigued by the terms *template* and *wizard?* You'll be impressed when you learn what they can help you do.

Templates are preformatted document layouts that contain preset margins, text fonts, line spacing, graphics, drawings, pictures, and so on. You can use templates to maintain a consistent appearance or to vary the appearance of your documents. Templates eliminate the need to reformat a plain document every time you want one that's all dressed up.

Wizards are technical geniuses that walk you through the steps for preparing certain types of documents or performing specific tasks. Wizards ask you questions and then use your answers to devise a fantastically complex solution. Don't hesitate to call on them when you're in a rush and need some extra help.

Training Works: The Common Elements

Although it's a fact that each Works module is designed to help you accomplish distinctive tasks, it's also true that most Works modules have many common elements. Only the Communications module differs extensively from the other modules. Consider your students for a moment. Isn't it true that although each student you teach is a separate individual, all students have common traits? Think about having a classroom of students who are all exactly like your most conscientious student — and then consider your day with a classroom of students who resemble Mr. or Ms. Troublemaker.

Table 7-1 describes some of the common features of the Works Word Processor, Spreadsheet, and Database modules.

Table 7-1	Works Windows Features and How to Use Them
Feature	*Description*
Menu bar	The Word Processor module and the Spreadsheet module have identical menu bars, and the Database module's menu bar has one different button.
Toolbars	The three Works modules display a common set of buttons in the toolbar, as well as a few module-specific tools. (Figure 7-2, which appears in the following section, identifies the toolbar buttons that are common to the three modules.)
Navigation buttons	The Word Processor and Database modules display a set of navigation buttons in the bottom-left corner of their document windows. This set of buttons provides an easy way to get to the first or last page of the document or database, and makes moving to the next or preceding document or page easier. (Figure 7-3, which appears later in this chapter, identifies the navigation buttons.)
Dialog boxes	The Open, Save, and Print dialog boxes contain basically the same options, regardless of which module you're using.

Tooling the toolbars

Look for the common buttons shown in Figure 7-2 in the toolbar of the Word Processor, Spreadsheet, and Database modules.

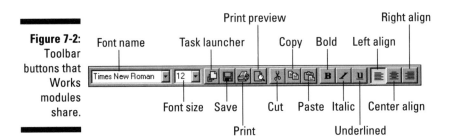

Figure 7-2: Toolbar buttons that Works modules share.

Don't know what a toolbar button is? Don't panic — Microsoft developed a neat little feature called *ToolTips* to help you out in a pinch. ToolTips appear when you point to a toolbar button and pause. A little square displays the task that the button performs. A more detailed description of the button's purpose appears in the status bar of your document.

Punching navigation buttons

Navigation buttons appear only in the Word Processor and Database module windows. Figure 7-3 identifies which navigation button is which.

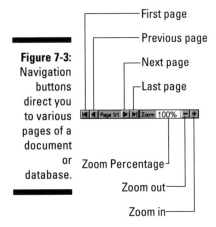

Figure 7-3: Navigation buttons direct you to various pages of a document or database.

Looking for an Open(ing) dialog box

The Open dialog box appears any time you do one of the following things:

✔ When you choose Open a Document Not Listed Here from the Existing Documents page of the Works Task Launcher

✔ When you press Ctrl+O while you are working in a module

✔ When you choose File➪Open from within a module

Regardless of what type of document you want to open, the Open dialog box looks like the one shown in Figure 7-4.

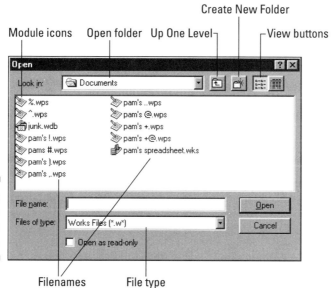

Create New Folder

Module icons   Open folder   Up One Level   View buttons

Figure 7-4:
The Works
4.0 Open
dialog box.

Filenames   File type

The Works module used to create each file listed in the Open dialog box is identified in two ways: An icon precedes the filename, and an extension follows the filename. Microsoft Works automatically adds the file extension to each file that you save, according to the following scheme:

✔ **.wps** for the Word Processor module

✔ **.wks** for the Spreadsheet module

✔ **.wdb** for the Database module

Using this file-naming scheme, when you save a document that you created in the Works Word Processor module by typing `Ch1Test`, Works automatically adds .wps to the end of your filename.

The default folder (you know — the automatic one) that Works opens when you use the Open command appears in the Look in drop-down list at the top of the dialog box. If you store your work in your own personal folder (which you should do to keep yourself organized), you can get to that folder by clicking the Up One Level button in the toolbar and then opening folders until you see the folder you want. If you need to create a new folder, simply click the Create New Folder toolbar button and type a special name for the folder.

Saving and then Saving As

Create a document, save it, open it, edit it, and then save it again. What a routine — but a routine you can live with much more easily than you can live with retyping complete documents. When you're working on a new document, recording grades in a spreadsheet, or adding records to a database, saving your work frequently is important. Imagine sitting for hours on Sunday afternoon plugging out those test questions for Monday's test, getting the test almost complete . . . when the power goes out, your system turns off, and you have to retype all your work. It has happened to us all, and it can make for a very late night. Save your work each time you stop to think of a new test question; you'll be glad you did.

The procedure that you use to save is the same in all Works modules; simply choose File⇨Save. If you haven't already saved the document, the Save As dialog box (shown in Figure 7-5) opens so that you can give the document a filename. If you already saved your document, the dialog box doesn't open because you've already assigned a filename.

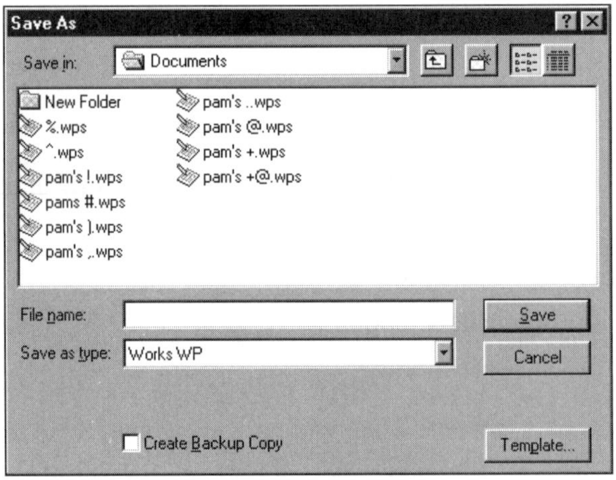

Figure 7-5: The Save As dialog box features are the same as the Open dialog box features.

Although this dialog box varies slightly, depending on the module that you are using, the main features and actions that you need to take to save your document remain consistent:

  ✔ Tell Works what folder you want to use to store the file.

  ✔ Tell Works what filename to use to store the file.

You also have to make additional decisions, which follow:

Saving to the hard disk

As a teacher, you need to decide how you want to set up the computer so that your students (and perhaps other teachers) can use the same computer without messing up one another's work. If students are storing their files on the hard disk, all they need to do to save files to their folders is to open their folders before saving.

When saving to the hard disk, you need to consider the following things:

- ✔ **Hard-disk space.** Is enough hard-disk space available to store all the program files and document files for all students and teachers who share the computer? If you aren't sure how much space you have available, check with the school's computer guru or technology coordinator. Although it may not be possible to estimate how long the hard-disk space will last (it's hard to determine how many files your students will create during the school year), the guru can at least tell you how much empty hard-disk space you have. Saving files to a hard disk also means that you have to clean off old files — quite a time-consuming task.

- ✔ **Security.** How do you plan to keep students from opening and nosing around in folders and files that they have no business opening? Do you want to set up a security procedure with passwords (which students will forget)? Then again, do you want to have access to student files?

- ✔ **File-folder location.** Where do you want to put student folders: at the base unit (C) or inside the Works folder as a subfolder? Are you going to allow students to create additional folder levels within their personal folders to sort out their documents by type and so on?

Saving to a floppy disk

Some schools request that students store their documents on floppy disks so that the hard disk is kept as clean as possible. If that's the case, another set of considerations comes up:

- ✔ Where will you store the disks, if they must be kept at school?

- ✔ Will the school provide a disk for each student, or will students be expected to provide their own disks? Who pays for these disks?

- ✔ What arrangements will you make if a student loses his or her disk?

- ✔ Can the students take their disks home?

- ✔ How do you keep students from using a disk that belongs to someone else?

- ✔ Do you have a good virus-checker to make sure that students' disks don't infect the system?

A virus can spread quickly if all students take their disks home. You can find out more about virus-checkers in Chapter 15.

Making a Template Decision

Choosing a template designed for the type of document that you want to create used to be quite a chore; you had to look over each template and then decide which one would be most effective in helping you accomplish your objective.

Mr. Wizard makes your template decision more flexible in Works 4.0. The final document structure is built as you answer Mr. Wizard's questions. You start with a basic category or document type and work your way up to a finished format. You'll find categories listed in the TaskWizards page of the Works Task Launcher; the categories range from Common Tasks to User Defined Templates that you design and create yourself. And wonder of wonders — could that be a Students and *Teachers* category listed among the TaskWizards? Quick — let's see what kinds of templates are already available just for you.

Choosing a template

To display a list of templates available in a category, follow these steps:

1. **Click the TaskWizards page tab in the Works Task Launcher window.**

2. **Click the down arrow in the Task Launcher scroll bar to review the available categories.**

3. **Click the category that you want to view.**

   For fun, click the Students and Teachers category. The list of formats that are useful to students and teachers is displayed in Figure 7-6.

Each document you create by using a wizard to design the template has no effect on other documents that you create by using the same wizard. You actually use the preformatted layout, fill in the blanks with your stuff, save the file by giving it a name, and then go on to the next task. As a result, if you create a class schedule by using the Schedule Wizard this semester and then need to create a new schedule next semester, you can use the same Schedule Wizard to create the new schedule. Simply choose the options that are available to you when the wizard asks its questions.

Browse through additional categories of templates you can create by using the TaskWizards. In Chapter 8, you actually create and save a template to add to the User Defined Templates category. Sound interesting? I think that you'll *love* applying your creative talents to something that you can use frequently.

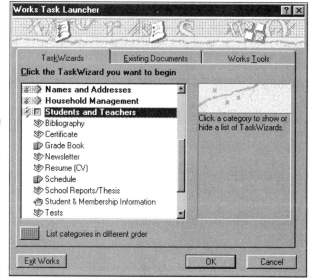

Figure 7-6:
Oh, how you'll love these templates found under the TaskWizards tab.

Working with wizards

Just to introduce you to how the TaskWizards work (sometimes, they pop up on their own), try selecting one of the Common Tasks Wizards, which appear at the top of the TaskWizards page of the Works Task Launcher window. Then follow these steps to get an idea of how these fellows work:

1. **Click the wizard that represents the document that you want to create.**

   I chose Letter from the Common Tasks list.

2. **Choose OK.**

   The Works Task Launcher dialog box opens (see Figure 7-7).

Figure 7-7:
Start answering questions right away.

3. Click <u>Y</u>es, Run the TaskWizard.

The first screen of the Works TaskWizard, which is designed to help you create a letter format, appears (see Figure 7-8).

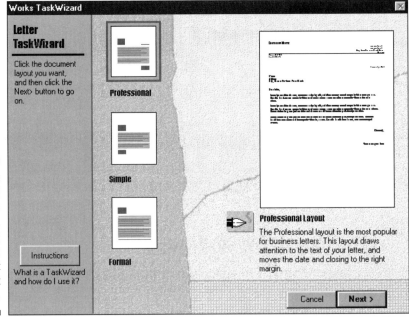

Figure 7-8:
Wizard
screens
differ,
depending
on the
document
type that
you choose.

If you want to continue through all the steps needed to complete the letter format, click the Next button and follow the directions given on each wizard screen. When you come to the last wizard screen, you see a Finish button instead of the Next button; click the Finish button to see your document format. To abandon the wizard, click the Cancel button in any wizard screen. It's sort of like leaving the playground when all the students are having so much fun!

Three cheers for a job well done!

Chapter 8

Documenting Words: Using the Works Word Processor

- -

In This Chapter

▶ Creating your first document

▶ Changing document settings

▶ Typing, editing, deleting, and enhancing text

▶ Saving your work to use again

▶ Getting your work back

▶ Using special Works Word Processor features

▶ Creating and customizing templates

- -

1 f you compare the different Works modules with the classes that you took in high school, you get a good feel for how the modules interact. Start with your English class, in which you learn to read, write, and speak well; then use these skills in your math, science, and history classes.

The techniques that you develop by using the Word Processor module resemble the skills that you learned in English class, and you apply many of these techniques in other Works modules.

By starting with a simple document, you learn the basic skills required to create, save, edit, retrieve, and resave documents. Your adventure is about to begin. Ready?

Taking the First Steps toward Creating Your Document

Okay, you're staring at the Works Task Launcher window of Works 4.0 and don't know what to do. Well, as you've discovered in most programs that are designed to run with Windows 95, you have a couple of options:

> ✔ In the TaskWizards page of the Works Task Launcher, choose a
> TaskWizard template and walk through the steps to create a
> preformatted document.
>
> ✔ In the Works Tools page of the Works Task Launcher, choose the
> module tool that you want to use to create your new document.

Calling up the Word Processor

To learn the basics (and find your way around a document), however,
starting with something simple makes better sense. If you use a template,
you may bump into some fancy things that are difficult to explain if you have
not yet learned the basics.

To create a "plain vanilla" document, follow these steps:

1. **Launch Works 4.0.**

   If you aren't certain how to launch Works, see Chapter 7. The Works
   Task Launcher opens automatically each time you launch Works and is
   ready to help you get started.

2. **Click the Works Tools tab in the Works Task Launcher.**

   You can also press Ctrl+Tab to access tabbed pages in a dialog box. The
   Works Tools page, shown in Figure 8-1, provides a rather intuitive way
   to select the Works module that you want to use.

Module buttons   Page tabs

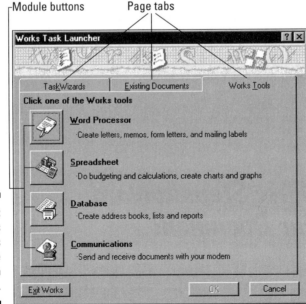

Figure 8-1:
Works
Tools helps
you create
plain
documents.

3. Click the Word Processor button.

There it is: your very first document in Microsoft Works! But whew —
what a complex window!

Dissecting the Word Processor screen

Actually, the window is not as complex as you may think. Take a close look
at the screen features identified in Figure 8-2.

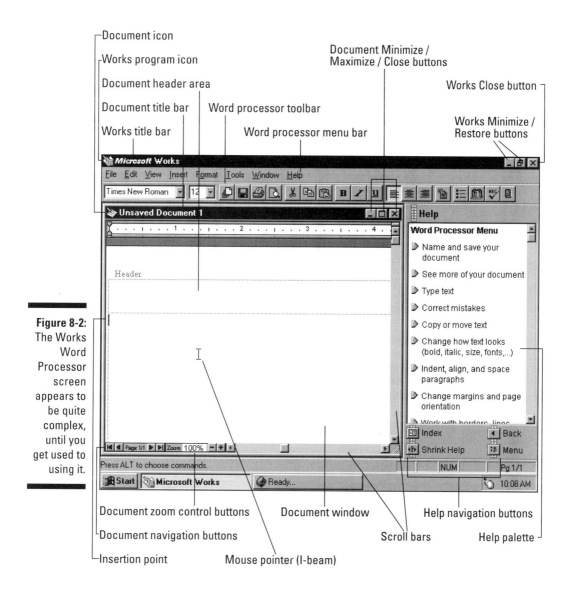

Figure 8-2:
The Works
Word
Processor
screen
appears to
be quite
complex,
until you
get used to
using it.

Most of the features that you see in the Works Word Processor window are standard Windows 95 program-window features. A couple features, however, are unique to Works and need a bit more explanation:

- ✔ The Help palette opens automatically the first time that you launch the Word Processor module (and other Works modules), to guide new users through tasks step by step. You have a decision to make before continuing: Do you want help from Help, or do you want to work on your own?

- ✔ The Document Header area is where you type information and text (such as page numbers, test chapter name and number, class period, student name line, and so on) that you want to repeat at the top of every page. Look at the information at the top of this page for an example of a header.

If you want to work on your own, you can hide the Help palette or shrink it. Hiding Help removes the Help palette from your window and maximizes your document work area; shrinking Help leaves it open and takes up part of your screen.

To hide Help, choose Help⇨Hide Help. You can always call Help back to the screen by following the procedure that you use to close Help. When Help is hidden, the command in the Help menu changes to Show Help.

Without the Help palette on-screen, you have the full screen as your document working area.

I usually advise new users of an application to click each menu option to get an overview of the available features of the program and how those features are organized. I'm usually in the classroom when I give users this advice, of course, so that I can help straighten things out when they find themselves with an on-screen mess.

If you feel confident that you can explore the menus on your own, go ahead — but remember that you're on your own. If you wander into uncharted territory (if you accidentally choose something from a menu that opens a dialog box or changes the screen in some way, for example), try one of these techniques to get the screen back to normal:

- ✔ Press the Esc key several times to see whether the dialog box closes.

- ✔ Click the document Close button and then launch the Word Processor again.

- ✔ Click the Works Close button to shut down the program and then relaunch Works.

Putting Pen to Paper: Typing

Adding text to paper is easy; all you have to do is type. You have a plain sheet of paper in your typewriter . . . I mean, right there on-screen, so you don't have to do anything else. Just type. Forget about errors; you can fix them later. Just type a long sentence to test word wrap and get the feel of your keyboard. If you can't think of anything to type, type this: **I can't think of anything to type, so the teacher gave me a practice sentence that's long enough to set word wrap into motion.**

Word wrap? What's word wrap? Ah, it's time to learn that some new typing rules apply to word processing. (For those of you who learned to type way back when you had to return the carriage by hand, you may find some of your old typing habits hard to break, but with time you'll be word processing like a pro.)

Pressing on and Enter

Watching Angela Lansbury use her handy-dandy typewriter during the opening sequence of *Murder, She Wrote* brings back fond memories for many typists. Why? Because remembering how we had to throw the typewriter carriage makes us appreciate the wonders of word processing so much more.

The developers of word processing programs came up with a neat little innovation known as word wrap (no, it's not a modern singing technique). Word wrap automatically moves the text that you type to the next line when you bump into the margin (wonder of wonders!). This automatic-return phenomenon helped rewrite the rules for throwing the carriage.

Here are some rules to follow so that you know when to end a line by pressing Enter:

- ✔ Press Enter at the end of short lines of text when you want to type text on a new line.
- ✔ Press Enter at the end of a paragraph to start a new paragraph.
- ✔ Press Enter to create a blank line.

Saving a space at the end of sentences

Another dramatic change that appeared on the scene with the advent of more sophisticated word processors involves the spacing that you place at the end of sentences. I never thought that I'd have to say this (being a business teacher and all), but you no longer have to press the space bar twice at the end of a sentence. There! I said it and need no disclaimer to restore my credibility among my peers.

If you're using a *scalable* font (a font that you can make bigger), word processing programs actually adjust the spacing of text, just as typesetters do. You no longer have to add an extra space between sentences. If you are not using a scalable font, go ahead and press the space bar twice at the end of each sentence; the rule hasn't changed for you.

To learn more about font types and sizes, see Chapter 6.

Correcting errors

If you make a mistake while you're typing, simply press the Backspace key to erase mistyped characters; then type the correct ones. (If you don't see a key with the word *Backspace* on it, look for a key marked with a left arrow at the right end of the number row in the standard keypad.) If you don't catch a typing error, don't worry; you find out how to correct errors in the following sections.

When you finish typing the text that you choose to type, your insertion point winks at you from the end of the sentence, because that's where you stopped typing. Because pressing the Backspace key erases characters, when you want to reposition the insertion point, you can use one of the following techniques:

- ✔ Press the arrow keys (they appear between the standard and numeric keypads) until the insertion point is where you want it. The left- and right-arrow keys move the insertion point one character at a time; the up- and down-arrow keys move the insertion point one line at a time.

- ✔ Position the I-beam mouse pointer where you want the insertion point to be, and click. If you don't click, you're only pointing, and pointing doesn't relocate the insertion point. You have to see the insertion point — not the I-beam — blinking where you want it. Otherwise, who knows where your text will go? After you click, scoot the mouse-pointing I-beam out of the way so that you can see what you're doing.

Inserting text

Adding characters to correct your typing mistakes or to restructure sentences and paragraphs involves inserting text. To insert text, position the insertion point where you want to add the characters and then type. If you put word wrap in charge of your paragraphs, any additional text that appears on the line where you're adding text scoots over to make room.

To get the hang of it, go ahead and position the insertion point between two words (or smack-dab in the middle of a word, if you like), and type something. Are you at a loss for words again? Then type **Wow! Neat!** before any word in the passage, and watch what happens.

Did your words move over to make room for the new stuff? Remember when you turned in a paper to the teacher and hoped she wouldn't notice that you left out a couple of words? Whether you were copying a poem for English class, doing a report for history class, or typing a letter for typing class, taking the chance that the teacher wouldn't read every word sure beat redoing the whole thing.

With word processing, adding words is not a problem — just do it!

Deleting text

The easiest way to remove text that you no longer need is to first select it. After you select the text, all you have to do is press Delete. Boom — the selected text is gone! If you already have some text on your page, skip Step 1 in the following steps. If you've been so caught up in my fabulous narrative that you have not yet typed anything (you're still staring at a blank page), type the sentence provided in Step 1 so that you have some text for practice.

To delete text, follow these steps:

1. **Type something.**

   If you can't think of anything to type, enter this: **The teacher gave me a Wow! Neat! practice sentence that's long enough to practice deleting text.**

2. **Position the I-beam on a word in the first line and double-click to select the word.**

   If you can't get the hang of double-clicking, try dragging the mouse over the text to select it. If that approach fails also, try holding down the Shift key and using the arrow keys to highlight the text. I selected the word *Wow* which appears highlighted in the figure shown here.

I can't think of anything to type so the teacher gave me a ▊Wow▊! Neat! practice sentence that's long enough to set work wrap into motion.

3. **Press the Delete key.**

   Your text disappears, and the insertion point stays put.

All that you did was remove the highlighted text. If you want to put the selected text elsewhere, you cut the text to the Clipboard and then paste it somewhere else. For more information about cutting, copying, and pasting, refer to Chapter 4, which gives you plenty of tips.

When you want to replace text with different text, select the text that you don't want and just start typing the new text. The new text replaces the old and saves you a keystroke or two. This method also explains why text sometimes seems to disappear when you least expect it.

For details about other techniques that you can use to select text, see Chapter 4. Practice each technique to see which one you like best.

Dressing characters to the nines

Once upon a time, you had to underline everything that you wanted to emphasize and underline the names of publications, because the typewriter offered no alternatives. Word processing programs have changed all that.

The left end of the toolbar contains buttons that help you to enhance your document. You can change the font and font size, apply boldface and/or italics, and underline text by using these buttons. (The same commands are also available in a menu, of course, but I know that teachers like shortcuts.) See if you can identify the buttons on the toolbar shown here:

ToolTips can help you identify the buttons in the toolbar. To display a ToolTip, simply point to a button or text box on the toolbar and pause; a rectangle appears to identify the purpose of the button.

Enhancing characters

Enhancing characters means selecting text — a single character, a word, or a number of words — and making them bold, italicizing them, or underlining them. Because these three features are the enhancements that people use most, they have prominent toolbar buttons for quick and easy access. To enhance text using these three buttons, try this:

1. **Select the text you want to enhance.**

   You can use the technique you like best to select your text. If you aren't certain what these text selection techniques are, refer to Chapter 4.

Make a mistake? Undo to the rescue!

If you accidentally press a key when text is selected, the Undo feature (Ctrl+Z or Edit⇨Undo) reverses actions as long as you don't do anything rash (such as panic when it happens). In some programs, you may find that you can reverse multiple actions. In Works, Undo reverses only the last action that you did. If you undo an undo what you really do is redo the undo, and soon enough, you'll be in deep . . . trouble!

2. Click the toolbar button which represents the enhancement you want to apply.

The button with the B on it represents **bold**; the button with the I on it applies *italics*, and the button with the U on it <u>underlines</u> the selected text. When you click a button, the button appears a little lighter in color and also appears pressed in (or recessed — no pun intended) so you can glance at the toolbar and easily identify the features that are active.

The enhancement buttons (bold, italic, underline) are *toggle* buttons, which means that you can turn enhancements on and off by clicking the buttons. You can have multiple enhancement features active at the same time, if you want to. If you activate enhancements before you type, the characters that you type are formatted with the active enhancements.

Sizing up fonts: It isn't pointless

To use the toolbar when you want to change the font or font size of existing text, follow these easy steps:

1. Select the text that you want to change.

Use the technique that you prefer to select the text. (If you don't know how to select text, see Chapter 4 for details.)

2. Click the arrow at the right end of the toolbar Font Name text box to display a list of available fonts.

You should see quite a few choices in your Font Name list. You can scroll down the list to review the available fonts and choose the font that you want to use. Remember that fonts are printer-dependent, so the font names that you see depend on the type of printer that you have. To review specifics about fonts, check out Chapter 6.

3. Click a font name.

Your selected text changes to the new font, unless you choose the font that is already active.

4. Click the Font Size drop-down arrow and scroll until you see the size that you want.

Font sizes are measured in points, so the larger the number, the larger the font. Text that appears after selected text moves over to accommodate the enlarged characters. Now are you convinced that word wrap is wonderful?

Setting Up the Document

Typing a document using a word processor is usually no problem if you know how to type. Controlling how the document looks is a bit more challenging than it is on the typewriter, though, because there are so many additional features you can use.

Rulings and the ruler: setting tabs and indents

You can display a ruler in the Word Processor module to help you identify and change tab stops and indents with the mouse. To display the ruler, choose View⇨Ruler. The ruler shown in Figure 8-3 appears at the top of your document window.

Figure 8-3:
You must use your mouse to change settings on the ruler.

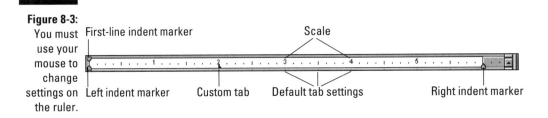

First-line indent marker   Scale

Left indent marker   Custom tab   Default tab settings   Right indent marker

Point to any position on the ruler, and the I-beam mouse pointer changes back to an arrow so that you can position it on the ruler where you want it.

Setting, moving, and removing tabs

Tabs are preset stop positions that mark the position to which the insertion point moves when you press the Tab key on the keyboard. The default tab settings appear every half-inch across your typing page. You can see these default tab marks on the bottom ruler border if you squinch up your eyes and get really close to the screen.

You set tabs, move tabs, move indent markers, and change other settings directly on the ruler. Here's some practice steps to show you how:

1. **Click any position on the ruler.**

   You've just set a custom tab. I set my custom tab at the 2-inch mark, as shown in Figure 8-3. Your custom tab may be at a different spot on the ruler.

   A couple of things change when you set a special tab on the ruler: The default tab marks between the left end of the ruler and your custom tab disappear, and an *L* marks the custom tab location. Works assumes that when you set custom tabs, you want the custom tabs to replace the default tab settings, so Works removes default tab marks on the ruler up to the last custom tab. The *L* indicates that the tab you set is a left tab setting.

2. **Drag the tab that you just set left or right along the ruler scale and drop it at a new position.**

   You can position custom tab marks anywhere on the ruler.

3. **Drag the custom tab straight down off the ruler.**

   Dragging the tab off the ruler removes a custom tab and restores the default tab settings.

Setting indents

How many of you had to type bibliographies when you were in school? Remember how many times you had to start over because you forgot to press the Tab key? And don't forget about those direct quotes of more than three lines that had to be indented $1/2$ inch from both margins and single-spaced, whereas the rest of the report had to be double-spaced?

Because the developers of word processing programs had to make bibliographies just like you did, they came up with a neat new concept: *indents*. Indents allow you to position lines of a paragraph to set them up for bibliographies and quoted material (and anything else that you may need to indent) and then return to the original margin when you're done.

Because the developers know how frequently users may have to adjust indents, the developers put indent markers right on the ruler so that you can get to them quickly and easily. They even broke the left indent marker in half so that you can indent the first line of a paragraph to a different position from all other lines of the paragraph. Study the paragraphs shown in Figure 8-4; notice how the indent markers are set to create the desired format.

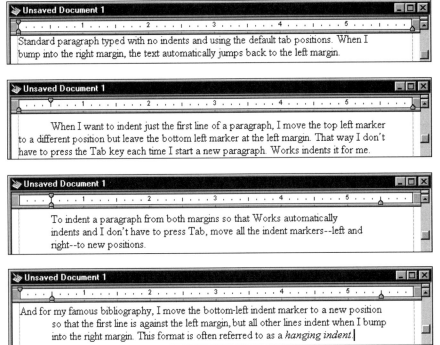

Figure 8-4:
See how
the indent
marker is
set for each
paragraph?

It's easy to confuse indent markers with margins, but they are not the same thing. Although you can move the markers in from both margins when you want to adjust the margins quickly and get a document out the door, you have not actually changed the margin settings; you've simply indented the entire document.

Lining up those paragraphs

Another exciting feature that's built into most word processors is a variety of alignment options. I often think of band directors and church secretaries when I think about the wonderful world of alignments — not because band directors have to make sure that students are lined up straight during those half-time shows or because church secretaries have to deal with pews. I think of these people because of concert programs and church bulletins.

You may have had to type a banquet brochure or another type of program yourself, right? Did you press the space bar repeatedly trying to get everything just so? Ouch! Your typing teacher told you to use the Tab key, not the space bar, to align things. With the features available in word processing programs, the Tab key becomes an even more important character.

Here's an example of how you can change the appearance of your paragraphs by using different alignment options in a word processor:

Left-aligned

When text is left-aligned, all lines of the paragraph appear even down the left edge. The right edge, however, is uneven. some people even call an uneven edge *ragged* because of the uneven appearance. Left-aligned paragraph format is the default for most word processing programs.

Right-aligned

When you want to get someone's attention, don't whisper: Right-align the paragraph so that the lines are even along the right edge. Right-aligned paragraphs receive far more attention than left-aligned paragraphs do, because of the ragged left edge.

Center-aligned

Centering lines of text often gives readers the impression that you've become poetic or that they are being invited to a special event. Use center alignment for your announcements and invitations to "Back to School" night.

Justified

How many of you went through the tedium of trying to justify a paragraph of text on an old manual typewriter? Remember having to count the number of characters and add spaces between words so that the lines were even along the left side *and* down the right side of the page? Yippee! Hurrah! Now a Justified setting does the calculations for you. As you can see, this fully justified paragraph has a proud bearing. Only lines that end with word wrap are actually justified when you format a paragraph by using Justified alignment. Pressing Enter at the end of a paragraph or single-word line prevents Works from spreading the whole word or a few words across the page.

So where do you find the buttons, knobs, and options to change your paragraph alignment? Well, all the alignment formats except Justify are right there in the toolbar. These buttons, which are just to the right of the enhancement buttons, display several straight lines (to represent lines of type). If you can't tell by looking at the lines on the buttons, ToolTips can help you figure out which alignment button does what.

 Unlike enhancement buttons, only one alignment button can be active for a given paragraph. If you have more than one paragraph, you can align each paragraph differently, but you can't align individual lines of a paragraph differently by using these alignment buttons.

Where did WYSI put her WYG?

A term that you will hear bandied about is *WYSIWYG* (pronounced *wizzy wig*). Basically, WYSIWYG means *what you see is what you get*.

What you find, however, is that WYSIWYG most often should be WYSIAWYG — what you see is *almost* what you get. Early word processors provided an "anybody's guess" approach to printing documents; you never

knew for sure exactly how your document would print.

Windows has improved screen resolution to such an extent that you can more reliably count on getting on paper what you see on screen. Sometimes, however, things are a little bit off, especially if you are in the habit of using the space bar to try to line things up.

You also can use keyboard shortcuts to change paragraph alignment. Simply hold down the Ctrl key and then press L to left-align, E to center align, or J to justify text.

To align text in a paragraph using the toolbar alignment buttons, follow these steps:

1. **Position the insertion point anywhere in the paragraph that you want to align.**

   If you want to format several paragraphs at the same time, select (highlight) the paragraphs. If you want to set the alignment before you type the paragraphs, click the alignment button and then type the paragraphs. The format that you choose stays in effect until you change it.

2. **Click the desired toolbar alignment button.**

Saving, Saving, Saving

Okay, are you about ready to produce something useful? I'm about to turn you loose, but first, I want to be sure that you realize that all the work you've done so far is volatile. *Volatile* means that your work is here today but gone tomorrow (or in a minute) if you don't save it. Every character that you've typed so far is stored in RAM, and RAM empties out and forgets everything that you tell it (like your students after the test). Therefore, you need to save your work so that you can get it back when you need it.

When should you save?

I know that many of you produce notes to send home and other documents that you need to print once and never use again. So when should you save them? I recommend saving documents in the following situations:

- **Save every letter until you actually mail it.** You may find a little error that you missed originally or think of something else that you want to add to the letter. If you don't save your letter, you get to retype the whole thing.

- **Save tests and review sheets until you no longer teach the course for which they were prepared.** I know that you often have to give tests that cover different material, but saving tests allows you to pull questions from more than one test and use the questions in a new test by cutting, copying, and pasting (refer to Chapter 4). This procedure is especially handy for creating a makeup test or a final exam.

- **Save all your work until you run out of hard-disk space (or floppy disks); then start purging.** You won't need many of those documents until you dump them, of course — it's Murphy's Law!

How to save

In Works, you can choose among several techniques for saving your work:

- Click the toolbar Save button.
- Choose File➪Save.
- Press Ctrl+S.

Regardless of which technique you use, the Save As dialog box opens. Remember that you need to tell Works where you want to save your document and what you want to name it. Go ahead and save this document for practice; in fact, name it Practice, and pick your own place to store it.

Close it up!

After you save, you can close your document. To close a document, you have several options:

- Click the document's Close button.
- Double-click the document's Control-menu button.
- Choose File➪Close.

✔ Press Ctrl+W.

✔ Press Ctrl+F4.

If you accidentally exit Works instead of closing the document, simply launch Works again.

When all documents in Works are closed, the document no longer appears on-screen, and the Works Task Launcher appears. Notice that your Practice document now appears on the Existing Documents page of the Task Launcher. Cool!

Get it back!

After you have saved and closed a document, you can open it, make changes in it, update it (sort or recycle it the next time that you need something similar), or copy information from it into another document. But first, you have to get the document on-screen — and if you didn't save it, it's retyping time.

Microsoft Works offers five easy options for opening documents that you have used recently:

✔ Double-click the filename in the Existing Documents page of the Works Task Launcher.

✔ Click the filename in the Existing Documents page and then press Enter.

✔ Click the Open a Document Not Listed Here button in the Existing Document page, and select the file that you want.

✔ Press Ctrl+O in any Works module, and select the file.

✔ Choose File⇨Open in any Works module, and select the file.

The first two alternatives seem to be pretty simple, but what happens when you choose one of the other options? These options all lead you to the Open dialog box. In the Open dialog box, you can open the folder that contains the document and then double-click the file to open it. (For details about the features of the Open dialog box, refer to Chapter 7.)

Go ahead — open a document that you closed to see whether it's still the way that it was when you saved it. Make changes, add more dressing, and fix it up nicely.

Applying Your Skills

There's no way to show you all the neat little things buried in the Works Word Processor module. For complete details on all these tidbits, pick up a copy of *Microsoft Works For Teachers,* also from IDG Books Worldwide, Inc. In that book, you find six chapters of goodies about the Word Processor module.

For now, get comfortable, relax, sit back, and enjoy — you're about to take off on a whirlwind tour of some of the great little features of the Works Word Processor. This journey tasks your creative talents. You learn how to use templates and wizards, and save your template design to use again. Pick a challenge and hop to it — the challenges are presented in no special order.

Challenge 1: Designing a letterhead template

Whether you need to send notes home to parents (as though they'd actually get there) or send out permission slips for trips, using a standard format that screams "IT'S FROM ME!" is fun. Besides, you may find the front office to be a little hesitant to give you a piece of its professionally printed paper.

Works' wizards help you create masterpieces that will be the envy of other teachers.

 The following quick and easy steps (you can always change your letterhead later if the parents don't respond) are technically sound and artistically liberal — like Republicans and Democrats riding the fence. Feel free to express your creative independence.

1. **Launch Microsoft Works, and display the Tas<u>k</u>Wizards page in the Works Task Launcher.**

2. **Click the Common Tasks category button to display a list of TaskWizards.**

3. **Click the Letterhead TaskWizard.**

4. **Click OK.**

   A Works Task Launcher dialog box displays two options: One enables you to run the TaskWizard and the other displays a list of documents already created using this TaskWizard. Because you want to create a new letterhead document, you want to run the TaskWizard.

5. **Click <u>Y</u>es, Run the TaskWizard.**

6. **Select one of the letterhead Format styles displayed in Figure 8-5; then click Next.**

   If you want to preview each of the styles before making your selection, go ahead and click the small page diagram to review each of the styles. If you select a style and then change your mind, you'll be able to come back to this page before you finish and select a different style.

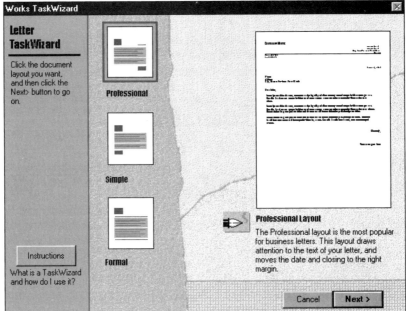

Figure 8-5:
Click a
style — see
a picture
of the
document.

7. **Click the Letterhead button.**

   The Letterhead window lets you tell Works whether you want to design a letterhead for your stationery or to use preprinted letterhead paper (the paper the school office divvies out conservatively).

8. **Choose I want to design my own and then click the Next button.**

   A list of different letterhead style appears on the next Letterhead screen. Click the option button beside different letterhead styles to display a sample that shows what the letterhead looks like.

9. **Select the letterhead style that you want to use; then click Next.**

   The options on this Letterhead page let you decide whether to add a company name or personal name or both to your letterhead. If you click the check box beside Personal name, a text box appears below the option so that you can type your name.

Continue making selections, adding information, following screen prompts, and clicking the Next button until you complete your letterhead.

Before closing the Letterhead window, review your document letterhead. My letterhead creation appears in Figure 8-6.

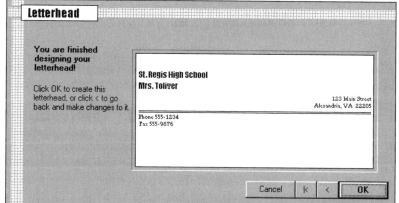

Figure 8-6:
Your
finished
letterhead.

Well, what do you think? Does the letterhead look the way you envisioned it? If not, click the Back button (the one with the < symbol) to back up to the page that you need to change. To return to the first Letterhead page, click the button with the |< symbol. Make the necessary changes, and then choose Next until you see the final product again. When your letterhead appears just right, continue.

10. Click OK to return to the Works TaskWizard window.

Before you tell the wizard that you're finished, you may want to change the text style. The other options in this page affect the actual text that you would add to a letter if you were really going to type a letter and send it. You're creating a letterhead template, so you don't need to worry about the other options right now.

11. Click Create It!

Review the checklist that the wizard presents; this is your last change to make changes before you see the actual document.

If you want to save just the letterhead part of the document as a template, return to the document screen (press Esc) and delete other text on the page. If you don't know how to select and delete text, refer to the "Deleting text" section earlier in this chapter.

Putting your students to work

Now that you've become an expert, have your students work on the computer, using Works. The students' work will be much easier to grade, and using the computer makes assignments seem like child's play.

What can you have your students do? Incorporate some of these activities into the lesson-plan format that your school requires (surely you can find several objectives that these activities can support!) and tailor them to fit the grade level that you teach. Here are some teacher-tested ideas. You can have your students:

✔ **Type a page of their notes** (assuming, of course, that they take notes). They can practice using formats such as bold and italic, changing font sizes and styles, and aligning the material in various ways to help them organize their material visually and logically.

✔ **Type their homework assignments.** Math and chemistry classes use the special formatting options.

✔ **Type a résumé, formatting it manually or using the Resume TaskWizard.** This exercise is good practice in personalizing a template and is ever so useful to high-school seniors.

✔ **Type a résumé for a famous person or a literary character.** This exercise is good practice for integrating your curriculum while you practice on a Works template.

✔ **Type a letter.** Students can type friendly letters to grandparents, for example (letters to friends can get out of hand), or persuasive letters that address various issues to a local school board or city-council member. Allow students to mail these letters. If your printer accepts envelopes, print them, too.

✔ **Type a report on a subject-specific topic.** Have students include a bibliography page to practice indenting and using italics.

✔ **Create a class newsletter,** using the same techniques that you used to create your stationery. Then have each student type an article for the newsletter. This activity provides lots of practice with fonts, columns, headlines, justification, and fitting copy to a prescribed space. It also is a good cooperative learning activity.

✔ **Write a script for a play,** using the tab-alignment features; make copies and present the play with friends or puppets.

✔ **Design an invitation.** The invitation can be for classmates, informing them about an upcoming event (a puppet show?), or for family members, informing them about open houses.

✔ **Create letterhead stationery for a literary, historical, or scientific character** (or even for a frog, butterfly, or foreign country). If possible, allow students to print the letterhead on colored paper in colored ink.

✔ **Write a letter that the literary, historical, or scientific person might send to Congress, the president, or to students of his or her day or time.** Students can write the text in longhand if there isn't enough lab time.

If this is the first time that you've used one of the wizards, you're bound to make mistakes. After you create your document, if you don't like it, it's very easy to start over — just don't let anyone know how easy it is, or they won't be nearly so impressed!

Challenge 2: Saving a letterhead as a template

When your letterhead is complete, if you want to save it so that you can use it over and over again, you need to save the letterhead as a template. Saving a document as a template means that each time you want to use the letterhead, Works makes a copy of the letterhead so that the original remains clean. You use the copy to create your letter and then save the letter as a document — not as a template.

To save your letterhead as a template, follow these steps:

1. **Click the Save button in the toolbar or choose File⇨Save to open the Save As dialog box.**

2. **Click the Template button to tell Works that you want to save this file as a template.**

   The Save As Template dialog box opens, allowing you to type the name of the template.

3. **Type a name for your template.**

   I generally try to use as descriptive a name as possible for my templates so that I'll know, when I use them, what type of templates they are. I typed **Pam's School Stationery** as the title of my letterhead, for example. That way, when I create a personal letterhead, I know which template is which.

4. **Press Enter.**

   Notice that when you save your letterhead as a template, you still see an unnamed document number in the document title bar. That's because you saved a template — not a document. To make sure that your template really is saved, check it out.

5. **Click the Task Launcher button in the toolbar (if you aren't certain which button it is, use ToolTips to help you locate it).**

   The Task Launcher window appears.

6. **Scroll the TaskWizards page of the Works Task Launcher until you see User Defined Templates at the bottom.**

7. Click User Defined Templates.

A list of templates designed by people who have used Works on your computer appears. Look through the list to see whether you see your template. It should appear right at the top of the list, because Works arranges templates with the newest ones first.

Go ahead, now — use your template, abuse it, but please don't lose it. Create a new document and type that note to your students. Let them know that you're becoming PC-proficient. Save the document and print it. Then see whether your template is still in the template pool for you to use again.

Three cheers! You did it — you created your first template. You're raring to go for your second one, right?

Challenge 3: Customizing test templates

Okay, it's your turn now. I know that you're just itching to get into those Students and Teachers TaskWizards, so here's your chance. See whether you can create the test format displayed in Figure 8-7 using the Tests TaskWizard from the Students and Teachers category. Substitute a test name for the one that I use, if desired, and of course, put your name where mine is. Add whatever standard instructions you use for your tests in place of mine.

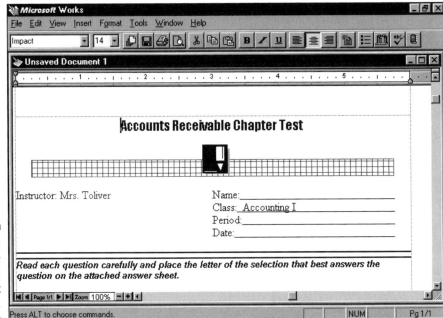

Figure 8-7: My customized test format template.

The proof(reading) is in the pudding

If you explored the menus, you may have noticed that the Tools menu contains commands that you can probably use. Included among the commands is Spelling, which helps you identify misspelled words.

It's true, I admit, that you can have Works check the spelling of words in your documents, and it does a fine job of checking them, too. But does the spell checker take proofing out of your routine? I don't think so; you still have to proofread your work. Look at this sample sentence:

> Sample sentence in you document the you decided you didn't need to proofread.

See any misspelled works? I don't, ether. But are their errors that need to be corrected? Yes. Get the pitcher?

Save your test format as a template; then use it when you prepare your first test. The only thing that you have to change when you use the template to create a test is the test name. By choosing the multiple-choice format, you can easily add true/false questions and essay questions to the end of the document. See what you can come up with — and be creative! Your students will love it.

Look for these great features

Here are a few top choice features that you'll want to explore when you're feeling stable on your Works feet. Look them up in the Help feature and then put them to use.

- **Easy Text** allows you to save frequently used phrases and formats and then insert them into other documents.

- **Footnote** makes creating references easy — and helps you avoid plagiarism.

- **Table** makes creating columnar text and aligning it even easier than fancy tabs do.

- **ClipArt** provides a gallery of cute pictures that you can add to your documents.

- **WordArt** changes your words into words of art.

- **Borders and Shading** add backgrounds and boxes to call attention to special messages.

- **Bullets** format lists to draw attention to specific points.

- **Easy Format** resemble templates but set up paragraphs by using standard formats.

- **Columns** divide your document into multiple-column layout for newsletters.

- **Envelopes** and **Labels** are great tools.

- **Thesaurus**, **Word Count**, and **Lookup Reference** are features that your students will come to depend on.

Chapter 9

Celling You on Spreadsheets

· ·

In This Chapter

▶ Identifying spreadsheet basics

▶ Creating your first spreadsheet

▶ Using spreadsheet templates

▶ Creating a spreadsheet lesson-plan template

· ·

Math teachers, social studies teachers, science teachers, elementary teachers, and all teachers in between celebrate their students' English skills each time they have to grade tests, decipher ink scratches on students' papers, or listen to their students try communicating verbally. Although it's the responsibility of each and every teacher, parent, and member of the community to encourage and reinforce communication skills (it takes a village, you know), quite often, we rely on English or Language Arts teachers to enforce the rules.

If you are skilled in software-application basics — typing, correcting, inserting, deleting, and enhancing text — you're ready to tackle spreadsheets. If you need to review these techniques, return to English . . . er . . . word processing class. Tucked into the pages of Chapter 8, you find neat tricks that you may want to use as you tackle spreadsheets.

Spreadsheets: An Overview

If someone were to ask you what comes to mind when you hear the term *spreadsheet,* what would you say? Do you envision flags flopping in the breeze or the linens on your bed? Maybe you think of spreading sheets by a pool of clear blue water.

If you're already familiar with spreadsheets, you know that a *spreadsheet* is a sheet of paper that contains columns and rows and that spreads out as you need more space — and more columns or rows. The column/row layout makes lining up numbers and other information much easier, and you'll be amazed by the types of information that you decide to store. A spreadsheet is like a page of your grade book or attendance register (if you keep them separate) that's been put on your computer so you can display it on-screen. You can use a spreadsheet to average grades, keep track of student attendance, and create a budget format to keep track of your finances. A spreadsheet is an electronic worksheet, similar in format to the ledger pages used by accountants when they kept records manually — *electronic* in that a spreadsheet keeps records on a computer.

The spreadsheet is used primarily in the business arena, but its column/row format makes it attractive in other professions as well.

Scratching Out Your First Spreadsheet

Many spreadsheet templates and TaskWizards are available in Microsoft Works, but you still need to know your way around the page. So how about creating a useful document and learning the basics of working with spreadsheets at the same time? Good; it's time to get down to the brass tacks of spreadsheets. To create one, follow these easy steps:

1. **Launch Microsoft Works and display the Works Tools page of the Works Task Launcher by clicking on the Works Tools tab.**

2. **Click the Spreadsheet button in the Works Tools page.**

   A clean new spreadsheet window like the one shown in Figure 9-1 opens.

Pretty simple, huh? But what do all the screen parts mean? Here are some guidelines to get you going on your spreadsheet:

✔ Each new spreadsheet that you create during your Works session is assigned a generic name and number (you must admit Unsaved Spreadsheet 1 is pretty generic) until you save it. You see similar generic document naming in each Works module.

✔ *Rows* are numbered; *columns* are lettered; *cells* are formed where rows cross columns.

✔ Cells are named by combining the column letter and the row number — A1, B6, and so on. This combination is called the cell's *address*.

✔ The *frame* of the spreadsheet is formed by the row numbers and column letters. You don't type anything in the frame. The numbers and letters appear on row and column buttons that you can use to select an entire row or column.

✔ All data and information (names, grades, check marks, and so on) is typed in the cells.

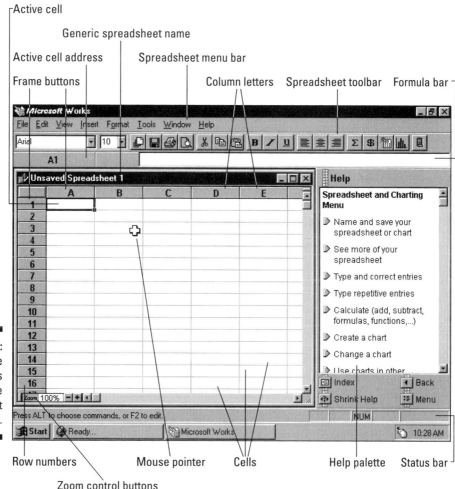

Active cell

Generic spreadsheet name

Active cell address

Spreadsheet menu bar

Frame buttons

Column letters   Spreadsheet toolbar   Formula bar

Figure 9-1:
The
treasures
of the
spreadsheet
window.

Row numbers   Mouse pointer   Cells   Help palette   Status bar

Zoom control buttons

- Cells are 10 characters wide and as tall as the characters that you put in them. You can change any column's width and any row's height.

- The *formula bar* contains three sections: the cell address, the edit area, and the entry boxes (you won't see these until you start typing).

- The *toolbar buttons* are primarily the same as those discussed in Chapter 8, but four of the last five are different.

- The *mouse pointer* is a broad, hollow plus symbol, and the *active cell* has a double dark border and a square in the bottom-right corner.

The Help palette takes up part of your screen real estate, and you won't need it to accomplish what the teacher has planned. Close Help by choosing Help⇨Hide Help.

Ah, that's better . . . and bigger, too. You can always get Help back when you need it by choosing the command again. When Help is hidden, the Hide Help command in the Help menu changes to Show Help.

Navigating the sheet

What you see on the screen when you activate the spreadsheet module is only a portion of the entire spreadsheet. You can click to select a cell that appears in the spreadsheet window or use the scroll bars to display additional cells. Clicking, of course, involves using the mouse to make cell selections. You can also use the keyboard to display cells. Table 9-1 identifies some great spreadsheet-navigation techniques that allow you to see how big the complete spreadsheet is. Try pressing some of the keys and key combinations and see where they take you.

Table 9-1 Navigation Keys to Move You around the Spreadsheet

Keystroke	Where It Takes You
Arrow key	From cell to cell, one at a time
Tab key	One cell to the right
Shift+Tab	One cell left
PgDn	One screen down
PgUp	One screen up
Ctrl+PgDn	One screen right
Ctrl+PgUp	One screen left
Ctrl+→	Last column
Ctrl+↓	Last row
Ctrl+Home	First cell (A1)

Well, do you think that you have enough columns and rows to hold your work? I would hate to have to type data in every single cell of the spreadsheet. By the time I would finish, I'd probably need an IV (that's also the name of the last column, which you find out in the next paragraph). And what about those rows? Whew! With 16,384 rows and 256 (trust me) columns, you'd need a spreadsheet to calculate the total number of cells!

You probably didn't look at every single column and row in the spreadsheet, so you missed the complex column-naming scheme (rows are much easier to number; they simply run consecutively). The alphabet was exhausted with the first 26 columns, so the double standard (very big grin, please) was adopted. Thus, you have AA, AB, . . . AZ; BA, BB, . . . BZ; CA, and so on. The 256th column is IV.

A grade book spreadsheet

Averaging grades is the perfect task to reveal the wonder of spreadsheets. Pull out your grade book and follow the steps shown in this section to get some work done as you learn, or if you'd rather just practice for now, use the sample stuff I've provided in the steps that follow. Be sure to launch Works and create a new spreadsheet (click the Spreadsheet module button in the Works Tools page of the Launcher) if you didn't create one as described earlier in this chapter at the beginning of the "Scratching Out Your First Spreadsheet" section.

Entering data into cells

To type data into cells, follow these steps:

1. Press Ctrl+Home to get back to cell A1.

Starting at the beginning is always a good idea.

2. Type the information that you want to place in the cell (just type; that's all).

Most spreadsheets contain a title of some type. I generally type my name and subject as the title of my grade book. You may want to identify your grade book by period or grade level. If you don't have your grade book handy, type **Mrs. Toliver's Algebra I Second Period Class.**

Notice as you start typing that your text appears in two places: in the cell and in the formula bar. If you look closely at the formula bar, you get your first glimpse of the entry boxes that I mention in the "Scratching Out Your First Spreadsheet" section earlier in this chapter. The entry boxes appear in the formula bar between the cell address and the text that you type.

As you continue to type, the text in cell A1 begins to scroll (just like a storm warning that appears at the bottom of your TV screen), but the formula bar shows all of what you typed.

3. Press Enter when you finish typing.

Does all the text appear in the spreadsheet cell? Remember that each cell, by default, shows you only ten characters. If nothing is in the cell next to the active cell, however, the cell contents spread out and take up space in additional cells, too (sort of as you do when the seat next to you on an airplane is empty!).

4. Move to the next cell in which you want to enter data.

5. Repeat Steps 1 through 3 until you have entered all data.

For practice, if you don't have a grade book available, try creating the portion of the spreadsheet shown in Figure 9-2. Substitute the names of your students where appropriate.

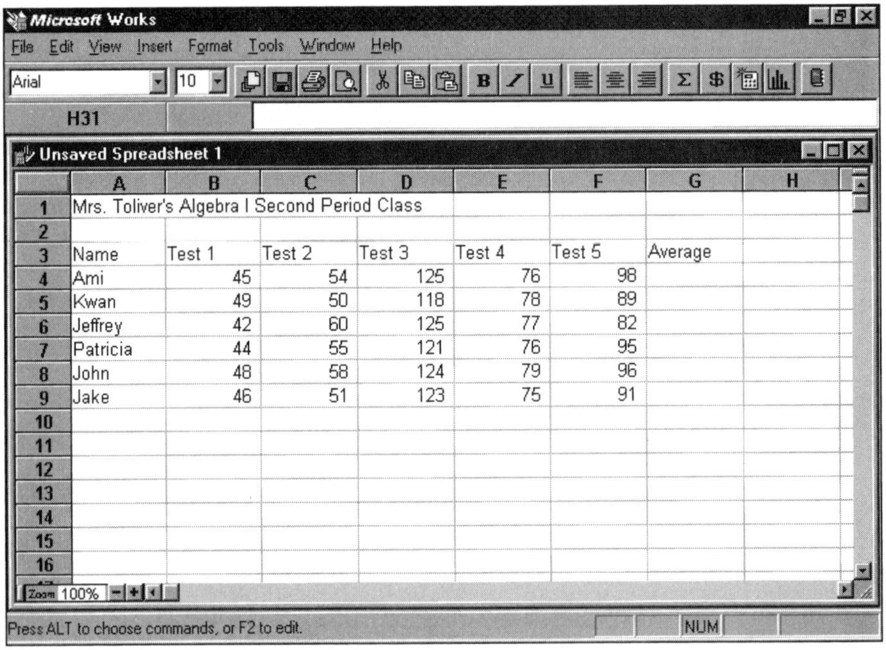

Figure 9-2:
Here's a
sample
spreadsheet
for you to
type.

Formulas, functions, dates, and data

You can enter more than just letters and numbers in your spreadsheet cells. In fact, unless you learn to enter formulas, it is difficult to get the spreadsheet to do your grade work for you. What you are able to do with the data that you add to your spreadsheets depends on what you put in the cells and how your data is organized. Here are a few guidelines to help you know when to enter what type of data to get the results that you want:

✔ *Alphanumeric* data contain alphabetic and numeric characters that you don't need to use in calculations. Names, addresses, and telephone numbers don't need to be added together, for example.

✔ *Numeric* data contains numbers as values that are used in calculations. Grades, money, grades, room dimensions, grades, and so on fit into this category.

✔ *Formulas* contain instructions to tell Works what to do with the numeric data. Instructions such as add, subtract, multiply, and so on are formula builders. B3+B4-B7*B1/2 is an example of a formula.

✔ *Functions* are built-in instructions that reduce the amount of typing that you have to do create a formula. Instructions such as Sum, Average, Minimum, Average, Maximum, Average, and so on fit this type of data. Functions begin with an equal sign (=). =Sum(B3:B10) is an example of a function.

✔ *Dates*. I won't insult you by explaining this type of data. Just remember those times when you have to calculate a student's age in years, months, and days!

Homing in on ranges

Range refers to a block of contiguous (touching) cells in a spreadsheet. You'll recognize a range when you select it, because it is highlighted. It's important to know the rules of the range:

✔ Ranges begin with the address of the first cell in the range.

✔ Ranges end with the address of the last cell in the range.

✔ The addresses of the first and last cells in the range are separated by a colon (:).

Put into pictures, a selected range appears as shown in the figure in this sidebar. Typed into a cell, the range appears as A4:C7.

Don't let the rules of the range have the ranger homing in on you!

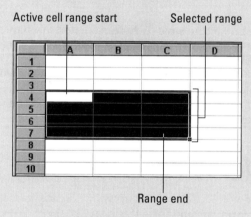

Active cell range start   Selected range

Range end

If you continue to add names to your list, additional rows scroll onto the screen automatically. Notice a couple of things about the spreadsheet:

✔ Each name lines up nicely along the left side of the cell. Alphabetic information left-aligns within the cell.

✔ Numbers line up along the right side of the cell. The ones line up under the ones column and the tens line up under the tens column, just as you were taught in elementary school.

Editing spreadsheet data

Just in case you see a mistake after you move to a different cell, you need to back up and correct it. Try each of the following techniques to determine which procedure is easiest for you:

✔ Click the cell that contains the error, and correct the error in the formula bar.

✔ Click the cell that contains the error, press F2, and correct the error in the cell.

✔ Double-click the cell that contains the error, and correct the error in the cell.

✔ Click the cell to make it active, type the new stuff, and press Enter.

Saving your work

Before you start messing around with your spreadsheet, you need to save it. That way, if something goes all awry, and you panic and can't find Undo, all will be safe.

 You can use any of the save techniques listed in Chapter 8 to save your spreadsheet work. The easiest way to save your work is to click the Save button on the toolbar.

Open the folder that you want to keep your spreadsheet in, and give your spreadsheet a neat name. Don't forget to save it again when you add some new information or change the format!

Formulating the sheet

 Before I turn you loose to dress up your spreadsheet, I want to show you how to add formulas and format the spreadsheet. With just a few quick steps, your grade book spreadsheet will be ready to go.

Entering formulas to get your grade book to work properly

To make the spreadsheet function properly, you need to add functions that add each student's scores and divide by the number of grades. Before you know it, your grades are averaged. Follow these steps:

 1. Make active the cell that is to contain the formula.

You can work with a spreadsheet of your own or open the spreadsheet named CH9-ss.wks on the CD-ROM that comes with this book. If you use the sample spreadsheet, make cell G4 active.

 2. Click the Easy Calc toolbar button.

The Easy Calc dialog box shown in Figure 9-3 opens.

3. Click the Average button.

After you click the Easy Calc button, Easy Calc examines your spread-sheet, finds that you've entered values in cells B4 through F4 of the current row, and assumes that these are the values that you want to average. It automatically selects the cells and creates the formula shown in the sample formula area at the bottom of the second Easy Calc window, shown in Figure 9-4. (I certainly wish that I were so accurate with my assumptions.)

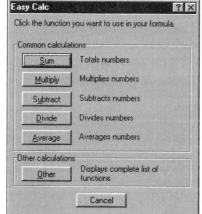

Figure 9-3:
Easy Calc
makes
calculating
a snap,
crackle,
click.

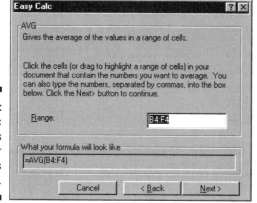

Figure 9-4:
Easy Calc
creates
your
formulas
for you.

4. **Click Next.**

A second Easy Calc window displays the cell in which Easy Calc plans to place the formula result.

Another great assumption on Easy Calc's part — but you had something to do with this decision, of course, because you chose the cell in the first place.

5. **Click Finish.**

Voilà — Ami's grades are averaged. Are they accurate? Pull out your handy-dandy pocket calculator and average the grades by hand to see.

You can use the same technique to create other function formulas listed on the buttons of the Easy Calc dialog box. If you don't see the calculation that you want to perform, click the Other button for a complete list — but watch out . . . you may be overwhelmed by the extent of the list!

Copying formulas

The formula that you create to calculate one student's grades is the same formula that you use to calculate averages for other students in the class. The only difference is that you want the computer to average the grades in each row separately. Believe it or not, this technique is not required exclusively of teachers. As a result, those marvelous programmers built in an automatic feature that adjusts the row number for formulas and functions that you copy from row to row or column to column. Ready for some new magic?

To copy a formula or function from one cell to a range of cells, follow these steps:

1. **Make active the cell that contains the formula you want to copy.**

   In the sample spreadsheet, cell G4 contains the formula.

2. **Position the mouse pointer on the tiny square in the bottom-right corner of the selected cell border.**

   When the mouse is positioned appropriately, the mouse pointer appears as shown in Figure 9-5.

Figure 9-5:
The mouse wants to fill your life . . . er, spreadsheet with formulas and functions.

CH9-ss.wks

	A	B	C	D	E	F	G	H
1	Mrs. Toliver's Algebra I Second Period Class							
2								
3	Name	Test 1	Test 2	Test 3	Test 4	Test 5	Average	
4	Ami	45	54	125	76	98	79.6	
5	Kwan	49	50	118	78	89		
6	Jeffrey	42	60	125	77	82		
7	Patricia	44	55	121	76	95		
8	John	48	58	124	79	96		
9	Jake	46	51	123	75	91	FILL	
10								
11								
12								
13								

3. Drag the square down to the last row in the column that contains values you want to calculate; then release the mouse button.

If you're using the practice spreadsheet, the last row containing student grades is Row 9. Presto — all grades are averaged. Notice that Works adjusted the row number for formulas in Rows 5 through 9 of the sample spreadsheet, so students get credit for their own grades — not Ami's.

Just in case you are using your own grade book and didn't take time to enter all your students' grades, you may find a few strange messages on the screen. Here's the deal: If you copy a formula to rows that do not contain grades, Works tells you that there must be some mistake and places an ERR message in the empty rows. The ERR message disappears as you start entering values for cells in the row.

One more point: When you copy formulas across a row (such as totals at the bottom of a spreadsheet), Works automatically adjusts the column named in the formula. As a result, using this technique on a financial worksheet gives you the correct total for each month or expense that you're tracking.

Laying out the spreadsheet

Spreadsheet layout is important, because it adds to the appearance and accommodates the information that you want to put in spreadsheet cells. Here are some techniques that you need to know to complete your grade book spreadsheet and to create your lesson-plan template in the "Applying Your Skills" section at the end of this chapter (in other words, it's on the test!), so listen up:

✔ Insert columns and rows to make adding that pop quiz between two existing test grades much easier, not to mention adding the new student that you get halfway through the first semester.

✔ Widen columns and heighten rows to accommodate those long last names and extra-tall characters.

✔ Enhance characters, shade, and border cells just to make the spreadsheet look pretty!

Inserting columns and rows

To add an extra assignment between two assignments that you've already entered in your grade book, or to add the student that you get right after you get your grade book all set up (in ink, of course), try these easy steps:

1. Click the frame button for the row or column that currently occupies the position of the new row or column.

Clicking the frame button highlights the complete row or column. If you're using the practice spreadsheet, select column B; adding student last names is good practice. (If you don't have a spreadsheet handy, open CH9-ss.wks, which you can find on the CD-ROM that comes with this book.)

2. Choose Insert⇨Insert Column.

Just so you know, Works realizes that you selected a column, so it offers only the option to insert a column. Had you selected a row, Works would offer the option to insert a row (finally, a feature that doesn't require you to make a choice!).

Notice that the other columns moved over to make room for the new column. Now you can add your students' last names.

Recycle these basic techniques to add a row and to delete a row or column:

✔ Click a row button and then choose Insert⇨Insert Row to add a new row between rows that contain data. (If you choose a row at the bottom of the spreadsheet, you won't see the effect.)

✔ Click a row or column button and then choose Insert⇨Delete Row or Insert⇨Delete Column.

Broadening columns and heightening rows

When a column of information extends beyond the 10 characters that Works allows, you need to widen the column to display cell data on-screen. When you want to add some space between rows in a spreadsheet, you can change the row height instead of skipping rows. Use one of the following techniques to change your column width or row height:

✔ Double-click the frame button for the column that you want to widen. This technique tells Works to make the column wide enough to fit the data — a Best Fit approach to formatting columns.

For practice, double-click the column frame button for column A.

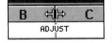

✔ Position the mouse pointer close to the column-frame button's right border so that the mouse appears as a two-headed pointer with the word Adjust below the pointer. Then click and drag the border to adjust the column's width.

✔ Position the mouse pointer close to the row-frame button's bottom border so that the mouse appears as a two-headed Adjust pointer. Then click and drag the border to adjust the row's height.

✔ Select the column or row and choose Format⇨Row Height or Format⇨Column Width to open a dialog box so that you can enter the height of the row or width of the columns that you want to use. You can also choose Best Fit to adjust rows and columns so that the data fits precisely in the cells or choose Standard to reset a row or column to its default setting by using the dialog box.

Putting it on paper: printing

Printing a spreadsheet sometimes does not deliver the expected results. The easiest way to ensure that you're going to get what you want is to preview the printout.

If your spreadsheet is large, Works puts as much information on each page as it can (which depends on the size of the paper, of course); then Works moves to the next sheet and prints the next group of columns and rows that will fit. The number of pages required for printing the spreadsheet depends completely on the size of the spreadsheet.

To be sure that the system prints only what you want, select the columns that you don't want to print and change the width of the columns to 0 (zero) so that they don't appear on screen. (If you aren't certain how to change the column width and row height, follow the steps in the section "Broadening columns and heightening rows" in this chapter.)

I know teachers who enter student ID numbers in addition to student names. When they print out their grade books, these teachers "hide" the student names and print the results by using only the ID numbers. That way, they can post the grade book and students can check their own grades anonymously. If that method doesn't suit your needs, you can set up page breaks and then tell Works which pages you want to print.

To add a page break, activate the cell in which you want to start the new page, then choose Insert⇨Insert Page Break. The Insert Page Break dialog box asks whether you want to start the new page with the active column or with the active row. Make your choice and then click OK.

As a final step, use Print Preview to verify that your printout is what you want.

Go ahead — drench it in dressing!

You're on your own — be creative. If you aren't certain how to accomplish some of the tasks that I've listed in this section, check out Chapter 8; you'll find that lots of font tips and tricks used in word processing apply to spreadsheet text as well. Try each of the following activities, or explore on your own to make your spreadsheet uniquely yours:

- ✔ Change the font for the title in A1, and make it really big.
- ✔ Click the frame button for column A to select all cells in the column, and change the alignment of the names to center them.
- ✔ Select the cells that contain grades (or the cells in which grades appear), and experiment with colors by choosing Format⇨Shading or Format⇨Border.
- ✔ Change the appearance of the numbers in column G by choosing Format⇨Number and choosing options.

Although you may think that some of these ideas are only window dressing for spreadsheets, think of the possible advantage of keeping grades for different types of activities in different colors: red for tests, blue for quizzes, yellow for homework, and so on. A glance can tell you that Susie would do better if she did her homework, whereas Tom could raise his grade if he performed better on tests. When it comes to managing teaching time, any shortcut helps.

When you finish, save your spreadsheet if you want to keep it for later use.

Applying Your Skills

I've formulated two challenges for you. One challenge uses templates, and the other starts from scratch. You can do both of them or pick the one that seems to meet your most urgent needs. I don't want to insult your intelligence, so I'm just going to throw you an idea and a picture or two, and allow you to experiment to achieve *your* desired results.

Just have fun — and don't be too creative, or you won't be able to stand yourself!

Challenge 1: Customizing the grade-book template

Use the Grade Book TaskWizard to create a grade-book format that you can use; then store it as a template in User Designed Templates, so that you can use it again next semester or next year, or once for each of your classes. You can create a template that is quite sophisticated and then change the format so that it more closely resembles the standardized grade sheet that you're required to use. (For a refresher on using the TaskWizards to create and save a template, see Chapter 8.)

Because I needed a weighted grade book format (tests count more than timed writings in a typing class, you see), I chose the Weighted format for the grade book shown in Figure 9-6.

Some points for customizing the grade book after you create it:

✔ Text that appears on-screen in red needs to be replaced with your own personal information.

✔ You can add students' names starting with the cell just below Students (cell A17 in the Weighted grade-book format).

✔ Many formulas have already been entered.

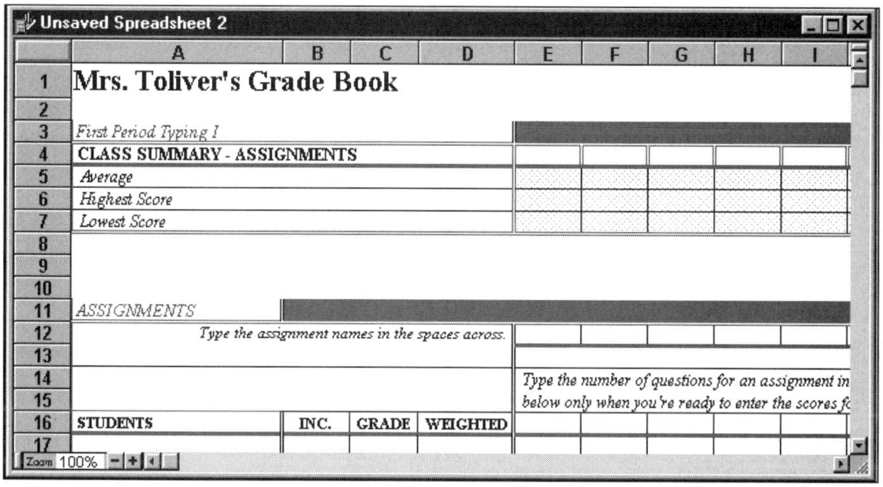

Figure 9-6:
My grade
book is *so*
charming!

Then look around the spreadsheet — see those sophisticated formulas? Aren't you glad that those template developers added these formulas for you?

You may want to print a copy of the grade-book template to show your supervisor before you type students' names and grades. Selling your supervisor on something new when a school-system standard is already intact may be more difficult than creating a new standard!

Challenge 2: What lesson-plan template?

A brief tour of the TaskWizards yields no lesson-plan templates! Does this mean that you are no longer responsible for performing those Sunday-afternoon tasks? You may wonder how can you have a TaskWizard category called Students and Teachers without lesson plans. Will you be expected to teach without a lesson plan?

Actually, the formats for lesson plans are so varied that trying to please everyone isn't worth the agony (and letters of complaint from all the teachers). So pull out your lesson-plan form; this is your chance to do it up the way that you've always wanted it (assuming, of course, that you are sure it's okay to use an alternative lesson-plan format at your school).

Launch the spreadsheet module of Works, and try to create a form that resembles the one that you use. I created the one shown in Figure 9-7. Feel free to copy it (this teacher won't mind) if you don't have one that you like.

If you reviewed all the features covered in this chapter, you already know how to set up the basic layout for your lesson plan template. Here are some additional features you may want to apply to get your template looking spiffy:

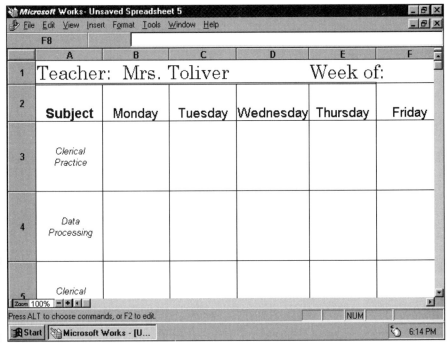

Figure 9-7:
An example
of a lesson-
plan format.

✔ Use the same text formatting (font, font size, enhancements) techniques identified in Chapter 8 to format text in the spreadsheet.

✔ Select cells that you want to outline with a border and then choose
Format➪Border to display the Format Cells dialog box. Choose a line
style, line color, and border style for selected cells.

✔ After you type **Monday**, you can use the same technique to fill in
Tuesday through **Friday** that you used to copy formulas. Simply drag
the fill handle in the bottom-right corner of the cell containing *Monday*
across the row.

✔ Select cells in which you want to center text vertically (as shown in
Column A of Figure 9-7) and choose Format➪Alignment➪Center.

✔ Select cells in which you anticipate that you'll type more than one line
of text (Columns B through F of Figure 9-7, for example) and choose
Format➪Alignment➪Top to start the text at the top of the cells. Click
the Wrap Text check box to tell Works to wrap text that extends beyond
the cell width to the next line.

Save your template by clicking the Save button and then click the
Template button in the Save As dialog box. Name the template in the
Save As Template dialog box and click OK.

You're done! Good job.

To use the template, simply double-click the template name in the User Defined Templates list. A new spreadsheet appears on-screen, formatted with the settings that you saved in your template — with words and everything!

As you create each week's lesson plans, save them under different filenames (I usually save mine by using Monday's date). Be careful, though — you have to use hyphens to separate the month from the day and from the year; the system doesn't like slashes.

Then dream of cutting, copying, and pasting to fix up your lesson plans for next week when you need to carry over an activity or lesson. Sometimes, all that it takes to prepare next week's plan is to change the date at the top of the lesson-plan file from last week!

Print out your work and turn it in bright and early Monday morning.

Putting you and your students to work

Is your head stuffed full of ideas for using spreadsheets? You'll find that brainstorming ideas with others (teachers, students, parents, and anyone else) can provide so many neat ideas for using spreadsheets that you won't know where to begin.

You can use spreadsheets any time you need cells to fill in. Sometimes, you print the spreadsheets and fill in the contents the old-fashioned way (by hand) later. Here are some tried-and-true ideas for putting spreadsheets to work for you and your students:

✔ Lists of book numbers assigned to each student

✔ Speech or research topics chosen by all the students in a class

✔ Seating charts and lesson plans for substitutes

✔ Study guides for a period of history or a science unit

✔ Rubrics for oral presentations or individual projects

✔ Progress charts in reading, vocabulary, keyboarding, or physical education

✔ Fund-raising efforts and results for the entire freshman class or the band or the PTO or . . . you get the idea

✔ Grammar practice in foreign-language classes

✔ Calculate formulas in math; write equations in science and home economics; figure out longitudinal or latitudinal measurements in geography; plot timelines in history; or gather statistics in sports or PE — you get the idea

Be careful when you start working with spreadsheets, though; it's easy to go overboard. Make sure that your activities are subject and age appropriate.

Chapter 10

Profiling a Database

. . . .

In This Chapter

▶ Identifying database terminology

▶ Setting up a database

▶ Adding information to the database

▶ Changing the database design

▶ Finding, sorting, and querying a database

▶ Merging data with documents

. . . .

So how many of you know what a database is? Have you never used one? Then close your eyes for a moment and imagine a visual tour of your classroom as it is now, and then keep them closed and picture your classroom as you *wish* it looked. Do you see any index-card files? How about student folders that hold all the important information that you need to know about your students: their histories, previous class performance, allergies, and those types of things?

If you can picture any one of these items, you're already familiar with databases — you simply don't know it. Hold these images close as you begin your database escapade; you'll find relating to databases to be much easier with friendly faces close by.

Database Ground Rules

Every once in a while, I find it necessary to get stuffy. Please bear with me during one of those stuffy phases while I define *database*. A *database* is a collection of data (facts, you know, just the facts) stored together to provide useful information about related items.

You've seen databases, you've used them, and now you're going to convert them to electronic files so that you can store them on your computer. Electronic databases provide a sophisticated way to organize large volumes of data so that you can search through information more efficiently. And how much space is required? Well, imagine your file cabinet compressed into a floppy little 3¹/₂-inch disk.

Without spinning many wheels, you can learn about databases and create something useful at the same time. You know that you have to keep records about students; you send forms home to parents and hope that the forms come back, so that you don't have to send letters asking for them or send another copy of the form. What you do with the forms when you finally do get them back may take a different avenue now that you've become computer-literate.

Plotting the Database Playing Field

Getting your database ready to use takes only a few minutes, and if you save your database as a template, you can use it again next year and save *more* time. A few terms help you get started. I use these terms throughout this chapter, so study them carefully:

- ✔ *Field* refers to each piece of information that you put in your database: first name, middle initial, date of birth, and so on. Each field has a name that should be descriptive (so that you know what the information you're looking at represents).

- ✔ *Record* identifies all the information about one person, place, or thing, such as your students. If you have 20 students in your class, you have 20 records.

- ✔ *File* pulls all the records together and stores them with one database filename. All students in one class, all students in all your classes, or all this year's students would each make up a separate database file. Many very powerful databases enable you to store several different tables of data in the same database file so that all your stuff is kept together.

To get started, you need to launch the Database module of Microsoft Works. Follow these steps:

1. **Launch Microsoft Works, and display the Works Tools page of the Works Task Launcher.**

2. **Click the Database module button.**

   Aren't the little Rolodex cards on the icon cute? Works may recognize that this is the first time you've used the Database module and offer help by displaying the First-Time Help window. Click the OK button to tell Works that you have help right here in this book and you don't need Works to help.

Defining your fields

When you start the Database module, the Create Database dialog box appears (see Figure 10-1) so that you can start telling Works what fields of data you want to put in your database. In addition, you see options that enable you to tell Works what type of data you plan to store in each database field.

For practice, how about creating a database that stores student information? Regardless of what subject or grade level you teach, you're bound to want to store student information, even if the information that you store in the database is the names and addresses of students who belong to a club that you sponsor. Try these steps to add the first field to your very first database:

1. **Type the first field name that you want the database to contain in the Field Name text box.**

   Breaking your data into smaller segments so that each segment is a separate field makes maintaining a database, sorting, selecting, and finding data easier. Make the field names descriptive (Field 1 is rather generic, don't you think?), so that you remember what you're supposed to type in each field when you start recording data in the database later.

   Field names can be up to 15 characters long. If you're using the student-information database idea, type **First Name** in the Field Name text box.

Generic field name

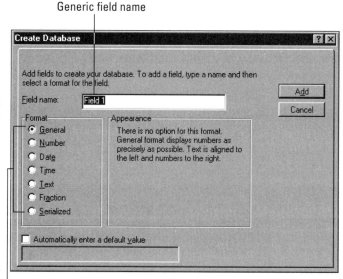

Figure 10-1: Type a field name and select a data type, and you're off and running around your database.

Data types

2. **Select a Format option that identifies the type of data that the field will contain.**

   For example (and I don't want to insult your intelligence here), identify fields that are to contain numeric values as Number fields, fields that are to contain text values (or numbers that won't be added) as General or Text fields, and fields that are to contain dates as Date fields.

   First Name should be a Text field.

3. **Press Enter.**

   After you press Enter, Works adds the field to the database and presents the next generic field name in the Create Database window.

4. **Continue to enter your field names and select data types for each field that you want to add to your database.**

   If you want to add more fields to the student-information database that I chose for practice, enter the following fields with their corresponding data types:

Middle Initial	Text
Last Name	Text
Nickname	Text
Street Address	General or Text
City	Text
State	Text
Zip Code	Number (integers with no decimal point)
Home Telephone	General
Parent/Guardian	Text
Parent Office	General
Comments	Text

5. **Click the Done button to complete the database.**

When you finish, you get your first peek at the full Database module window, shown in Figure 10-2.

Saving your database creation

 Save the database by using the same techniques you use to save files in other Works modules and Windows applications. Click the Save button on the toolbar to save your database. Then open the folder where you want to keep your database and give your database a neat name — maybe My 199x Students. Now you can start adding data to the database.

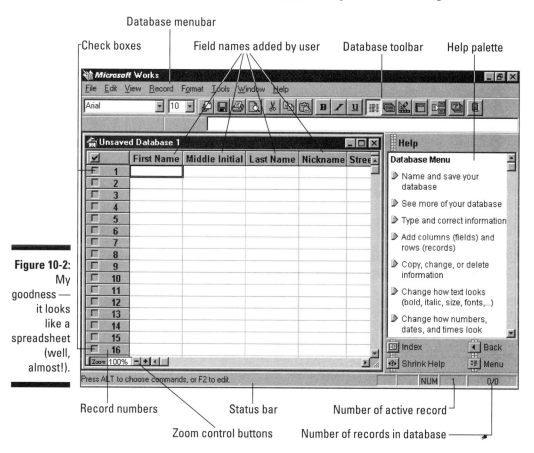

Database menubar

Check boxes   Field names added by user   Database toolbar   Help palette

Figure 10-2:
My
goodness —
it looks
like a
spreadsheet
(well,
almost!).

Record numbers   Status bar   Number of active record

Zoom control buttons   Number of records in database

And don't forget to save the database again after you add some new information or change the format!

Viewing data differently

The default view that Works uses to display your database is List View, which displays multiple records at the same time and makes reviewing records more efficient. To display only one record on-screen at a time, you can switch to Form View. Yet another view, Form Design, lets you rearrange the fields in the form (like rearranging desks in a classroom) make them more accessible. To switch views, use one of the following techniques:

✔ Click the toolbar button for the view that you want to display.

List View   Form View   Form Design

Fee fie field fo(rmats)

Are you concerned about the number of field-format types that you can choose? Here's a guide to help you filter field types so that you can get the most from your database:

✔ **General:** Text and numbers that you won't be using for calculations.

✔ **Number:** Numbers to be used in calculations. (You can choose a format for the numbers from the list in the Appearance box that appears when you choose Number.)

✔ **Date:** Dates (duh!). (But you can select a variety of data formats for displaying your dates.)

✔ **Time:** Time down to the second, in a format that you like.

✔ **Text:** Text and numbers that you won't be using in calculations.

✔ **Fractions:** Numbers that use a slash (/) to create fractions so that the database won't divide.

✔ **Serialized:** Incremented records, in a format that you like. (When you use this field type, each new record contains a field with a number automatically assigned to show you the order in which you entered the record.)

✔ Choose the View menu and then select the view that you want to display.

✔ Press F9 for Form View, Shift+F9 for List View, or Ctrl+F9 for Form Design.

Regardless of which view is active, data that you add in one view automatically appears in any other view; you're still working with the same database, after all.

Putting Data in the Field

You have a couple of options for adding information to your database after you set it up. Some people like adding records for students by using Form View; others are more comfortable using List View. I find List View to be more efficient, because I'm used to working with spreadsheets. Regardless of which view you choose, a couple of hints help you move from field to field:

✔ You can enter data in both Form View and List View.

✔ Press Tab, right arrow, or down arrow to move to the next field.

✔ Press Shift+Tab, left arrow, or up arrow to move to the preceding field.

Adding records to your database List View

To view or not to view or which view to view. Decisions, decisions . . . decisions and options are continually cropping up. You have to decide your own preferences; all I can do is acquaint you with your choices.

The easiest way to determine which view you like best is, of course, to try both views. Enter data for your favorite student to create the first record (row 1) in List View. Press Tab to move from field to field. If you make a mistake and need to go back to a field, click the field or press Shift+Tab and then use the same editing techniques that you use to correct errors in spreadsheet cells. What? You don't know how to edit spreadsheet cells? Well, you find all the details in Chapter 9.

After you enter the data for the last field of your first record, Works automatically returns to the first field but makes the first field of the *second* record active. Figure 10-3 shows you a completed record in List View.

Figure 10-3:
Database data can be entered into a spreadsheet-like format.

✓		First Name	Middle Initial	Last Name	Nickname	Street Address	City	State
□	1	John	R.	Smith	Johnnie	142 Highland Ro	Alexandria	VA
□	2							

Third Grade Students 1997.wdb

Adding records in Form View

Switch to Form View, and fill in the form blanks with data for your son, daughter, another student, or (if you can't think of anyone else) yourself to create the second record of your database. Figure 10-4 displays another record in Form View.

When you press Tab after the last field, a new, clean record form appears, so that you can enter the information for the next student. You can keep this up all day, and sometimes you do! Feel free to complete your student list, if you have time, but don't forget to learn how to fix the database design to fit your data, as described in the following section.

Be sure to save your database again before going on to the next page.

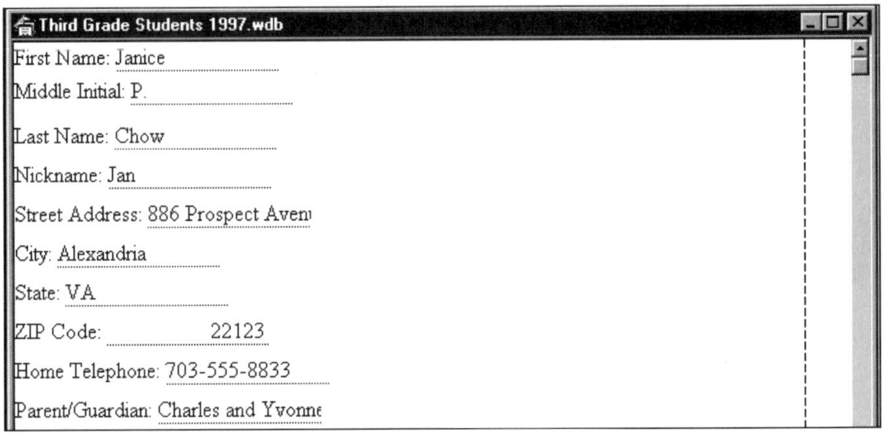

Third Grade Students 1997.wdb

First Name: Janice

Middle Initial: P.

Last Name: Chow

Nickname: Jan

Street Address: 886 Prospect Aven

City: Alexandria

State: VA

ZIP Code: 22123

Home Telephone: 703-555-8833

Parent/Guardian: Charles and Yvonne

Figure 10-4:
In Form View, you shoot from one blank entry field in the form to another blank field.

Changing the Database Landscape

Rearranging fields in Form View enables you to position fields so that they look exactly like the paper forms that you send home and ask parents or guardians to fill out and return. Form View default settings simply list fields down the left edge of the screen. You have to admit that there's nothing special about that! And what about those fields that need more space to adequately display your data?

Putting your creative talents together with those of Works, you can turn a bland format into something a bit more aesthetically pleasing and make changes in the field length at the same time, as shown in Figure 10-5.

Moving fields in a form

To get your Form View to appear the way that you want it, follow these easy steps:

1. **Click the Form Design toolbar button to display your Form Design.**

   (See the toolbar button in the section "Viewing data differently," earlier in this chapter.)

   You use Form Design simply to rearrange your form — no data entry here, please. Form Design displays fields as shown in Figure 10-6.

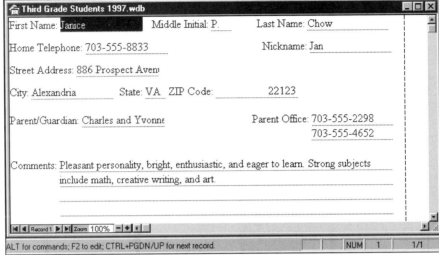

2. Click the name of the field that you want to move.

The field name is highlighted, as shown in Figure 10-6. I chose the
Middle Initial field so that I could move to a position next to First Name.

Selected field data line   Size handles   Mouse pointer

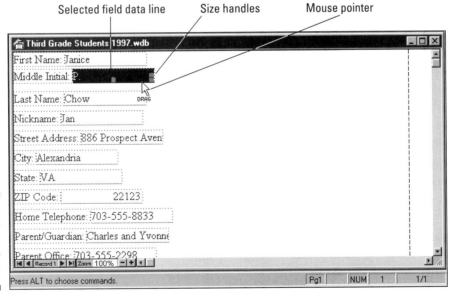

3. **Position the mouse pointer close to the edge of the selected field so that the word** DRAG **appears.**

   When the mouse pointer tells you to drag the field to its new position, you can drag the field to its new position or use the arrow keys to position it more precisely where you want it.

4. **Drag the field to a new location.**

   If you're creating the information sheet shown in Figure 10-5, position the Middle Initial field to the right of First Name.

5. **Follow the procedure outlined in Steps 2 through 4 to position other fields as you want them.**

   When you want to move more than one field at the same time, hold down the Ctrl key while you select additional fields. Then drag one selected field and watch the other selected fields tag along.

Sizing fields in a form

To change the size of a field's data area so that it better fits the information that it contains, you can drag a size handle. Works tells you when you have the mouse positioned just right by displaying the RESIZE message. Here are some techniques you can use to change the size of fields on the form:

- Drag a side handle until the field-data line appears to be the proper width.

- Drag a top or bottom handle to add lines to the field box (as shown for the Comments field in Figure 10-5 earlier in this chapter). Then, when you need to add information to those extra lines, press Shift+Enter to move to the next line or allow word wrap to take charge.

- Drag a corner handle to size vertically and horizontally at the same time.

Adjust the field lengths for fields in your database. If you're using the practice database, see whether you can get your fields sized and positioned just like mine in Figure 10-5. Got it? Does your form look *anything* like the one in Figure 10-5? If not, and if you want to try again, close the database without saving your mess; then reopen it. (You *did* save it originally, didn't you?). Your form should look like it did before you started moving things around.

Renaming fields

When all is said and done, you want to be sure that your field names describe the data that they contain. When adjustments to field names are required, follow these steps to change the field name but leave the data intact:

1. **Display List View or the Form Design and select the field you want to rename.**

2. **Choose Format⇨Field.**

   The Format dialog box displays the field information sheet you saw in the Create Database dialog box shown in Figure 10-1.

3. **Type a new field name.**

4. **Click OK.**

When you get everything set the way that you want it, save the changes — or you get to repeat this whole exercise the next time you open your database!

Adding and removing fields

If we were able to think of everything and anticipate any eventuality, we wouldn't need to add fields or remove fields from our databases. Because we're human, however, we *do* need to make such changes. Adding and removing fields from databases is quite straightforward. Follow these six easy steps:

1. **Display the Form Design.**

   For a review of what a database Form Design looks like, see Figure 10-6.

2. **Click the Form Design screen at the position where the new field should appear.**

3. **Type the field name, followed by a colon (:).**

   The colon (:) tells Works that the information you typed is a new field.

4. **Press Enter.**

   The Insert Field dialog box opens after you press Enter.

5. **Select a field type from the Insert Field dialog box.**

6. **Click OK.**

After you add the field, display List View or Form View, and enter field data for each record. Practice this technique by adding the Date of Birth field to your database.

Deleting fields removes not only the field, but also the information contained in the field in *all records* of your database. Some easy steps get those unwanted fields out of there:

1. **Display Form Design View.**

2. **Select the field that you want to delete.**

3. **Press the Delete key.**

   Works displays a message to warn you that deleting the field removes data contained in the field from all records in the database.

4. **Read the message and then click OK to delete the field or Cancel to keep the field.**

Picking and Choosing Database Players

If you've ever wondered how sportscasters come up with some of the trivia that they spout off the top of their heads during a broadcast, I'll let you in on a little secret: They really don't know *all* that stuff about *every* player on *every* team in *every* sport! They have access to a humongous database!

Locating data in an electronic database file is infinitely more rewarding than searching through stacks of papers and drawers of file folders. Learning some of the ways to home in on specific data within a database gives you a glimpse of the power behind database technology.

Finding records

To practice finding records, you may want to use a larger database. I put one on your CD-ROM (and named it CH10-db.wdb) just so you can use it to practice finding data. If you created a database and have entered plenty of records in it, feel free to use your database instead. Then use the sample database to find data by following these steps:

1. **Open the database that you want to search in List View.**

   Works allows you to find information in the database in either List View or Form View. You see the results of your search more readily in List View. (If you don't have a database of your own, open the database on the CD-ROM that comes with this book.)

2. **Choose Edit⇨Find.**

The Find dialog box opens.

3. **In the Find What text box, type the data that you want to find.**

4. **Choose a Match option to tell Works what records you want to search.**

For practice, try finding records that contain the data 70817 in All Records.

5. **Click OK.**

Whoa — what happened to all your records? Don't fret — Works displays only those records that contain 70817 (or the value that you entered) in any database field. The other records are still there; they're simply moved out of the way (hidden, sort of) so that you can focus on the records that you told Works to find.

To leave all records displayed and tell Works to simply move to the next record and field that contain the data that you want to find, choose Next Record in the Match section of the Find dialog box.

Redisplaying records

To see all your records again, just to prove that they really are still there, try this:

1. **Choose Record⇨Show.**

The Show submenu enables you to choose what you want to see.

2. **Choose 1 All Records.**

See, there they are — all neatly set up the way you left them.

You'll find more tips and tricks on working with databases in another title of mine, *Microsoft Works For Teachers* (IDG Books Worldwide, Inc.). Check it out, and go for the database gold! You'll be glad you did!

Applying Your Skills

One delightful feature of Microsoft Works that you can enjoy is seeing how the modules work together. You can pull data from one module and plop it right into the middle of a document, alleviating the need to retype the data. You also find that sharing information makes your student profiles more portfolio-like. Try the challenges in the following sections, and see what you think. You meet some new database friends along the way.

Challenge 1: Merging data into a letter

The Word Processor module is specifically designed to create documents (letters, reports, and so on), whereas the Database module is used to create and enter detailed pieces of information, each of which can be used separately. You can pull information from these two modules and create a new document by using a procedure commonly known as a *merge*.

Merging information from your database with a letter, note, or some other document allows you to identify the specific fields of data that you need (using the field names that you assigned) and to place those fields of data in the document appropriately.

Each of you have bells and whistles going off in your head about now; you're simply overwhelmed with ideas about how you can use this feature. But keep this first taste simple — just a note to parents, inviting them to attend your Back to School night. You need a Student Information database for this activity. If you don't have one, that's okay; I placed a practice database on the CD-ROM that you can use.

Follow these steps to merge a database with a document:

1. Create a new blank document in the Word Processor module of Works.

If you have stationery that you plan to use, feel free to create a document by using your stationery. If you need help in creating a document, see Chapter 8.

2. Position the insertion point at the top of your document, and choose Insert⇨Database Field.

If this is the first time that you have used this feature, you may see the First-Time Help window (again!). Just press Enter to close the window.

The Insert Field dialog box, which is pictured in Figure 10-7, opens. You can use this dialog box to tell Works what database to use and to gain access to a list of the fields in the database.

3. Click the Use a Different Database button.

The Use Database dialog box appears, listing the databases that you created by using Works. You can select a database of your own or use the CH10-db.wdb database on the CD-ROM that comes with this book. To open the practice database, click the Open a Database Not Listed Here button and then select the file from the Use Another File dialog box.

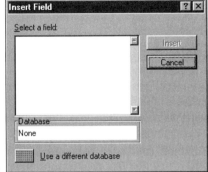

Figure 10-7:
If you
haven't
chosen a
database
yet, no
fields
appear.

4. **Select the database file that you want to use.**

5. **Click OK.**

   Finally, you see the Insert Field dialog box, shown in Figure 10-8. Does the dialog box list the fields that you entered in your database?

Figure 10-8:
Ah, there
are the
fields I
entered
in my
database!

6. **Select the field that you want to add to the letter, and click Insert.**

   I chose Parent/Guardian as the field that I wanted to add to my document.

7. **Repeat Step 6 to insert additional fields from the database into the document.**

8. **Press Esc or click Close (the Cancel button changes to the Close button after you insert a field into the document) to return to the document.**

   You have two options when you add more than one field to a merge letter: You can insert all the fields and then go back and rearrange them on-screen; or you can insert each one, close the Insert Field dialog box, reposition the insertion point, and repeat all the steps again. Whichever approach you choose, see whether you can insert and position fields as shown in Figure 10-9.

Notice that each individual field is marked with double brackets on each side. Works uses the brackets to show that it's supposed to pull the real data from the database rather than display *First Name* and so on. Be sure to include any spacing or punctuation that you would normally place in a typed document, such as a comma between the city and state.

You can add your own special note or use the one shown in Figure 10-9. Add the pieces of information that you like to see in notes: date, time, and so on. Then preview the document before you complete the merge. Previewing the document gives you a glimpse of how the data will appear in the printed document. You can make any spacing and punctuation adjustments after viewing the document and save the hassle of reprinting.

9. **Click the Print Preview toolbar button.**

   A message window appears.

10. **Click OK to acknowledge the Works message window.**

When the merged documents are ready, print them. You have an original document — not a photocopy or a ditto — individually addressed to each parent, with the correct student name as part of the letter.

Figure 10-9:
See if you can arrange your fields like these.

Putting your students to work

Your mind is probably working overtime with ideas for using databases with your students. Jot those thoughts down quickly, because you won't remember them tomorrow. I thought I'd share the ways that I've seen databases used in a classroom.

✔ Students can research different subjects in the curriculum and then create a database to contain records about their research topics. Obviously, databases get more complex as students gain experience and knowledge.

✔ Create a class master database. Then students can add to the database as they learn about anything from trees, presidents, authors, and chemical elements to great Internet sites.

✔ Teachers can create a database to keep track (inventory) of textbooks, school supplies, audiovisual aids, and anything else that comes to mind and then have the students keep it up to date.

✔ Students can build genealogical files and fill in records to trace their family histories.

Coming up with generic field names to account for all genders, races, and so forth enhances students' thinking skills. You can easily spot those students who think ahead.

Be careful to include ideas that appeal to both the guys and the gals in your classroom. Also vary the age level of topics to appeal to a wide range of interests.

Challenge 2: Profiles to portfolios

Having your students use different modules of Microsoft Works to complete their work makes pulling samples of their work together into portfolios easier and more efficient. If they store their work in the same folder or on the same floppy disk, adding documents, spreadsheets, and other things to their database record is easier. You find lots of objects listed in the Insert menu (the menu that you use to insert database fields).

Although I don't have any real samples of student work (my son is away at college, so I borrowed a pretend work sample as his), I can simulate attaching a document — a book report, in this case — to the record in the CH10-db.wdb database on the CD-ROM that comes with this book. You can practice using your own database or create a portfolio of your own work! Here's how:

1. **Launch Microsoft Works, and open the database into which you want to insert files.**

   Again, feel free to use CH10-db.wdb, on the CD-ROM.

Strategic planning

Last night, not long after dark, I heard what sounded like explosions close by. After a few moments, I heard the sound of fire trucks, police cars, and emergency vehicles as they arrived at the scene of a fire just across the street. As I watch the fire from the front window, I wondered whether the poeple who lived in that house had an inventory of everything they owned. Preparing such an inventory of your home or school is a great way to build something useful as you learn about databases.

Your mind may already be working overtime with other ideas for implementing this new card-file system of storing data. Take a moment to jot down some ideas that you'd like to implement; you never know when you'll need them.

Here are a few ideas to get you started.

- ✔ Student information files
- ✔ Student cumulative-record information
- ✔ Teacher/administrator phone book
- ✔ Personal directory or address book
- ✔ Holiday-card address file
- ✔ Recipe file
- ✔ Test-question data file(by subject or grade level)
- ✔ Computer-time log information
- ✔ Textbook-inventory data form
- ✔ Cartoon card file(subject-appropriate, if you please

2. **In Form Design View, display the database and record into which you want to insert the file.**

3. **Position the insertion point just below the Comments field on the left side of the form.**

4. **Choose Format⇨Insert Page Break to create a second page for the record.**

5. **Choose Insert⇨Object to open the Insert Object dialog box.**

   As usual, Mr. First-Time Help may offer assistance; click OK to get him out of the way.

   You can use the Insert Object dialog box to attach different object types (such as a sample of each student's work for a portfolio) to records.

6. **Click the Create from File option button.**

7. **Click the Browse button and find the file that you want to attach to the record.**

8. **Double-click the file to place the filename in the File text box of the Insert Object dialog box.**

Choose any document or spreadsheet that you've created so far, for practice.

9. **Click the <u>D</u>isplay As Icon check box in the Insert Object dialog box.**

10. **Click OK.**

The file appears as a graphic item below the page-break line in the record. When someone wants to review the student's work, the reviewer can double-click the document icon to view the complete document in the module of Works that you used to create it.

11. **Close the document and the database, responding <u>Y</u>es to save the changes to the file and OK to the warning message that may appear.**

If your system doesn't have the program that was used to create the document or file attached to a record, you get a message telling you that no application is associated with the file. As a result, you are not able to open the file. What's the lesson? Determine a standard for the teachers to use or a method of converting different file types to something that can be used readily on most systems.

Imagine what your friends missed if they didn't do these homework assignments!

Chapter 11

Publish It and Present It!

· ·

In This Chapter

▶ Using presentation and publishing programs

▶ Using Web-authoring programs

▶ Adding ClipArt to publications

▶ Creating WordArt

· ·

*H*ow many of you have had a teacher's pet? Now, be honest. Haven't you had that *one* student who was enthusiastic, talented, personable, and sensitive, and who had great dimples — that special student with whom you bonded? I have! You're about to meet my teacher's pet, so be nice and don't say anything bad.

My teacher's pet is presentation programs. Presentation programs are wonderful, marvelous, simply delightful . . . and the most fun applications that you will probably ever use! (Okay, that's my opinion, but convincing you was worth a try.) And although presentation programs are near and dear to my heart, publishing programs — programs that are designed to help you plot and lay out your newsletters, school papers, bulletins, brochures, and just about everything else that you usually send to the print shop on the corner — are close behind presentation programs.

So put on a smile and prepare to shake hands; you want to make a good impression on some really friendly tools.

Using Perky Presentation Programs

Presentation-software applications are programs that you can use to create brilliantly colored visuals designed to enhance your presentation — attention-grabbers. Use the programs to create remarkable transparencies, capture students' attention, and dress up your lecture (yes, your students consider everything that you have to say to be a lecture). Presentation programs provide you with a new approach to getting your point across. Allow the computer to explain a new concept or review the important points that you covered yesterday when Johnny was absent.

A presentation consists of a number of slides containing whatever you want to put on them: text, pictures, bullet points, review items, sound clips, video clips, movies, charts, graphs, tables, organization charts, and so on. Each slide is created separately and stored as part of the presentation.

Presentations generally contain anywhere from 1 to 99 slides. When you need to include additional slides in your presentation, you can take *detours* (by using an advanced technique known as *branching*, which you can learn more about in your application manual) to other presentations from any slide in the parent presentation. As a result, the number of available slides appears to be unlimited — but remember, you have RAM to consider. If your presentation gets too big, RAM won't be able to handle it. Most of these programs require a minimum of 8MB of RAM and really need 16MB to store presentations that contain graphics. Lack of RAM is an increasing problem when you want to go beyond the basics.

Are you becoming interested in this teacher's pet? Good. Then you'll appreciate some of the ways that presentation programs allow you to view your presentation. Check out the views in this simple but power-packed sample of what you'll see when you create a presentation by using PowerPoint 97. Challenge 1 in the "Applying Your Skills" section at the end of this chapter provides the steps for creating basic presentations.

- ✔ **Slide view** (shown in Figure 11-1) displays slides on-screen one at a time so that you can type text, add graphics, create art, view charts, and edit in this view.

- ✔ **Outline view** displays text in a notebook-like format without drawings and art so that you can focus on presentation content. When you complete the text for all slides, switch back to Slide view and then add art, color, and other objects to enhance the slides.

- ✔ **Slide Sorter view** displays small images of numerous slides on-screen at the same time. It's the most efficient view for reorganizing and rearranging your presentation.

- ✔ **Notes Pages view** places each slide in a presentation on a separate page and reduces the image size. This lets you use the space below the slide image to jot down any notes that you want to review while the slide is on-screen.

Is that all? Of course not. You also have *handouts* — and although a handout is not a view, it is something that you can print so that your audience has miniature images of your presentation slides. Handouts are a good way to get your points across graphically, and you can even add lines to the sides of the slides so that your audience (even students!) can take notes. Students may even find this technique to be relatively hassle-free and (if you don't mention it) interesting.

Standard toolbar   Presentation title   Slide   Formatting toolbar

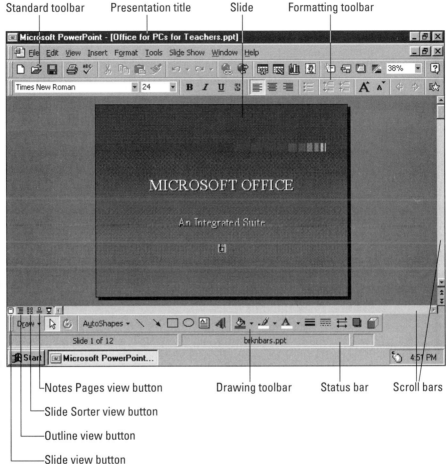

Figure 11-1:
A slide
awaits your
presentation.

Notes Pages view button   Drawing toolbar   Status bar   Scroll bars

Slide Sorter view button

Outline view button

Slide view button

Although my favorite presentation software program is Microsoft
PowerPoint, you can find lots of presentation software on the market. Each
presentation-graphics program has a unique approach to accomplishing
basically the same thing. Regardless of which presentation program you
choose, it is sure to delight you. Here are some fascinating packages to
watch for:

- ✔ Adobe Persuasion
- ✔ Alpha Bravo
- ✔ Freehand
- ✔ Harvard Graphics
- ✔ Lotus Freelance
- ✔ Microsoft PowerPoint

In addition, a number of independent software developers have similar products on the market. Look for these products in the software section of the local computer store. Take Challenge 1 in the "Applying Your Skills" section at the end of this chapter to learn the basics of creating a PowerPoint presentation.

Desktop Publishing: A Proliferation of Programs

Desktop-publishing software applications were initially designed simply as *layout programs* — that is, they took articles, stories, and typed text from word processing applications and provided the means to position the text in a predetermined space on the page. After the text was placed, if it didn't all fit into the desired area, the leftover text could be placed on another page. Today, desktop-publishing and word processing programs wear one another's hats. Most word processing programs are now more like desktop-publishing programs, and publishing programs offer word processing features.

To give you an idea of what you can do with a desktop publisher, I created the calendar shown in Figure 11-2 by using Microsoft Publisher. Why did I choose Microsoft Publisher? Because it was the only desktop publisher that I had available at the time I needed it. (In other words, it was already up and running, and I didn't have to buy it and install it. Might this be a familiar situation in your school?)

Be sure to learn the basic word processing techniques before you try to tackle a desktop-publishing program. A quick overview of Chapter 8 will help get you started on your publishing prowess. Please don't make Microsoft Publisher the first program that you learn.

In the world of desktop publishing, the power packed into programs varies — and the more power you have, the more fantastic your publications will be. Unfortunately, more power also means more hardware capabilities and more time required to learn the application. Because of the power packed into Microsoft Works' Word Processor module and the templates that you'll find there, you may discover that you don't really need a desktop-publishing application at all.

If you do decide to try a publishing program, try one of these:

- ✔ Adobe PageMaker (the program used to lay out this book)
- ✔ Corel Ventura 7
- ✔ Microsoft Publisher

✔ PosterWorks 4.0

✔ Print Shop and Print Shop Deluxe

✔ Quark Xpress

Wizards in Microsoft Publisher use magic to create publications quickly and easily. Learn how to get the wizards working for you in Challenge 2 of the "Applying Your Skills" section at the end of this chapter.

Generic document name   Publishing rulers

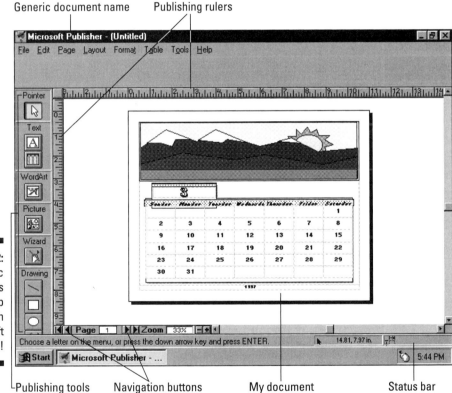

Figure 11-2:
Dynamic publications are a snap with Microsoft Publisher!

Publishing tools   Navigation buttons   My document   Status bar

Web Weavers: Web Page Authoring Tools

Web-authoring software applications take publishing one step further by formatting the documents that you create and saving them in a format that you can use to broadcast your document on the World Wide Web. These special programs help you design Web home pages and create hyperlinks — things that you need to know about before you start creating the documents, right?

When you want a program to help you design a power-packed page for the World Wide Web, you have a wealth of new tools to check out, including the ones in the following list:

Adobe Acrobat	HomePage Wizard
Adobe PageMill	Microsoft FrontPage 97
Astound	NETCOMplete
Astound WebMotion	NetObjects Fusion
Borland IntraBuilder	OmniForm
Claris Home Page	WebBase
*Click*Book	WebPrinter
CorelWEB Data	WebSeeker
DeltaPoint QuickSite	WebSite Professional
HomePage Publisher	WebWhacker

Then again, you may just want to see what you can create by using regular applications, such as Word, WordPerfect, Lotus, and Microsoft Works. There's a built-in feature that enables you to save your document in a format that the Internet and World Wide Web like. You can find instructions for saving Works documents in different formats in Challenge 3 of the "Applying Your Skills" section at the end of this chapter.

Playing with More Works Pets

If you're an *artsy* kind of person, you're going to *love* the goodies that Works is hiding among the folds of basic features. If you're not an artsy kind of person, perhaps working with Works' special features will make you more crafty (groan, groan!). No publication or presentation would be the same without *these* little pets.

Saying it with pictures

They say that a picture is worth a thousand words, but to a teacher, anything that grabs the attention of your students and/or their parents is priceless. As a result, adding pictures to your documents and database forms can send a message that screams, "IT'S FROM ME!"

Creative moderation

When you start working with presentation and publishing software, you most likely will have visions of uninhibited displays of grandeur. Remember the old saying, "Less is more." Here are some tips to help make your presentations and publications more effective:

✔ Keep titles and bulleted lists short and to the point.

✔ Limit graphics, and make them meaningful instead of using them as fillers.

✔ Graph numeric data. This data is easier to summarize and has greater impact when it's presented visually.

✔ Limit each slide in a presentation and each published article to one point or a small group of related points.

✔ Watch your color. Consider the method that you'll use to deliver the presentation or the printer that you'll use to print the publication, and adjust color to fit the product.

✔ Remember that color prints in shades of gray on black-and-white printers.

✔ Choose a black-and-white template for transparencies if you have a black-and-white printer. You'll get visuals that are easy to read.

✔ Remember that clutter is distracting; simplicity is enhancing.

You've probably seen those booklets that are chock-full of cheerleaders, football players, club symbols, and classroom objects that you can clip out and paste in school programs and other documents. If you have, you know that cheerleaders come in all sorts of costumes, with some jumping high and others way down low, and the football players are running, throwing, or crouched and ready. Well, computer programs have those booklets stored inside, ready for you to open them.

The Clip Gallery on your computer (see Figure 11-3) is shared by all Microsoft programs. Many Microsoft programs come with a special set of clip art images that are added to the Gallery when you install the program. As a result, the more Microsoft programs you have on your computer, the more clip art images you see in the Gallery.

How do you get those images out of the Gallery and into your documents? That's easy: Position the insertion point in the document or on the slide where you want to place the clip art image. Then look through your menus and see whether Clip Art is listed. Most likely, the Clip Art command is in the Insert or Edit menu. Then again, you may find it in the Format menu. I'm confident, though, that you'll find it somewhere. When you do, choose the Clip Art command to open the gallery. Then browse the gallery just as you would browse an art gallery. When you find an image that you like, click it and press Enter. Presto — the image is part of your document.

┌Media types on tabbed pages   Thumbnail images

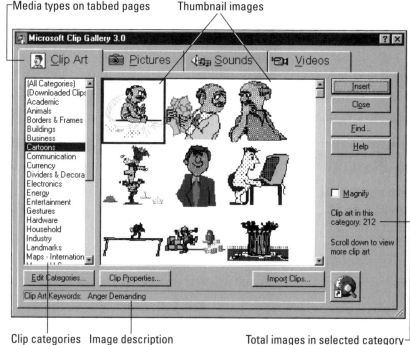

Figure 11-3:
Aren't these
Clip Art
images
cute?

Clip categories   Image description   Total images in selected category┘

When you want more than a snapshot of your clip art, you can change the image size and move it to a new location in the document. Following are a few notes about selecting and working with an image:

- Click an image to select it.
- An image has handles (little squares) on the sides and corners when it's selected.
- Read your mouse pointer to tell whether you're about to move or size the image. The mouse pointer says DRAG when you point to any part of the selected image except the handles; it says RESIZE when you point to any handle.
- Drag a side, top, or bottom handle to distort an image.
- Drag a corner handle to change the image size so that it retains its appearance.

Doesn't that sound easy? Try dragging a handle to see how you can distort the image so that it looks nothing like the original image. Neat, huh?

Before you try to move the picture to another location in the document, you need to tell Works that you absolutely, positively want the picture to be moved to a specific location; otherwise, the image won't budge. Just follow these steps:

1. **Select the picture.**

2. **Choose Format⇨Picture.**

3. **Click the Text Wrap page tab.**

4. **Choose Absolute.**

You'll have your images sized and positioned precisely where you want them in a jiffy!

Incidentally, you'll find collections of people clip art images and animal clip art images on the CD that came with your book. Check these images out when you're looking for something different in the clip art area.

Creating words of art with WordArt

Pictures are great, and drawings can be, too, if you're artistic. But when you want to create something really special, it's time to call out the natural talent of WordArt. Now, I may be an uninspired artist of the drawing persuasion, but I can create masterpieces with WordArt. You can, too.

Just position your insertion point in your document where you want to add gorgeously designed text; then look through the menus to see whether you find a command such as WordArt, TextArt, or something similar. In Works, you'll find WordArt in the Insert menu. When you find what you're looking for, choose it and then type the text that you want the program to draw for you. See if you can create a design similar to the one shown in Figure 11-4 by using Works tools.

When you finish typing the text, you're on your own. I'm not leaving you in a lurch, though. Here are some tips for editing and formatting your WordArt:

✔ To change the size of your WordArt box, click the WordArt and drag a handle.

✔ To edit WordArt, double-click the WordArt.

✔ To format WordArt, double-click the WordArt and then explore the WordArt toolbar buttons.

✔ To add special symbols such as ©, ®, and ™, click the Insert Symbol button in the Enter Your Text Here dialog box and then select the symbol that you want to add.

You may want to keep this wonderful feature a secret for a while. Your students will consider it to be a challenge to figure out how you accomplished such fascinating feats — especially if you're as inartistic as I am!

WordArt menu bar   WordArt typing palette   WordArt toolbar

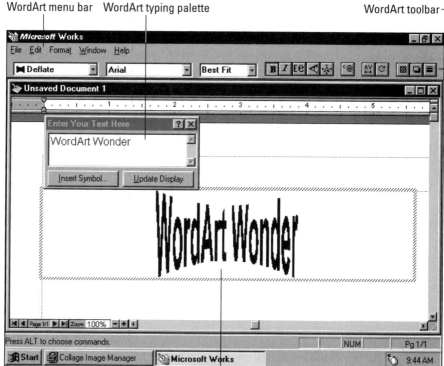

Figure 11-4:
Here it is —
my WordArt
creation!

WordArt object in document

Adopting Fresh Ideas

Have I persuaded you to adopt my teacher's pets? The next time that you have to prepare an outline or lesson with transparencies, why not create a presentation? For your next note home, try a publishing program. And when you decide to go online, creating a Web page that students can check for homework assignments is a great way to get them involved in using the computer as well. The following sections have some ideas to get you started. Add your ideas to the bottom of the list before you forget the great things that are churning through your head!

For teachers

As teacher tools, presentation and publishing programs are invaluable. Here's how I've seen them used most effectively:

✔ Overview course material during Back-to-School Night.

✔ Sell an administrator on a new theory (such as computers).

✔ Impress supervisors during those never-ending observations.

✔ Report to the school board about a new curriculum.

✔ Introduce new material and display bulleted items to aid student note-taking and then use again to introduce the same topics to students who have been absent.

✔ Present material at workshops, conferences, and in-service programs. (Audiences always love the handouts.)

✔ Introduce a unit of study to your students. Include daily assignments, related items of interest, and even a bonus problem for those who read the newsletter carefully.

✔ Create a brochure or newsletter with headlines or major divisions already filled in so that students can flesh out the text (by hand) as a review or as a test.

✔ Make a last-minute card for the principal on any special occasion. Share the beauty of these programs!

✔ Post information on the World Wide Web for your school's home page to tell other teachers and students what you're doing in class.

For students

Now that you have an idea of what *you* can do with presentation and publishing software, you're probably reeling with ideas for putting your students to work with it. You may want to do the following things:

✔ Allow students to create presentations or publications to prepare reports, and then present their reports in class or distribute their publications.

✔ Have students type their notes about a lesson or topic in a presentation or publication, and then use students' presentations and publications to present the topic to next year's students.

✔ Allow students to create flyers to send home, notifying parents of meetings, or to post around school (some of the same ways that students have used Print Shop in the past).

✔ Have students create special colors by blending primary colors in the color palette (pretty advanced topic).

✔ Allow students to create brochures about the material that they're studying, in the form of either a book report, an advertisement to promote a certain animal, or an overview of a time period or of a geographical location.

✔ Assign students articles to make up a newspaper that is representative of a time period in history or that reports news about a character and an event in literature. The newspaper can be the business section for an economics class.

✔ Encourage students to dress up their report covers.

Applying Your Skills

After you have an idea of the differences among presentations, publications, and Web-authoring tools, you might want to test your artistic skills by putting some of these tools to work for you. If you have a presentation program available, create the simple presentation outlined in Challenge 1 that follows. For up-and-coming publishers, put your talents and your software to the test with Challenge 2, later in the chapter. And those of you who are interested in publishing worldwide can use the Word Processor module of Works to create a Web page in Challenge 3, later in this chapter.

Challenge 1: Creating a simple presentation

What are you planning to teach tomorrow? Do you have an outline? If you do have an outline, use it to prepare your presentation. If you're giving a test or having a field day (I know that you are all well prepared for class tomorrow, even though you may not have an outline; I'm giving you an out!), you may want to use the example that I provide. In effect, you kill two birds with one stone: You learn to use the program, and you start a presentation that your students can use.

Getting started: Creating the first slide

I use Microsoft PowerPoint 97 for the pictures that you see and the instructions that I give, but you can use these basic steps to create a presentation in most presentation-software programs (you'll notice only slight differences in the button clicking; the concepts are the same):

1. **Launch your application, using standard Windows techniques.**

2. **Choose the option to create a blank presentation if a startup window of any type appears.**

   If no welcome-type window appears, the program may automatically create a plain presentation; if not, choose File➪New to create a new presentation.

Some applications present another opening window, which enables you to select a layout for the slides in your presentation. The formats generally contain objects (such as tables, charts, titles, and bulleted lists) that users like to include in slides.

PowerPoint includes a separate window that appears each time you create a new presentation, followed by another window that displays the layouts you can use to create the first slide. PowerPoint automatically selects a Title format.

3. Click the Title slide AutoLayout for the first slide in the presentation.

4. Click OK.

Your blank title slide appears as the first slide in the presentation (see Figure 11-5). Notice that PowerPoint assigns a generic presentation name to the new file, just as Works does when you create a new document or spreadsheet.

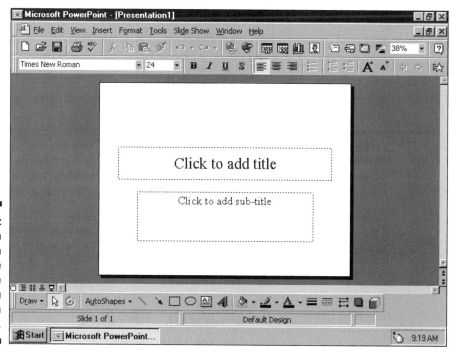

Figure 11-5:
You see a plain-vanilla title slide like this one when you launch PowerPoint.

5. Follow screen directions, and type Microsoft Works Modules **as the presentation title.**

6. Follow screen directions, and type A Brief Tour **as the subtitle.**

Your first slide is finished; now you need to add a slide to the presentation. Perhaps you already have enough computer savvy to figure this one out on your own?

Adding more slides

Presentations generally include more than one slide, and a variety of options for adding new slides to presentations is available, depending on the product that you use. Because adding slides is a pretty common task, most programs include a toolbar button or a status-bar button to make adding a slide easy and most efficient.

1. **Click the New Slide button in the toolbar and select a bulleted-list format for the slide.**

   The New Slide window opens each time you create a new slide in PowerPoint, so that you can choose the format that contains place-holders for the things that you want to put in the slide.

2. **Type** Four Modules of Works **as the title of Slide 2.**

3. **Type** Word Processor **as the first bulleted item and press Enter.**

4. **Follow the procedure outlined in Step 3 to create additional bullet points for Spreadsheet, Database, and Communications.**

Slide 2 is complete. See how easy this is? You can continue clicking the New Slide button to create additional slides, you can switch to Outline view and type the title and body text for each slide in a notebook page, or you can quickly format your two-slide presentation to make it stunning.

Applying dressing

I'll cut to the chase here because I want to get to the fun stuff. If you have read Chapters 7 through 10, you found out what a template is. For those of you who didn't get to those chapters yet, a *template* is a preformatted document that contains color, text format and alignment, graphics, and any other object or information that you want to include in every page of your document. Templates are designed by professionals, so use them! The templates that you find in presentation programs are much fancier than the templates that you use in Works, and they can save you hours and hours of work.

To apply a design template to your presentation, follow these steps:

1. **Press the PgUp key to return to your first slide.**

2. **Click the Template button (it may be called a Design button in your particular program) in the toolbar to open the Presentation Designs window.**

If you don't see a status-bar button or toolbar button for templates, look for the feature in the Format menu first. If you don't find it there, look in the other menus.

Most programs include a preview area of the template window so that you can see what the different template designs look like. Explore the templates until you find one that you like.

3. Select the template that you want to use.

4. Click OK.

The computer buzzes, whirs, and spins for a few seconds before presenting your slides in their fancy togs. Pretty neat, huh?

Now, how long did that take? Maybe five minutes. See how quick and easy preparing a presentation can be? That teacher's pet is getting to be more tempting; I can tell.

Adding fun to your presentation

When you master the basic features of presentation-graphics programs and are comfortable creating simple presentations, you may want to explore your application and try to locate more fun stuff. See if you can find ways to apply these features in your presentation program:

✔ **Create "build" slides** to present one bulleted item at a time as you show your presentation — displaying one bullet point at a time keeps students from madly copying all the bullet points at once and missing your narrative.

✔ **Add special effects** to change the way that a slide appears on-screen or leaves the screen — scrolling from the left, raining on, dissolving, and fading in or out are a few of the most commonly available effects.

✔ **Insert photographs** to personalize your presentation by including scanned images of people and places that are familiar to your audience.

✔ **Include sound and video clips** to professionalize your presentation and help capture your audience's attention.

✔ **Hide slides** to include extra information in case someone asks for more details; show the hidden slides only when they are needed.

✔ **Branch out** to take your presentation down a different path or vary the template to subdivide your presentation. (Other audiences are as bad about getting you off track as your students are!)

You may even discover that your presentation program has special features of its own. Here's a tip: Save your presentation on a floppy disk. Why not use the presentation again next year, when you again introduce sonnets or amphibians or the digestive system or . . . ?

Challenge 2: Publishing your work

I'm going to have you take the reins to complete this activity. I want you to produce something that you will find to be useful. When you see how easily wizards create your publication, I have a feeling that you'll be so enthusiastic that you'll have your students working with this application in no time.

I use Microsoft Publisher for this challenge. You can use the program you have available or launch the Newsletter TaskWizard from Works 4.0. Launch the application from the Start menu to get the program up and running, and you're off. You'll need just a bit of guidance.

Choosing your Assistant

The Startup window in Microsoft Publisher presents a list of PageWizard Assistants that you can use to create your document. Because these Assistants take their names from the types of publications that they create, you shouldn't have any problem determining which Assistant you want to use.

If you click an Assistant, a sample layout for the selected publication type appears in the Preview window of the Startup dialog box. I chose the Newsletter Assistant to help me create my journal. If you want to see the same screens pictured in this chapter, you may want to choose Newsletter Assistant for your first publication.

Following the Assistant

Have you chosen your Assistant? Good. Your Assistant is going to present you with a bunch of options. Each option is designed to create a publication that is uniquely yours (and by the time you finish your publication, you may think that no one else would want it). Experimenting is fun anyway.

If you chose an Assistant other than the Newsletter Assistant, the screens that you see, the questions that the Assistant asks, and the layout topics may vary. The beauty of working with Assistants is that they phrase their questions in words that are easy to understand. You should be able to tell what you need to do without my help; if not, simply accept the option that's already selected. In most cases, the selected option is the most popular for the publication that you are creating. The first screen or two may simply provide information. Then you'll see some screens that allow you to make choices.

The following items discuss some things to watch for, in no specific order.

✔ **Document style**: Most Assistants want you to select a style for your document. Select a style to preview it; then select the next one and preview it. When you find the one that you want to use or one that is close to the one you like, leave it selected and then click the Next button.

✔ **Basic layout:** Depending on the Assistant that you choose, you may have to provide additional information about the document layout. Review the available options and make your choices. If you choose the Newsletter Assistant, for example, you have to specify the number of columns for your newsletter and how you want to lay them out. In this case, do you want strictly structured columns (like lining up students' desks), or do you want a varied column layout (like arranging students' desks in different patterns)?

✔ **Adding a title:** A title can be a company (school, in this case) name and address and other pertinent information, or a document title (for your newsletter, for example).

✔ **The rest of the story:** Other screens that you may bump into (and the decisions that you may have to make) include:

Whether the publication will be printed on one side of the paper or two (front and back).

Whether the document will have a back cover, where you can add a mailing label.

The number of pages that you expect the document to contain. (A rough estimate is good; you can add pages later, if you need them.)

Additional parts that you plan to include in your document. If you're creating a newsletter, for example, do you want to include a table of contents, fancy initial letters, the date, or volume/version information?

Didn't realize that you had so much to think about when you create a publication, did you? When you make your decisions, the program actually creates the newsletter and keeps you informed of its progress, telling you what it's doing while it's doing it. Watching the progress report is fun, because you can appreciate what you *don't* have to do.

Figure 11-6 shows you my almost-complete newsletter. (All that I still have to do is create some articles — and I believe that I'll have my students do *that*.) Have fun!

Saving your work

As soon as you create your publication, before you do *anything* else, save your work.

To become better acquainted with publishing techniques, pick up a copy of *Desktop Publishing & Design For Dummies* by Roger C. Parker (IDG Books Worldwide, Inc.). You'll find that the author has packed lots of tips and tricks and terminology to help you through your publishing tasks.

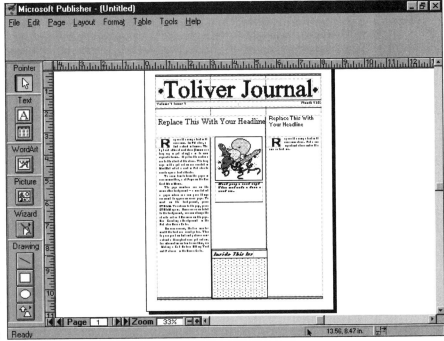

Figure 11-6:
Here you can see the front page of My Journal.

Challenge 3: Reaching out to the World Wide Web

Creating your document by using the Newsletter TaskWizard in Works has an added advantage over using Microsoft Publisher. Works 4.0 has a feature that enables you to save your document in a format that you can use to post the document to the World Wide Web. Here's how:

1. **Create a new document, using the Newsletter TaskWizard in Works.**

   Or choose a different TaskWizard, if desired.

2. **Make the document look pretty.**

3. **Add the articles that you want to include.**

4. **Change the newsletter name**

   This ensures that everyone who reads the newsletter knows that it's from you.

5. **Get the newsletter just the way that you want it.**

6. **Save the document, using standard save procedures.**

After you save the document as a Works document, save it again in an HTML format, using the following procedure:

1. **Choose File⇨Save As to open the Save As dialog box.**
2. **Click the arrow beside Save As Type to display the drop-down list.**
3. **Choose HTML Document.**
4. **Type a new filename in the File Name text box.**
5. **Click Save.**

Works 4.0 takes a bit longer to save the document in HTML format because it has to add a whole bunch of instructions about the document. Just be patient and wait. When Works is done, you can close the document, which is now listed among the documents in the Existing Documents page of the Works Task Launcher (but it has an .htm extension in the filename).

Now all you have to do is check with the person who's in charge of your school's Web site to find out how to upload the document to the site or to your Internet Service Provider.

Posting a document to the world

When you create your Web-page design, what are you going to do with it? That's what I thought! Seems as though something's missing here, doesn't it? Well, here's the scoop.

When you save your document in HTML format, you can view it from your own little computer by opening it in the Internet window without logging on. That doesn't really take you far, though, does it? To post something on the World Wide Web, you have to have a server. Most school systems have a server that they will gladly allow classes to use. All you have to do is find your niche . . . and your space on the server. Then your students will be able to upload their creations and tell the world what they are doing.

Check with the systems administrator or technology coordinator at your school for specific instructions.

Part III

Communicating with the Outside World

"No, Thomas Jefferson never did 'the Grind;' however, this does show how animation can be used to illustrate American history on the Web."

In this part . . .

*S*urfing is a powerful term for a graceful ride. And *surfing* is an apt word for exploring the Net, because it requires a number of ups and downs, highs and lows, wipeouts . . . and near-drownings. The power behind the Net builds gradually and eventually leads to a capping of velocity that thrusts you forward, only to drop you dramatically when you reach the end of the path (or wave!). You've heard of getting hooked on surfing or becoming a beach bum? Well, surfing the Net can be just as addictive as surfing the waves — and just as costly. And, of course, there's also the chance that you'll get tangled up in the World Wide Web.

Before you go off the deep end, you need to identify the hardware that you need to connect to the Net, compare the available online services, explore ways to protect your students (and yourself) from surfing into waters that are too deep (no, no land), and find out how to send and receive e-mail. You may even want to identify reasons for getting involved with the Net in the first place and find out how to tell when you've entered the Web. The chapters in this part are designed to help you wade into these topics — yet prevent you from getting in so deep that you're thrown back to shore!

Chapter 12

Connecting to the Net

. . . .

In This Chapter

▶ Identifying modem features

▶ Exploring Internet basics

▶ Locating online services

▶ Reviewing tips for effective communicating

▶ Setting up a schedule for connecting

▶ Identifying tools to set surfing limits

. . . .

Cyberspace! Cyberspace? The first time I heard the term, I was captivated. Cyberspace is similar to la-la land — it's everywhere and yet nowhere. Cyberspace is that place where all things seem to come together that no one can find. Now are you confused? *Cyberspace* is simply a term that refers to the online world created by the interconnecting of computer systems. When you communicate though the Internet, you are sending information through this boundless virtual space. (*Cyber* refers to something electronic, by the way.)

Oh, Dem Modems!

How does cyberspace link or connect to the computer? Through a modem.

Modems are hardware units that connect to standard telephone lines and transmit signals to other computers. Three basic types of modems exist: internal, external, and PCMCIA-card modems.

The ins and outs of buying a modem

Space, size, location, and use all control the type of modem you decide to buy. Here are your choices:

✔ **Internal modems** fit inside the computer and leave the telephone-cord outlet exposed. Only one cord is needed to connect an internal modem to the telephone outlet. The modem is contained on a little circuit board that is about the size of your checkbook (see the illustration in Figure 12-1).

✔ **External modems** are contained in a "little black box" that sits outside the computer and can be connected to different computers. External modems require two wires: one to connect to a port in the back of the computer and one to connect to a power source. External modems vary in size but generally are about the size of a paperback book (see Figure 12-1). Some external modems are as small as a box of breath mints.

✔ **PCMCIA-compliant (Personal Computer Memory Card International Association) modem cards** can be kept inside or outside your computer. When you want to connect, simply insert the card into the card slot on your computer and connect the cord that comes with the card to the telephone outlet. The cards are about the size of a credit card and just a bit thicker (see Figure 12-1), and they are popular with laptop computers.

Each type of modem can connect you to cyberspace, and each type of modem is available for sending data only (*data modems*), as well as for sending faxes and data (*fax/data modems*). Some of the most modern modems even serve as answering systems, have caller ID, and offer voice transmission so that you can actually talk to your computer instead of picking up the receiver, holding the telephone to your ear, and speaking into it.

It's baud, not Maud

I once attended a teacher in-service workshop where the keynote speaker was a motivational type. I'll never forget that she told us that we'd know we had an eating problem when we stood in front of the microwave and said, "Hurry up!" I feel the same way about transmitting data through a modem.

Modems come in a variety of shapes and sizes, and a term that you will often hear when people talk about modems is baud. *Baud* simply refers to the speed at which information is sent and received through a modem. Modem speed is measured in *bits per second (bps),* and the higher the number used to refer to a modem, the faster the modem works — and believe me when I tell you that you need lots of speed when you start surfing the Net!

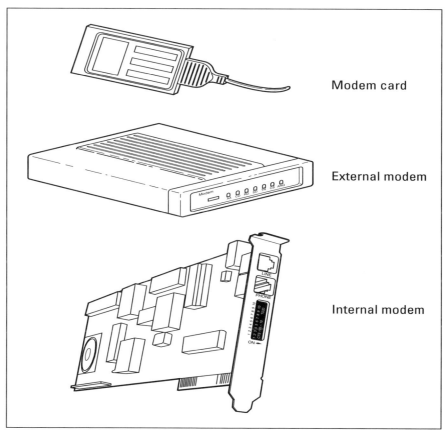

Figure 12-1:
Three
different
types of
modems.

Modem card

External modem

Internal modem

Modem speeds range from 1,200 to 115,200 bps, with the most popular speeds today ranging from 14,400 to 33,600, but faster speeds are being developed every day. My slowest modem is 14,400 and my fastest is 33,600, but I'm itching for more speed. When more online services start supporting 57,600 and 115,200, I'll jump right in and get a faster modem.

Advice? Buy the fastest modem that you can afford — and if you're running Windows 95, don't buy anything slower than 14,400. If you currently have a modem that's slower than 14,400, replace it with a faster modem pronto.

Modeming the fax

In addition to modems of various types (internal and external) and different baud rates, you can also buy a modem that acts as a fax machine. Chapter 6 talks about printing to a fax/modem by using the same procedures that you use to print to a printer. Well, to transmit a document by printing to a fax, you must have a fax/modem. Fax/modems generally are a bit more expensive than data modems, but fax/modems can save you money by eliminating the need to buy a separate fax machine.

Fax/modems enable other people to transmit documents from their separate fax machines directly to your computer system. When you receive the document, you can save it, edit it, print it, or discard it, just as you would a document that you created on your system. The main difference is that you must turn on your system and set it up to receive the fax.

Talking to a modem: the soft stuff

Modems come with software that you install to tell your system that you've added a piece of hardware and to enable you to use the modem. If you're running Windows 95, the moment you plug in the modem card and turn on the computer, *Plug and Play* (an industry standard that allows computer equipment to work together) polices your machine and pops up to tell you that you just installed a new piece of equipment (as if you didn't already know). Plug and Play asks whether you want to use the modem. If you say yes, it instructs you to insert the disk that came with the modem (sort of like real police asking for a driver's license or the principal asking for a note from a parent).

The disk that comes with your modem is sort of like your license to use the hardware (modem). The disk contains the communications software that bridges the gap between you (on the computer) and the modem, to allow the two pieces of equipment (your computer and your modem) to talk to each other. The instructions for installing the software are specific to the particular modem that you purchase, so follow them closely to set up your modem.

Locating your modem

Okay, you have your modem, you have it installed on your computer, and now you're ready to connect the modem cord to the phone line in your classroom. What? No phone line? That dilemma is quite common — and solvable if you have a "connected" principal who understands the importance of connecting every classroom. The next decision involves deciding where to locate the computer with the internal modem or which computer to connect to the external modem. Consider these important factors:

> ✔ **Will your administration permit additional phone lines?** Generally, administrators can be sold on the idea of running phone lines at least to strategic locations that can allow access to many users if a phone line can't be placed in each classroom.

> ✔ **Is there a media center that already has a telephone line available?** If so, the media center usually has more room for you to work with the computer in a quieter setting — and often without the confusion of your normal classroom.
>
> ✔ **If you choose to connect via a media center, can you safely send your students there to work independently?** Be sure that there is sufficient supervision in the media center and that the media-center coordinator doesn't mind working with individual students when you need to be with a class.

Connecting via a telephone line actually ties up the telephone line, just as it does when you have a teenager at home. As a result, if you plug the modem into the wall jack, you are unable to use the telephone until you disconnect the modem and plug in the telephone.

Now picture where the wall jack for your telephone is located. Ah! Now you see it. Unless you like crawling around on your hands and knees, you may want to purchase a modem that has a specific jack for the phone line. If your modem doesn't have such a jack, purchase a splitter, plug it into the wall jack, and plug the modem wire into one jack and the telephone wire into the other. That way, you have access to either piece of equipment without a lot of fuss.

Online Services: New Ways to Reach Out and Touch Someone

When you get your modem set up, you can use it to connect to cyberspace by using a variety of services. Connecting to the service is referred to as *going online* — you are actually using a line to connect, so you're online.

If you have a *host computer* (the main computer to which other computers are connected), you can go online directly by connecting to the host, which in turn passes you through to the Internet. If you are not connected to a host, you can use one of the variety of online services that are ready and waiting to escort you to the Net. The number of online services varies from location to location because of the number of local providers. In addition, you'll find lots of national and international services available.

Routes to the Net: online services

As a beginner using a home computer, you are most likely to connect to the Net by using a commercial service. Several commercial services are available, and experimenting with each one doesn't hurt. The table in the "Rates you can live with" sidebar provides an overview of the costs of the most popular services. By the time you read this book, these rates may be different, but the information gives you an idea of services that are tried and true — tested and found to be reliable. You can find out how to surf the Net in Chapter 14. For now, I focus on the different types of online services.

Routes through the Net: browsers

Online services provide information and services that do not involve actually connecting to the Internet — information and services that are available only to subscribers to the service. Bulletin boards and forums enable you to post messages to other subscribers of the online service without actually tying into the Internet.

ON THE CD

Rates you can live with

Most school accounts that have online services are set up to limit the number of hours per month that students (and teachers) can travel about online. You may find that this time is insufficient (especially if you become an online junkie). Before going out and buying additional hours at the commercial rate, you might try checking with the service to see about lower pricing for educational institutions. (See the table in this sidebar for a comparison of online service fees.)

CompuServe recently initiated a program to offer its software free to schools and is challenging other companies to join the push to get everyone online. The CompuServe program provides a safe environment that offers information and chat lines that are geared only to children.

Set up accounts for each class, and make sure that both students and teachers stay within their allotted time — or charge them overtime (like a library fine).

When America Online offered unlimited online time for a flat fee, the company was not quite prepared for the popularity of the service or the repercussions that resulted — many users were unable to get online because the phone lines were tied up due to demand. Other online services are eager to follow AOL's lead in providing unlimited access and time for a flat fee but are moving forward more cautiously. They're guarding against the technological insufficiencies that AOL experienced in order to guarantee their customers easy — and equal — access.

You'll find a copy of AT&T WorldNet Service software on the CD-ROM that comes with this book. Pull out the CD-ROM and install the program; AT&T offers several hours of trial time online.

Service	Monthly Cost	Hours Included	Additional Hourly Rate
America Online	$19.95	Unlimited	N/A
CompuServe	$9.95	5	$2.95
Microsoft Network	$4.95	3	$2.50
Prodigy	$9.95	5	$2.95

Note: *Rates are as of this writing and are subject to change.*

To reach the Internet, whether you have a direct line or go through an online service, you need a browser. *Browsers* enable you to hop from place to place on the Internet — like browsing through a department store or art gallery (and by the way, both these activities are possible on the Internet). Popular browsers available include

- ✔ Internet Explorer 3.0 (4.0 is on the horizon)
- ✔ Netscape Navigator (free to teachers)
- ✔ NetLauncher

A Forrester Research report quoted in the Feb. 26, 1996, issue of *USA Today* predicted that online services will peak in 1998, with 15.8 million subscribers, and that the number of surfers who will get direct Internet access accounts will grow to 32 million from 5 million today. Online services are predicted by the experts to be with you into the next century.

Net-picking netiquette

As is true of most things, online communication has guidelines that help keep things straight and clean. These guidelines, as they apply to the Internet, are often referred to as *netiquette* (network etiquette).

Microsoft Network lists only six rules, and I believe that they are good ones. These rules apply to messages displayed in *chat rooms* (places where you can "chat" with other people who have connected to the same room at the same time), as well as to e-mail messages that you send to others, either anonymously or by design. Keep in mind that e-mail messages can be printed and might be used in court!

I've broken the Microsoft Network six rules into eight rules. I think you'll find the following rules direct and to the point:

- ✔ No profanity.
- ✔ No racist remarks.
- ✔ No threats toward guests or hosts.
- ✔ No ASCII (American Standard Code for Information Interchange) art to create special characters such as © or ®.
- ✔ No scrolling the screen by *laaaaying* down on a keyboard character while chatting online. It transmits a series of repeat keystrokes and prevents others from getting a message on-screen.
- ✔ No TYPING IN ALL CAPITAL LETTERS — it means you're SCREAMING!
- ✔ No harassment of guests or hosts by another guest.
- ✔ Respect the wishes of others, and always act as though children are in the room.

How to Divvy Up Online Time

"That's not fair!" said one student to the teacher. "So-and-so's been on the computer for over an hour and won't let any of us have a turn." Sound familiar? If it doesn't yet, it probably will. How do you handle scheduling time on the computer? Well, the answer depends on the subject you teach, the grade level, and, of course, the number of computers that you have available!

Setting limits

Wouldn't it be nice to have a computer for every student in your class? Even if you could, how many of you believe that you would have 25 or 30 phone lines available so that all students could go online together? In your dreams!

If you aren't one of the lucky teachers who work in a school that has already implemented direct links to the Internet, you need to set up a schedule for computer time. The following are good practices for allowing students to go online:

- Be sure that students are well supervised while they're online.

- Overview rules and procedures with small groups to introduce students to the system and to the online places where they can go.

- Post the rules on posterboard — in large print — above the computer center.

- Situate the computer so that you can see the monitor from any location in the classroom. (You don't need to be a rocket scientist to figure out why.)

- Keep track of online time by having students enter time on/off in a log book.

- Post students' online entitlements on a poster so that entitlements and online time can be monitored by everyone and coordinated by you.

- Assign a student to monitor and coordinate online time and entitlement and to report any "advances" for points not yet earned.

Controlling online time

For those of you who do not have a computer for every student in the class, here are a couple of ways that I've seen teachers control (or reward) students' online time and encourage the best work from students at the same time:

✔ **Assign a set base time.** Require each student to log a basic amount of time — say, a couple of hours a month — and then reward additional time by using other procedures.

✔ **Set up a voucher system.** Award grade-equivalent points for daily assignments, double the grade-level points for quizzes, and triple grade-level points for tests. The scale can be 4 points for a daily assignment on which the student got an A, 3 for a B, and so on; 8 points for an A on a quiz, 6 for a B, and so on; and 12 points for an A on a test, 9 for a B, and so on.

Most students have a favorite way to use the time that they accumulate. Give students online time — so they can read a book, play a game, or whatever — equivalent to the number of points that they have. If you grade in points anyway, give students time equivalent to their total score (within reason), especially for daily assignments. You also can award points for special projects, tasks, and other things to help those students who can't accumulate as many points as they would like through their grades.

✔ **Assign timed tasks.** Develop a set of tasks that you want your students to accomplish; then have students demonstrate their abilities to perform the tasks by assigning them something to find online. Give each student a different topic or subject, and set a time limit. This approach ensures that *all* students spend time online exploring and experimenting before being tested. (By the way, this approach is also an excellent way to have students locate information that you may want to look up to update a lesson plan for the following week.)

✔ **Allow students to make decisions.** Allow students to devise a fair system for setting online (or on-system) time. They often come up with innovative ways to earn points that you and I don't think of.

✔ **Set up accounts.** Setting up accounts is a good way to teach students accountability. But be careful — they quickly learn how to barter time with other students. (Some students actually earn lots of extra spending money by selling their computer time.) They also may start trying to set up charge accounts and issue charge cards!

Screening the Net gaps for safety — and surviving!

Although the Internet can be a fascinating place to visit, you want to avoid certain parts of town, and your students should not "accidentally" wander into other streets and avenues. Before connecting your students with the Internet, have students and parents sign an acceptable-use agreement, telling the parents and students that there will be consequences for inappropriate use of the Internet.

In addition to relying on users' self-control, most of the online services offer screening software that's designed to control the Internet sites that students can visit. Check these products out if you subscribe to an online service. To protect students on school computers, look for some of these products:

✔ **Cyber Patrol** (http://www.cyberpatrol.com). This product ($34.95), from Microsystems Software (800-828-2608), enables parents and teachers to choose categories that they want to block and prevents the transmission of personal data, such as names, addresses, and phone numbers.

✔ **CYBERsitter** (http://www.solidoak.com). Solid Oak Software (800-388-2761) developed this product ($39.95) so that parents and teachers can customize a list of unapproved sites and categories to block by entering specific words and phrases.

✔ **Microsoft Plus! for Kids** (http://www.microsoft.com/kids). From Microsoft (800-426-9400), this product ($24.95) packages security features for parents with fun programs for kids. The software includes password-protected parental controls similar to those in the Internet Explorer 3.0 browser and other security features that enable you to password-protect desktop files.

✔ **Net Nanny** (http://www.netnanny.com). Net Nanny Ltd. (800-340-7177) created this product ($39.95) so that it can be set to log the sites that users visit or to shut down the system if users attempt to visit unapproved sites. The software also monitors and prevents the use of unauthorized floppy disks and CD-ROMs that contain unsuitable material (such as violent games).

✔ **Rated-PG** (http://www.ratedpg.com). You can get this Windows 95 program ($54.95) from PC DataPower (800-404-9913), in Christian bookstores, or by mail order. The product allows parents and teachers to block Web sites, CD-ROMs, and floppy disks that are not preapproved, and it restricts computer use during certain hours. The software also generates reports showing what times the computer was used and what sites were visited. Rated-PG is ideal for classroom monitoring and control.

✔ **SurfWatch** (http://www.surfwatch.com). This product ($49.95), from Spyglass (800-458-6600), screens Web sites, newsgroups, and other areas of the Net and automatically updates its list of blocked sites as new sites are added.

You might want to pass this list of sites and products along to parents so that they can protect their children at home, too!

Chapter 13

Going Online with Microsoft Network

- -

In This Chapter

▶ Choosing an e-mail program

▶ Logging on

▶ Connecting with the e-mail system

▶ Creating and sending an e-mail message

▶ Addressing e-mail across online services

- -

E-mail is the No. 1 reason why most people connect to the Internet. At least e-mail is the reason why I connect — sometimes two, three, or four times a day. When you discover the advantages of e-mail, you'll be hooked, and you'll have started down the entrance ramp to the Information Superhighway.

The network of roads on the Information Superhighway is vast, and you can pick the road that you want to take. I chose Microsoft Network (referred to hereafter as MSN) for your tour in this chapter because it comes free with Windows 95. You may have chosen a different road for your e-mail travels, and that's okay. Many of the same concepts and techniques that you would use to travel MSN apply to other roads as well. If you want to explore the MSN road with me, you can explore, learn about, and get lost in cyberspace for 30 days — free, regardless of how many hours you spend online.

E-Mail: An Overview

E-mail, simply put, is a modified acronym that stands for *electronic mail.* E-mail consists of messages, letters, documents, and any other communication transmitted electronically from one computer to another.

E-mail goes to a mailbox, just like mail delivered by the U.S. Postal Service. The difference is that the e-mailbox is not physically located at the end of your driveway or hanging outside your front door. Your electronic mailbox is located at a specific location on a computer controlled by the online service that you use to transmit and receive messages. You give your mailbox an address when you install the program software and use the address to tell your computer who you are each time you connect to the online service. When you get your address set up, you can exchange messages with others who have electronic mailboxes.

MSN is an online service (one of those I mention in Chapter 12) but is not by any means the only online service that has e-mail service. All online services have features for sending and receiving messages. In fact, each online service mentioned in Chapter 12 offers a way to exchange messages with the other online services as well as with the Internet. Perhaps it's time to rename the Information Superhighway so that it really reflects the extent of its growth — maybe the Information Super-duper Highway.

What's the advantage of using e-mail? Speed. You can send an e-mail message, and within seconds, the message is received and distributed to the other person. That's why e-mail is so popular — everyone is about as patient as I am (not!).

Getting Set Up — and Liking It

If you're running Windows 95 on your computer, you most likely had a small icon on the desktop when you installed Windows 95 (or when you received your computer) that allowed you to install and set up MSN. Then again, you may have received a copy of "The New Microsoft Network" CD-ROM in the mail. If you have not yet received your free copy of "The New Microsoft Network," call 800-386-5550. Microsoft will be glad to send you a copy.

You can install the program by following the easy instructions that appear on the CD-ROM folder. Just put the disc into the CD-ROM drive and watch what happens.

MSN even provides a preview video to introduce you to some of its great features. Take the tour to see what all the hype is about; then go ahead and install the program. A cute little guy keeps you apprised of the installation progress, and somewhere along the line, MSN needs to restart your machine (and it's *so* automatic!). When the computer is running again, MSN wraps the installation up tightly, and the little guy on-screen throws streamers in the air to tell you that setup is finished. Then you have to make some choices about signing up:

  ✔ If you have neither an MSN account nor an Internet account, you can choose the first sign-up option and get two accounts for the price of one.

> ✔ If you already have an Internet program (such as Internet Explorer or Netscape Navigator), choose the second sign-up option.
>
> ✔ If you already have an MSN account and are simply upgrading to the latest and greatest version of MSN, choose the last sign-up option.

Make a note on the calendar that you logged on to MSN today, so that you won't lose track of your 30-day free trial. Believe me, MSN won't forget, and the clock starts the minute you go online.

Regardless of which online e-mail service you choose, somewhere during the installation process, the developers and the people who monitor the online service (much like the school principal) will ask you for information — key information, such as your online name and your password. You need to provide the information so that the keepers of the network can get you all signed up.

Naming yourself

If you've ever wished that you could change your name, this is your chance. Regardless of the online service that you choose for your e-mail service, you have to pick a name. The name that you enter as your e-mail name is the address that will appear on your e-mailbox online. Other people will use that address to ensure that your e-mail messages are delivered to *you* and not to someone else. MSN calls your name your member ID but asks how you want others to address you online. Is that an open invitation or what?

Naming yourself can be fun, though. As you consider different names, be careful — you have to remember how or what you named yourself each time you go online or give your e-mail address to a friend. Forgetting your own name is significantly more embarrassing than forgetting a student's name.

Passing the word

When I think of passwords, I usually recall with a smile the group of people I taught to operate a customized system for processing special forms. They had to type their worker IDs and passwords as they started work each day, as well as after a break or lunch. Unfortunately, their system *assigned* passwords to them; they couldn't pick their own. As a result, employees often had difficulty remembering their passwords. What did they do? They wrote their passwords on sticky notes and stuck them on their monitors so that they wouldn't forget them!

The word to pass is that students should *not* pass their passwords to other students, teachers, or anyone else — and neither should you. Passwords allow access to an online account, and time spent is also money spent. You'll be surprised by how quickly you'll use up any free hours or days offered by the online service that you're using, so be selfish and hog them all yourself.

Here are some tips for selecting a password:

✔ Select a word that has meaning for you and is easy to remember.

✔ Use the same password for all your personal accesses, so that you don't have to try to remember which password you used for which service or whatever. Don't, however, use the same password for all your students; allow them to determine their own.

✔ Keep your password short (fewer than ten characters). Lengthy passwords are difficult to remember.

✔ Don't ever, *ever* give your password out, not even to another teacher or family member, but especially not to a student. Would you give anyone your PIN number for your bank ATM?

Your password is not part of your e-mail address. You should never be asked online what password you are using. If you are, please report it to the service immediately so that the service can investigate.

Sometimes, the online service assigns you a name and a password to use the first time that you go online. If you haven't yet been asked what name and password you want to use, the program tells you where to find the name and password that's been assigned to your disk. Use the assigned name and password the first time you sign on. You'll be given a chance to change your name and password when you're online.

Connecting close to home

After you provide all the information requested during installation, click the Sign Up button to go online for the first time. Follow the screen prompts to learn how to proceed. You may be asked who you want to be (your online name) and what password you want to use, if you were not asked during installation. In addition, MSN (and other online services) allow you to connect by using an 800 number the first time you sign on, give you a chance to tell the service where you are (your area code and phone number), and locate local access phone numbers within your area.

Pick the number that's closest to your home to make connecting easier — and much less expensive. You may also want to pick a backup number to use in case the first number that you choose is busy when you try to sign on. Some services present a page of options that enable you to tell the computer to dial 1 for long-distance calls or how to disable call waiting each time you go online. Choose the options that you want to set.

Anatomy of an e-mail address

Naming yourself is important; your name is your link to other online services and to the Internet. If you're a member of an online service, other users of the service can contact you directly simply by typing your online name. When users of other online services need to contact you, they have to cross a bridge or go through a gateway. The Internet has made crossing bridges and passing through gateways much easier.

Most online services are attached to the Internet, so when their users send e-mail to you or when you send e-mail to friends on other services, you need to include the online service's name and account type with the user's address — sort of like providing the city and state part of your real address. Look at how an MSN address compares with a CompuServe address:

Soft-Spec@MSN.com

72724,656@CompuServe.com

Notice that both addresses end with .com. *.com* stands for *commercial*, which identifies the type of account.

Students at educational facilities usually can choose their own IDs as well. For example, you'll find addresses at educational institutions that look like these:

PRT304@students.psu.edu

The post office (the space allotted to e-mail addresses on a server) or account group (students, in this case) varies from facility to facility. I communicate with students at several universities; some have students as their account type, whereas others have email, a computer name or acronym, or another code set up by network administrators.

If you get to choose the facility name for your school, make it distinctive and exciting — something that people will remember!

When you finish choosing a phone number, MSN signs you out and logs you back on, using the number that you chose. This procedure helps verify that the number is accurate and opens up the long-distance line to other new customers. If the number doesn't work, an error message appears; you need to log back on, using the 800 number again, to verify the number or to choose a different number.

Accounting matters

When you log on for the first time, your online service may quiz you (or grill you, as the case may be!). The service wants to know where to send the bill in case you get hooked and those free hours (or the 30 days) are gone before you know it. You may want to look at the costs of going online the first time that you sign on, just to get a feel for what could happen if you go over the allotted free time. Your school may have already checked out the costs. Check with the technology coordinator to be sure and also to identify the limits allowed for each class or teacher that signs up.

After you answer all MSN's questions and read all its preliminary information (you did read each of those screens, didn't you?), you hit the Information Superhighway.

Plunging Directly Online

Okay, you're all set up, you've answered all your network's questions, you've renamed yourself, and you've entered a password. What do you do the next time you want to connect? That's easy . . . with MSN as well as with other online services.

Sign on, please

Each time you want to sign on, follow these steps:

1. **Double-click the online service's icon on the desktop.**

   MSN sets up this icon for you during installation, and so do many other online services. If you don't see an icon for your online service, choose Start⇨Programs and then choose the program from the submenu.

   When you double-click the MSN icon, the MSN Sign In window appears, as shown in Figure 13-1.

2. **Type your Member ID and Password in the appropriate text boxes.**

   If you're using a different online service, your screen will be arranged differently, but the information requested will be basically the same.

Figure 13-1: You won't need much help figuring out what to do here.

Password entry box   MSN Member ID   Command buttons

As you type your password, only asterisks appear in the Password text box. The asterisks prevent someone from looking over your shoulder and stealing your password. The asterisks help maintain secrecy, individuality, and privacy.

Also notice the check box that tells your computer to remember your password. If you check the Remember My Password check box, anyone can sign on to MSN by using your name and password — and I don't even let my husband do *that*. He could get my account into a real mess! Protect yourself — don't check the check box.

3. **Click Connect.**

You may think that someone left the phone off the hook when you hear the sounds that come from your computer after you click Connect. The procedures that your computer has to follow to get you online are the same procedures that you have to follow to call your friends and family members: Pick up the phone receiver, listen for a dial tone, dial the number, and listen for the brrrrr to signal that the phone on the other end is ringing. Hearing these sounds coming from your computer is a real treat.

When the computer that you're calling answers, you hear a high-pitched noise, followed by a lower pitch, followed by a ca-thunk, ca-thunk, whsh-whsh-whsh. The Sign In window shown in Figure 13-1 displays messages telling you about the logon progress. Finally, your screen fills with something resembling the window shown in Figure 13-2.

If you're lucky and have a sound board in your computer, the magic of music accompanies you on your tour.

Hi, good morning, welcome

Whether your online service greets you verbally or simply presents options for you to choose, the screen that you see when you first go online is designed to welcome you. MSN puts you "On Stage" (the default location identified at the top of the screen) each time you sign on and notifies you when you have mail by providing the number of new messages that you have in the top-left corner of the window (alas, I have nothing).

Other programs display their welcome screens differently; just look around your window to see what's available. Look for a feature that might be the road to your e-mail feature; you need to know where it is if you plan to become an e-mail whiz.

Navigation buttons   Communications options   MSN menu

Figure 13-2:
Ah . . . now I
have proof
that I'm
online!

Preview channels

Communicating across Party Lines

Now that you're online, you may feel like partying; and then again, you may simply want to join the party that's already online. One of the first things that new users want to learn is how to deal with their mail — e-mail, of course.

Have you located your mailbox yet? Because e-mail is so popular, the feature usually is easy to find; and as you may have guessed, the Communications menu in MSN provides easy access to e-mail.

If you're using AOL, the Post Office is listed in the Main menu. Double-click the mailbox icon to access your e-mail.

If you're using CompuServe, look for a Mail Center button on the Home Desktop, as shown in Figure 13-3. The Home Desktop appears each time you launch CompuServe. Notice, too, that CompuServe has a Mail menu you can use to get to your e-mail. When you click the Mail Center button on the Home Desktop, a list of e-mail messages appears automatically.

See how easy it is to find your e-mail? Now that you've found the mail, you need to open your messages and read them.

Home Desktop   Mail menu

Figure 13-3:
CompuServe
has a really
neat and
very
colorful
Main Menu.

Mail Center button

Reading your mail

Reading your mail on the computer is a great deal more satisfying than
wading through everything that gets stuffed into your mailbox at school.
Check e-mail out and see whether you agree. Here are some directions to get
you started:

1. **Click Communicate in the MSN menu bar.**

   If you're using a different service, click the icon or menu item that leads
   to your e-mail feature. The MSN window appears similar to the one
   shown in Figure 13-4. You'll discover when you first start using e-mail
   programs through an online service that the windows are updated
   frequently. As a result, the window I see today will not necessarily be
   identical to the window you see when you're reading this book.

2. **Click the start e-mail button at the top of the window.**

   Unless you have the most up-to-date version of Microsoft Office, the e-
   mail program that MSN opens is Microsoft Exchange. If you have Office
   97 installed on your computer, MSN opens a new feature called Outlook.
   (Pick up a copy of *Microsoft Office 97 For Windows For Teachers* by Neil

E-mail options   Message Center   E-mail address   Active communicate indicator

Figure 13-4:
Wow! My
screen
name
actually
appears on-
screen (but
alas, I have
zero
messages).

J. Salkind for more information about Outlook.) If you're using a different online service, the window that opens resembles the one pictured
in Figure 13-5.

3. Double-click any message to open it.

The message opens in a separate window, as shown in Figure 13-6. Use
the scroll bars to display the part of the message that appears off-
screen, or maximize your window to view more of the message.

After reading the message, explore the buttons in the message-window
toolbar and see whether you can determine how to display the next message, how to send a reply to the open message, and how to forward the
message to someone else.

Do you think that you have the hang of this e-mail thing? I *knew* you could
handle it! Now see whether you can close the message that you have open —
remember, X marks the spot. (It's the character that's on the Close button.)

E-mail menu bar   Attachment clips   E-mail toolbar

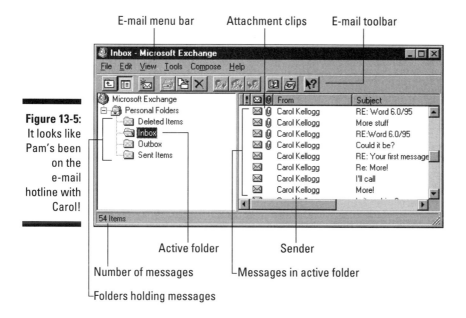

Figure 13-5:
It looks like
Pam's been
on the
e-mail
hotline with
Carol!

Active folder   Sender

Number of messages   Messages in active folder

Folders holding messages

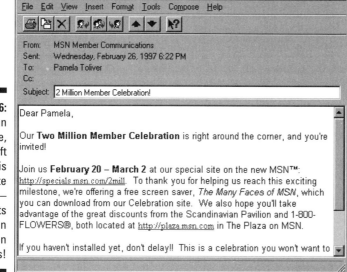

Figure 13-6:
As you can
see,
Microsoft
Network is
quite
popular —
it boasts
more than
2 million
subscribers!

Creating and sending your first message

For your first message, type a letter to someone whom you already know is online: your spouse, another teacher, your students, or me. You can mail a letter to me by using either of the following online addresses:

  ✔ 72724,656@compuserve.com

  ✔ Soft-Spec@msn.com

Whether you're reading e-mail or sending e-mail, when you're online you're communicating. And whether your online service calls communicating Communicate, Post Office, or something else, the procedure for sending an e-mail message is the same. (Be sure that your students know the difference between the online "post office" and the party game of the same name; they may convince you that they can communicate by using both!)

To create a new e-mail message, follow these steps:

1. Open your e-mail window and click the New Message button.

In AOL, click the Compose Message button; in CompuServe, choose Mail⇨Create/Send Mail. In MSN, the New Message window opens (see Figure 13-7).

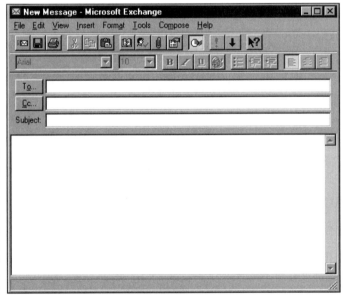

Figure 13-7:
The New Message window resembles an interoffice memo.

The insertion point is in the To text box when you get started. Before you can e-mail someone, you need to add that person and his or her address to your address book.

2. Click the To button beside the text box.

The Address Book window, shown in Figure 13-8, opens.

Names selected to receive message

Buttons to add selected names to list   Address book name

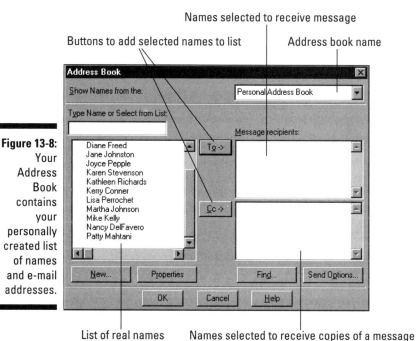

Figure 13-8:
Your
Address
Book
contains
your
personally
created list
of names
and e-mail
addresses.

List of real names   Names selected to receive copies of a message

3. **Click New.**

   A New Entry dialog box lists different e-mail entry types.

4. **Choose Internet over the Microsoft Network from the entry type list.**

5. **Click OK.**

   The New Internet over The Microsoft Network Properties dialog box opens (see Figure 13-9). If you aren't certain what information to place in the dialog box, read the example provided at the bottom of the dialog box. It shows you where to type the person's e-mail name, *domain* (the information that follows the @ sign), and real name. If you use my address as an example, **Soft-Spec** would go in the E-Mail address text box, **msn.com** would go in the Domain name text box, and **Pam Toliver** would go in the Name text box.

6. **Type the requested information in each text box.**

7. **Click the To button to place the address in the message window.**

   The name is added to your Address Book and to your message at the same time. You can add names and e-mail addresses as you need them or build your Address Book when you have spare time.

8. **Type the subject of your message in the Subject text box.**

9. **Type your message in the message window.**

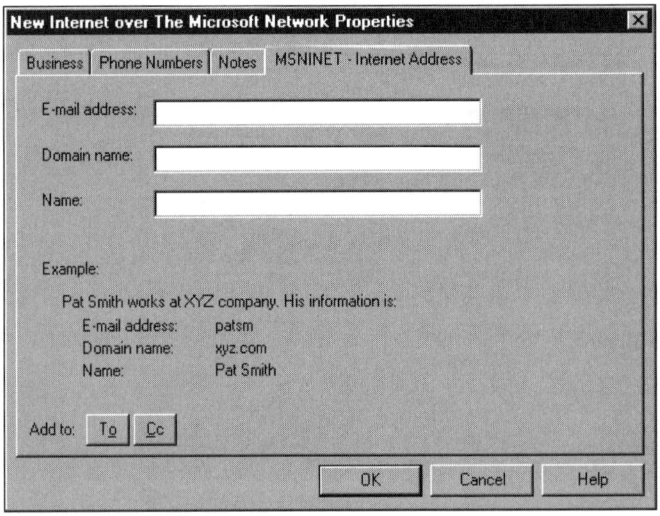

Figure 13-9:
Read the
example to
see what
goes
where.

As you type, use the same procedures to edit and correct text in the New Message window that you use to correct errors in Microsoft Works. Be sure to ask the person you're addressing to respond so that you'll know that he or she got the message — that way, you'll get e-mail, too!

10. **Click the Send toolbar button (the button with the envelope on it) to get your message off and running.**

The all-in-one e-mail address

Imagine a world in which you can choose one e-mail address to access from any online service. Sound interesting? It's actually quite exciting, and according to a recent article by Kevin Maney in *USA Today*, it's only a URL away.

According to the article, MailCity (www.mailcity.com), a service unveiled by an Internet-directory service called Who-Where, allows a user to register on a Web site; picks a name for his or her mailbox (such as PToliver or CKellogg), which is located at @mailcity.com; and identifies addresses used on other services so that mail sent to other addresses is automatically forwarded to the MailCity address. You still need a password to collect your mail, but you won't have to log on to several services. (At one time I had *four* services at the same time!)

What's even better is the fact that the service is *free*! MailCity sells ads that scroll across the top of your screen while you are online (like the severe-weather info on your television set), however, but you can ignore these ads, which are the electronic equivalent of junk . . . er, business mail.

That's all there is to it. Now log off (shut down, go off-line, or whatever you want to call breaking the communications connection). Then sit back and relax. One of two things is bound to happen: The person who receives your e-mail will respond (in a day or two), or the network administrator will return the message with a "Return to Sender. Address Unknown. No Such Server. No Such Phone." (My apologies to Elvis.)

And by the way, if you subscribed to one of the services that has a limited amount of time attached to your monthly payment, you may find that creating your e-mail messages off-line reduces the amount of time that you spend online composing your notes. Simply launch your program and then press Esc or click Cancel to tell your program that you want to work with the program a bit before going online. Try it; you'll open many of the same windows off-line that you open online, without the clock ticking!

Chapter 14

Surfing the Net

• •

In This Chapter

▶ Discovering Internet origins and technicalities

▶ Touring special Net road maps

▶ Locating forums and other favorite places for teachers and students

▶ Exploring ways to limit student access online

▶ Evaluating Web sites

▶ Designing online searches for students

▶ Sampling school policies and guidelines for going online

• •

*I*t's everywhere! It's everywhere! What am I talking about? Why, the Internet, of course. And whether you refer to a jaunt through cyberspace as being an excursion on the Internet or a trip around the World Wide Web, you'll want to be everywhere at once!

Many of the questions that may occur to you as you begin your journey through cyberspace are answered in this chapter. The rest of this chapter is devoted to whetting your appetite — simply getting you started. After you learn the basics, I have every confidence that you'll swim, not sink (unless, of course, you get deeper and deeper and . . . well, you get the picture). I use the Microsoft Network, along with its Web browser, for my examples, but feel free to use any online connection that you have available.

The Internet: Facts to Know

Have you ever wondered whose brilliant idea led to this phenomenon known as the Internet? Well, I'm about to provide you some basic facts that I think you need to know before you get caught up in the Net (that's short for Internet).

Defining the Net

The *Internet* is a gigantic network of slightly smaller networks located all over the world. Each smaller network consists of literally millions of computers, all using a common language of signals known as an *Internet Protocol (IP)* to communicate. The Department of Defense originated the Internet when it developed a network called ARPAnet (Advanced Research Projects Agency) back in the late '60s — before many of us had color TVs, microwave ovens, and personal computers. When the Defense Department allowed the National Science Foundation to join its network, other agencies (primarily universities and other government agencies) soon followed suit. As a result, the Internet quickly established a culture of free exchange of information and ideas.

The commercial arm of the original Internet was created when the *Commercial Internet Exchange* (CIX) joined the Net and determined to make the Internet a money-making enterprise. You've heard the debates recently about censoring information on the Internet and so on. Well, it's amazing that this problem has only recently (within the past year) surfaced. The Internet has no one in charge, although the Internet Society (ISOC) tries to coordinate the Internet and maintain viability. Can you imagine your school without a principal? (Okay, maybe that's not such a good analogy, but you get the idea!) Suffice it to say that no one owns and operates the Internet.

Setting up a Net niche

To get your own little niche on the Net, you need to buy a *server* (sometimes called a *host*) computer: a large-capacity computer that you can leave on all the time. After you get your server all set up, you need to contact InterNIC (the group in charge of assigning IP addresses) and ask for your own IP address. Many schools already have servers that their students and staff members are using to access the Internet. Check with the school's technology coordinator or central-office staff to find out whether your school system has such a server and to learn the IP address.

If you don't have a host that enables you to connect directly to the Internet, you can use an *Internet Service Provider* (ISP) such as CompuServe, America Online, and so on, to connect to the Internet, but you usually have to pay a fee.

Untangling.Internet.strings

When you start using the Internet, you're going to run into a bunch of bizarre strings of characters, such as `http://stsimonshs.is.edu` and `Ptolivr@stsimons.com`. These strings of characters identify locations on the Internet.

You may be wondering what `http` means, why it's followed by a couple of slashes and a colon, and why you need all the periods, right? Here's a decoding session that will have you, too, talking in riddles . . . er, strings.

- ✔ **@ (at symbol):** Identifies a location — in this case, a computer location. `@msn` means that the computer is connected to the Microsoft Network, for example; `@aol` means that the computer is connected to America Online.

- ✔ **HTTP:** Stands for Hypertext Transfer Protocol, a special language developed by the Swiss (here's where we go international!) that enables you to click a word and jump to a new Internet location that's linked to the word. (Just think of hypertext as a *hyper* student who jumps all over the classroom.)

- ✔ **FTP:** Stands for File Transfer Protocol, a special format for placing information on the Internet or World Wide Web sites. Each server has a specific protocol (language) that it uses to transfer files.

- ✔ **:// (colon and two slashes):** Is a randomly selected set of characters used to divide the protocol from the rest of the Internet address. Now aren't you glad that no one decided to use ^%##& as the characters?

- ✔ **. (period, but pronounced *dot*):** Separates your computer name from its *domain*, which usually identifies the type of account you have (`.edu` for educational facilities, `.com` for commercial, `.gov` for government agencies, and so on).

- ✔ **~ (tilde):** Separates the main site's address from a person's or business's home page.

- ✔ **/ (slash):** Separates folders contained at Internet sites so that pages stored at the site can be grouped.

If you compare the Internet strings with your home address, they make more sense. The main difference is that Internet addresses separate pieces of the address by using keyboard characters and periods, whereas pieces of your home address appear on separate lines. As a result, you have:

> Your name
> Your street
> Your city, state, and ZIP code

versus

```
Yourname@yourcomputer.yourdomain
```

An Educator's Wonderland

Many of you may have already dipped the areas of the Internet when you explored other avenues of Microsoft Network. (If you're seeing Microsoft Network for the first time, you may want to check out Chapter 13, for an overview of using Microsoft Network.) In this chapter, I want you to focus on business — educational business.

By introducing you to the procedures that you can use to locate information in the educational arena, I'm really showing you how to work with the other features available on the Internet as well. If you're connecting to the Internet by using Netscape Navigator, Internet Explorer, or some other direct line to the Internet, the techniques discussed in this chapter work for you, too.

Special education — for teachers only

No, you don't need to be in special ed to enjoy your tour through the special education feature in Microsoft Network and other online services. Most online services display menu buttons that provide an easy way for you to access special *forums* — places on the Internet that group information about topics of interest to special groups.

You can follow different paths to get to Microsoft Network's special spot for teachers. Sign on to MSN and then choose one of the following roads to locate lesson plans for your subject:

- Click the Essentials list arrow; then choose MSN Classic, Custom Page, Classic Categories. Then you can open folders that contain information you want to explore by double-clicking the folders.

- Try opening MSN Classic Categories, Education & Reference, Technology in Teaching; then open the folder that most likely contains lesson plans for your teaching level or subject matter.

- Click the Find list arrow; then choose Search MSN and the Web. When the Find screen opens, click the Subject tab to display a list of subjects. See Education listed there? Good. Click Education and then choose For Teachers (or a grade level, if you want to explore more). Following this route, you'll be able to get to your lesson plans by selecting a series of hypertext links that jump you to the spot that you want.

  Figure 14-1 shows how MSN displays teacher topics. To display the next page of topics for teachers, click the Next navigation arrow at the bottom of the window. To return to the preceding listing, click the Back navigation arrow.

- Type the URL (Uniform Resource Locator) of the site that you want to visit in the Address box, and press Enter.

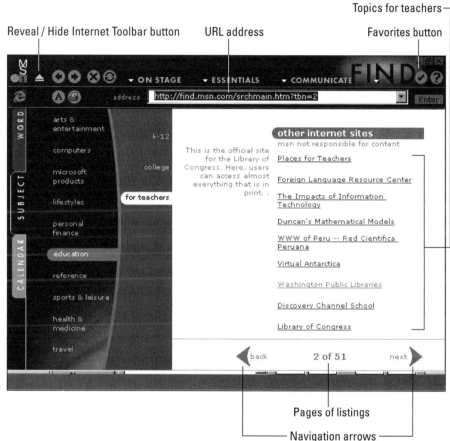

Topics for teachers

Reveal / Hide Internet Toolbar button   URL address   Favorites button

Figure 14-1:
Teachers
have a
special
place on
MSN.

Pages of listings

Navigation arrows

The first few routes to Internet sites provide a roundabout way to get to where you're going, don't they? To go directly to a site that you like to visit, you may want to try the route that the crow takes (the old "as the crow flies" approach) outlined in the last route (the one in the preceding list). You may also want to develop a list of favorite folders or sites. When you find an area or site that you like, click the Add to Favorites button in the toolbar. The next time you sign on and want to go to a location stored in your Favorites folder, all you have to do is click the Favorites button on the toolbar and choose the site from the Favorites list.

Internet special features: forums, bulletin boards, and newsgroups

Your exploration of the Internet will lead you to some unique sites, and sometimes, the connotation used to identify different sites may be misleading. The Internet and the World Wide Web have three basic types of message-posting spots, and you can use all three types to post information or to read notices and information posted by others.

Here's a quick guide to help you separate the acronyms from site types and help you identify the sites that you may want to visit:

- **Forums:** Online areas devoted to special-interest groups in which people can post messages, requests for help, and bits of information designed to help other users who are interested in the same topic. Forum discussions sometimes take place live in *chat rooms* (sort of like on-line teacher lounges where you can converse live with other people who are also online and in the same "lounge"). Forums are usually identified with the term *Forum* to make them easy to find.

- **Bulletin boards:** Another type of message-posting forum used for sharing information and special notices. *Bulletin board* is often abbreviated *BB* or *BBS*.

- **Newsgroups:** Special areas of the Internet where you can post special-interest messages. Many newsgroups also hold live discussions and share information about related and special topics. Some newsgroups also require that you join the group. Be sure to check membership fees before signing up.

Do you notice a sameness in the meanings of these three special features? I thought so. Just be aware that you can use any site type to call for help or information! But be careful — some forums, bulletin boards, and newsgroups are appropriate for adults only. Watch your students carefully so that they don't wander down inappropriate pathways.

Downing loaded stuff

When you find a lesson-plan file that you think you can use or discover useful information in a bulletin board or forum, you may want to *download* the file (copy the file to a disk). Teachers have contributed their lesson plans and programs to software libraries using a wide range of formats. As a result, the completeness (you know, objectives, procedures, list of supplies and materials, and so on) varies from plan to plan. Sometimes, the lesson plans that provide the greatest benefit to your class are among the simplest plans that you find. Other lesson plans are quite detailed.

Depending on the service that you use to connect to the Internet, downloading files may be free, but be aware that some services charge you for the time that it takes to download the file.

Imagine what you might find if every teacher in the country posted just one technology-related plan online. Isn't it time that you thought about posting one of yours? Most online services provide a way for you to contribute or compose a message and then attach your lesson plan so that others can use it. Check out the online help feature to find out how to contribute to libraries in your service.

Protecting Everyone from Online Danger

Before showing you where to find neat stuff for the students (okay, I admit I enjoy kids' stuff, too), you need to get serious about the dangers that you and your students may encounter online. If it hasn't done so already, this warning should trigger some red flags and you should be hearing sirens about now.

You've heard the concerns about the unsuitable material some students have encountered online; they're all over the news. Many times, the concerns are overblown; many times, they are not. Protecting your students also helps you protect yourself. Congress has even taken action to help protect children and what they may encounter as they venture onto the Net. Here are steps that two online services are implementing:

- ✔ America Online's Parental Controls feature enables you to limit students' access to specific areas of the Internet, as well as to newsgroups.

- ✔ CompuServe's Parental Controls Center enables you to restrict access to Internet services that you feel are unsuitable. You can restrict students' access to newsgroups and file transfers, as well as their access to services on CompuServe. You can also download Cyber Patrol software without charge. This software, which works with Windows 3.1, Windows 95, and Macintosh System 7.x, helps patrol the information that your students can access. The Go word is Controls.

You also can buy special software that is designed to block students' access to certain areas of the Internet and World Wide Web. These programs basically work the same way as the online information blockers provided by online services but can be attached to any online or Internet access program. You find a more comprehensive list of these programs in Chapter 12.

If you don't want your students to go directly online, consider an off-line browser such as WebWhacker. (There can be many reasons for a concern about students working online: the number of Internet connections available to your class at one time, a limit on the amount of time you have online, the amount of time you have to supervise students while they're online, and so on.)

Citing online sites

Now that you've got that up-to-the-minute information stored, edited, and printed, you probably want to use it in a report or some other paper. How do you give credit where credit is due? (I *know* that you've heard the term *plagiarism*.)

As sources of information from the Internet and the World Wide Web become more widely cited in student papers and other documents, citations change as well.

Here are a couple of citations that appeared in the February 7, 1996, issue of *USA Today* that serve as examples of how to cite a source:

✔ **Footnote/Endnote** from Kate L. Turabian's *A Manual for Writers of Term Papers, Theses, and Dissertations:*

William J. Mitchell, *City of Bits: Space, Place, and the Infobahn* [book on line] (Cambridge, Mass.: MIT Press, 1995, accessed 29 September 1995) available from `http://www.mitpress.mit.edu:80/City_of_Bits/Pulling_Glass/index.html;` Internet.

✔ **Bibliography** from Janice Walker's *MLA-Style Citations of Electronic Sources* (found on the World Wide Web at `http://www.cas.usf.edu/english/walker/mla.html`):

Burka, Lauren P. "A Hypertext History of Multi-User Dimensions." MUD HISTORY. `http://www.ccs.neu.edu/home/lpb/mud-history.html` (5 Dec. 1994).

PC Magazine Online recently reviewed as many as 16 programs that allow you to download Internet sites and then let your students browse the material as though they were actually online and surfing. This way, students can browse only the sites that you select, avoiding the accidental link to less appropriate material.

Just remember, though: The two major ingredients in monitoring students' access to the Internet in the classroom are a teacher who is alert and involved in what his or her students are doing on the Internet, and students who take responsibility for their actions. For more information about how some schools tackle this issue, check out "Laying down some online rules" later in this chapter.

Before going online with your students, you may want to get a brochure from the National Center for Missing and Exploited Children to increase your awareness of hazards. Contact this organization at 2101 Wilson Blvd., Suite 550, Arlington, VA 22209-3052 (`74431.177@compuserve.com`).

Student Fun

If you've already explored the Kids Only section of your online service, you have a good idea of what you and your students can find online. I thought that I'd mention a few tips for having your students work more efficiently (in other words, reduce time online and save money). Teachers are using online features to supplement out-of-date textbooks and to research current events so that they can provide students up-to-the-minute information. Students can simply gather information or become interactive and then dissect a frog without enduring the smell of formaldehyde.

You may find, however, that what kids consider to be top spots may not always be the same as the top *educational* spots for kids. Table 14-1 lists a few sites that you may want your students to enter (but be sure to explore the sites before recommending them to your students).

Table 14-1	Top Educational Spots for Kids
Site	*URL*
ABC News	`http://abc.com`
C-SPAN	`http://cspan.com`
CNN Newsroom	`http://cnn.com`
Compton's	`http://comptons.com`
Discovery Channel School	`http://school.discovery.com`
Encarta Schoolhouse	`http://encarta.msn.com/schoolhouse`
Global Schoolhouse	`http://www.gsh.org`
HotTopics	`http://www.reedbooks.com.au`
Library of Congress	`http://lcweb2.loc.gov/ammem/ndlpedu`
Microsoft	`http://microsoft.com`
National Geographic	`http://www.nationalgeographic.com`
NBC News	`http://www.msnbc.com`
Reference Dictionaries	`http://dictionary.com`
Scholastic	`http://scholastic.com`
Schools Online	`http://www.sol.com.sg`
White House	`http://www.whitehouse.gov`

Learning to Spot Good Sites

Because new Web sites are being posted constantly, it is essential that we, as educators, help our students learn to evaluate these sites as they do their research. I found a site — where else but on the Internet! — that provides evaluation tools posted by five prestigious universities.

Obviously, media specialists and technology coordinators will find value in Web site evaluation tools. So will classroom teachers who want to help students understand that *anyone* can post practically *anything* on the Internet. These tools include checklist questions about the author of the article, the reputation of the organization or institution affiliated with the article, the timeliness of the information, and so on. Just because something is in print (or on a computer screen) doesn't mean that it is accurate or valuable. A healthy skepticism is essential when using the Net.

Teaching students how to search the Net before requiring them to do independent research is worthwhile, too. Many *search engines* (tools to help you search the Web) are out there; some are better for younger students (HotBot, for example), whereas others are more comprehensive (such as AltaVista). One interesting new engine, called MetaCrawler, searches several other search engines for the best results.

By designing Web searches for your classes (which are sort of like the old neighborhood treasure hunts that we used to love), you can help your students learn to navigate the Net with greater results. Dr. Bernard Dodge of San Diego State University has created WebQuest, which is an inquiry-oriented activity that enables learners to interact with information that comes from resources on the Internet. Check out his excellent framework for designing your own successful Internet activity at `http://edweb.sdsu.edu`.

Informing Others of Online Rules

How many of you know whether your school has rules, regulations, guidelines, or policies regarding student use of computer online time? If your school doesn't, perhaps you should create some and be sure to include the following:

> ✔ A note or form advising parents that their students will be using online services. I don't want to call it a permission slip, because you are probably going to require students to go online for their assignments. Parents sign the note to tell you that they saw it. You can ask parents what services their children have at home (sort of gather information) and tell them that you're available to discuss their students' online work with them at any time.

Laying down some online rules

Students need to be aware of the dangers that they may bump into online (give them just a hint about these dangers without scaring them). Here are points that you may want to include in your agreement with your students:

✔ Students shouldn't give out personal information (name address, phone number, parents' work or phone numbers, or school name and phone number) without teacher permission.

✔ Students should inform a teacher or parent when they come across information that makes them feel uncomfortable (or that they are sure that their teachers or parents wouldn't want them to see).

✔ Students should never agree to get together with someone they meet online unless a parent or teacher goes with them.

✔ Students should never send pictures of themselves to anyone without teacher permission.

✔ Students should notify the teacher or a parent immediately if they run across mean messages, and they should never respond to those messages.

✔ A set of guidelines (a few key items to include appear in "Laying down some online rules" later in this chapter) that students must agree to live with.

✔ A set of guidelines that teachers should follow (such as being sure that students are supervised at all times while they are online).

✔ Information regarding the school system's time available, as well as each teacher's allotment of that time. Include charges to be made when teachers go over their allotted time. Spell out the rules; teachers will try to find a way around paying.

Part IV

The Softer Side of Computers: Software

The 5th Wave   By Rich Tennant

"I found these two in the multimedia lab morphing faculty members into farm animals."

In this part . . .

1f you're ready to explore the different types of software that can *really* enhance your classroom's learning environment, it's time to go shopping.

Before you go, though, browse through a couple of software catalogs — you'll find them in the library of your school, floating around the teachers' lounge, or on the technology coordinator's desk in the computer lab. You may even have received some software catalogs at home — and promptly dropped them into Round File 13.

Software manufacturers were quick to notice when the educational world turned toward computers. One catalog, for example, lists more than 8,000 titles. What's a busy teacher to do — plan lessons, grade papers, contact parents, serve on school-improvement committees, sponsor the junior/senior prom, and also become a software expert? Somehow, all of June, July, and August don't provide enough time to stay current.

In this part, I hope to come to your rescue. If I can't get you comfortably into the swim of things, maybe you'll at least be able to keep your head above water. In this part, I suggest programs that many teachers have learned to love. You may want to start with these programs, and then be sure to ask around for other recommendations. Don't forget to actually these programs yourself; what works well for someone else may not fit your needs. Ready? Dive in!

Chapter 15

Software Musts for Educators

• •

In This Chapter

▶ Tips for buying software

▶ Educational programs guaranteed to please

▶ Publications that keep you up to date on new software releases

• •

*I*f you've read the previous chapters in this book, you've explored so many exciting advancements in your classroom, thanks to the computer. You've created newsletters, stationery, grade books, and lesson-plan templates. You've decided how to get your students using word processors and databases. You've even hopped onto the Internet.

Would you believe it? There's more! As soon as you enter the world of software, you can be overwhelmed again. Seemingly thousands of titles and hundreds of catalogs are waiting in your mailbox. How do you make sense of all this material? Where do you go for help? Keep reading.

Software-Buying Tips

Before starting your search for software titles, think about what you want to accomplish in your classroom. Dazzling as it is, technology should support the curriculum just as worksheets, projects, textbooks, and tests do — yet everything still needs to be educationally sound.

After reviewing your curriculum and identifying the places where you could use help (technological, that is), you can get your feet wet by wading into what some people consider to be deep water. The major question: With so many choices, how do you find out what software you should buy? Here are some tips:

> ✔ One obvious source is other teachers. Find out what the teachers on your grade level find to be useful. Visit their classrooms to see that software in action. As we all know, there can be a big difference between the promotional material and what real students can do with the program.

✔ Another helpful source is your state department of education, which may offer sites for previewing and using software.

✔ Local colleges and universities may have technology available for their own teacher training; ask about the accessibility of their materials to local educators.

✔ Ask vendors whether you can try their software or get demonstration copies. It is to vendors' advantage to have happy customers who spread the word.

✔ Software catalogs arrive at your school regularly, and a likely place to find them is the media center. Check with your technology coordinator, too; tell this person that you want to be included in purchase decisions.

✔ Educational journals, both technology-oriented and subject-specific, regularly review new and popular titles. These journals typically describe the software and offer recommendations for use.

✔ The Internet and services such as America Online, CompuServe, Prodigy, and Microsoft Network can keep you informed.

✔ Technology conferences invite vendors to demonstrate their products. In addition to hosting sessions on how to use various technologies in the classroom, these conferences put you in touch with educators from all over. Now we're back to the first suggestion: Your best bet is always a fellow teacher.

Just remember: Determine what you want to accomplish in your class and then find the software that meets your needs. As always, curriculum should come first. Before you know it, teachers will be visiting *your* classroom to see a software wizard in action, and you'll be speaking at next year's technology conference!

Getting a Taste of What's Out There

Educational software falls into several categories: drill and practice, productivity, multimedia, and simulation. Some catalogs divide their material into many more listings, but most programs fit into these categories. In addition to these instructional tools, programs offer management tools for grade reporting and attendance. You can find course-scheduling and GPA-calculation programs that can help sell administrators on the value of purchasing computers and software. I've included an average price for each title in the following sections. Shop around; even your local discount stores often carry some of these titles. Purchase orders ready?

Note: All prices listed in this chapter are as of this writing and are subject to change.

Drill and practice

As teachers, you're told to go back to basics. But at the same time, you're supposed to foster the creative sides of your students, engage their left brains as well as their right brains, and challenge their critical-thinking skills. All this responsibility can be overpowering. Recent television coverage touts the benefits of drill, drill, drill, particularly in those subjects in which memorization is essential. This kind of practice in the classroom, however, often falls into the category of drudgery, both for the student and for the teacher (no wonder some people call it *drill and kill*).

Rescue! Many software programs take the chore out of drilling students in fundamental skills; they allow the learners to progress at their own speed while freeing the teacher to work with students individually or to create lessons. Drill-and-practice programs also give the student encouragement, immediate feedback, and remediation; it all depends on the program. But one thing's for sure: These computer programs have great patience, even on the Friday before Christmas vacation!

Good examples of skill-building programs are those that provide practice in mathematics, language, reading, study skills, and GED, SAT, or ACT preparation. Programs that serve as tools for providing reinforcement include:

- **Advanced Automated Accounting** (International Thomson Publishing, $90, secondary): Offers accounting instruction.

- **All Star Drill** (Tom Snyder Productions, $69.95, all grades): Drills the entire class by using a baseball-game format to review any material that the teacher chooses.

- **Electronic Bookshelf** (Electronic Bookshelf, $399.95, primary through middle): Quizzes students on books read.

- **Grammar Computerized (French, German, Italian, Latin, Spanish)** (Lingo Fun, $59.95, middle and secondary): Reviews common grammar lessons.

- **Mavis Beacon Teaches Typing** (Mindscape, $59.95, all grades): Teaches keyboarding skills.

- **Number Munchers** (MECC, $59, primary through middle): Provides game atmosphere to teach basic arithmetic.

- **Play It by Ear** (Alfred Publishing, $79.95, elementary through secondary): Provides practice in ear training through an on-screen piano keyboard.

- **Pronunciation Tutor for Chinese, French, German, Spanish** (Learning Company, $40 each, middle and secondary): Introduces students to pronunciation through use of native speakers.

- **Reader Rabbit** (Learning Company, $50, pre-K and primary): Introduces beginning reading skills.

✔ **Speed Reader** (Davidson & Associates, $59.95, middle and secondary): Helps students increase reading speed and understanding.

✔ **Super Munchers** (MECC, $69, primary through secondary): Instructs students in various subjects, such as geography, biographies, and nutrition.

✔ **Word Attack 3** (Davidson & Associates, $79.95, elementary): Offers a game that provides practice in spelling and vocabulary.

Feeling creative? You can try converting a database that you and your students develop into a drill-and-practice program!

Productivity software

Whether you realize it or not, you've been using productivity programs as you've traveled through Parts I and II of this book. Microsoft Works, Microsoft Publisher, and PowerPoint are productivity programs; they allow you to create a product. From results that can be viewed on a computer screen and saved to disk, to full-color printouts, to presentations shown on a projection unit, students and teachers can produce fantastic results by using various software programs. These titles are popular with teachers:

✔ **Children's Writing and Publishing Center** (Learning Company, $45, primary through middle): Provides writing activities and allows for desktop publishing.

✔ **PageMaker** (Adobe Systems, $199, middle and secondary): Provides professional-looking layouts for student newspapers, playbills, and so on.

✔ **Print Shop Deluxe** (Brøderbund, $69.95, all ages): Students, teachers, and PTA members all can use this program to design greeting cards, stationery, certificates, and banners. Science-fair students in particular get mileage out of this program, which is a favorite for schools.

✔ **Slide Shop** (Scholastic New Media, $75, middle and secondary): Creates computer slide presentations.

✔ **TimeLiner 4.0** (Tom Snyder Productions, $89.95, elementary through secondary): Produces a printed time line for whatever data is entered.

The following specialty programs fall among the productivity packages and are worth a glance:

✔ **Lotus Organizer** (Lotus Development Corporation, $85, secondary): Keeps your calendar in an appointment-book format, makes lists, and schedules meetings.

✔ **Quicken** (Quicken, $40 and up, middle and secondary): Tracks your club finances and shows students ways to plan their budgets.

✔ **TurboTax** (Quicken; $35 and up, depending on the sophistication of the package that you buy; middle and secondary): Helps you introduce students to the phenomenon of paying taxes.

Multimedia software

This category of software is literally exploding, and it is as easy to find multimedia CD-ROMs as it is to walk into your local discount store. A more detailed list appears in Chapter 16, but allow me to tempt you a bit first.

Multimedia programs span the educational spectrum. Career materials, for example, can help a person explore various career choices, create résumés and cover letters, practice interviews, and so on. Multimedia encyclopedias include sound clips of Neil Armstrong's speech (remember "That's one small step . . ."?) and video displays of how to play basketball. Databases include all the works by Shakespeare and allow the user to search by topic or word. Talking books entice beginning readers. Are you interested? Silly question! Here is a sampling of multimedia resources:

✔ **HyperStudio** (Roger Wagner Publishing, $112.95, middle and secondary): Allows you to create your own multimedia program, complete with text, graphics, and video and sound clips. You can even connect to the Internet.

✔ **Cinderella** (Discis Knowledge Research, $25, primary and elementary): Provides beautiful illustrations, sound effects, and bilingual pronunciation. Other titles are also available.

✔ **Thinkin' Things** (Edmark, $44.95, primary and elementary): Develops critical-thinking skills.

✔ **Compton's Interactive Encyclopedia** (The Learning Company, $45.95, all ages), **Encarta 97** (Microsoft, $69.95, all ages), **Grolier's Multimedia Encyclopedia** (Grolier, $49.95, all ages), and **World Book Multimedia Encyclopedia** (World Book, $105, elementary and middle): Provide what you'd expect from encyclopedias, but with sound and video links. Some of these products even link directly to the Internet.

✔ **Shakespeare on Disk: Electronic Text** (Shakespeare on Disk; $75–$175, depending on the number of plays; middle and secondary): Allows you to search by theme, word, and quotation and to print scenes.

✔ **Trudy's Time and Place House** (Edmark, $44.95, pre-K to primary): Helps students learn time and geography.

If these titles sound exciting, read Chapter 16 for more titles and ideas for using these programs in your own classroom.

Simulation software

Another term for simulation software is *interactive software* — in other words, the user helps direct the outcome of the activity. You are in charge. You're the director. Kids love these programs. Well, who's kidding whom? Teachers love them, too. In the future, giving up lunch time or staying after school may not be the sign of a devoted teacher so much as an indication that the computer is running a really great program.

Although these activities are delightful, they are, in fact, educational games (okay, we'll be honest here). Remember all the requirements that your community expects you to fulfill: back to basics, critical thinking, affective domain, and so on? Well, these interactive programs, if carefully selected, do all these things — plus they (dare I say it) *teach*. But who's telling? Check out some of these teacher-tested titles:

- ✔ **Choices, Choices: On the Playground** (Tom Snyder Productions, $99.95, primary and elementary): Provides decisions that youngsters must make about the new kid in school.

- ✔ **MayaQuest** (MECC, $79, elementary through secondary): Turns students into high-tech explorers on a trip to the Mayan ruins.

- ✔ **SimCity 2000, SimAnt, SimLife, SimFarm** (Maxis, $34.95 to $47.95, elementary through secondary): Probably some of the best-known simulation programs; enable students to experience designing modern cities, building ant colonies, creating life forms, and running an agribusiness.

- ✔ **Africa Trail** (MECC, $79, elementary through secondary): Puts kids in charge of a bike trek across Africa; based on an actual 1992 trip.

- ✔ **Where in the World Is Carmen Sandiego?, Where in Space Is Carmen Sandiego?,** and **Where in Time Is Carmen Sandiego?** (Brøderbund, $43.95, elementary through secondary): Invite students to become detectives and, using clues, to trace the whereabouts and era of Carmen.

- ✔ **Decisions, Decisions:** overview (Tom Snyder Productions, $149.95 each, elementary through secondary): Simulate various historical or current-issue situations in which have students decision-making roles.

Management programs

Every time I watch a student teacher struggle with all the demands of teaching — following the curriculum, responding to 150 or so students each day, filling out the proper forms for the administration, keeping track of textbooks, grading papers, and maintaining a personal life (yes, Virginia, there really is such a thing as a personal life, or so I've heard) — I am amazed by the demands on educators.

When you think about it, being a teacher is a *huge* job. Is anyone present who wouldn't appreciate a little help? All of you who didn't raise your hands are probably too busy and didn't hear the question!

Some software programs record attendance, generate tests, average grades, keep track of discipline, help you plan lessons, create crossword puzzles, and even teach you how to use computers. Don't assume that all software-program purchases must be for the students exclusively. You may find programs that release you from the tedium of teaching and provide you more time to be creative, to evaluate your students' work more carefully, or maybe — just maybe — get you out the door a little earlier on Friday afternoon. Check out these teacher aids:

- **Coach's Assistant** (McCarthy-McCormick, $49.95 per sport): Prints sign-up sheets, tournament grids, and other necessities for coaching. Titles deal with specific sports: girls' volleyball, girls' and boys' soccer, girls' and boys' basketball, and so on.

- **FormBuster** (Virtual Reality, $99.95): Allows you to scan or fax forms — ranging from school forms to college-scholarship recommendations — into your computer and then fill them out quickly.

- **Grade Busters: Making the Grade** (Jay Klein Productions, $99.95): Allows grades to be weighted, dropped, excused, and (of course) averaged immediately.

- **Grade Machine** (Misty City Software, $65.95): Makes keeping grades easier, including reports that the teacher can customize.

- **IEP Writer Supreme** (Super School Software, $170.95): Assists the special-education teacher in keeping track of IEPs on the computer.

- **Portfolio Assessment Kit** (Super School Software, $167.95): Evaluates students' progress over time by using graphics, sound, color, and video; offers mini portfolios for specific subject areas.

- **SportsPro** (Micromedia, $150 per sport): Stores the following types of information: statistics on individual players (even game-by-game performances), team stats, information about opponents, medical files, rosters, and coaches' comments.

- **Teacher's Helper Plus** (Visions, $59.95): Helps you create activity sheets, tests, and word searches, all incorporating your favorite graphics.

- **Visual Planner** (Edunetics, $49.95): Provides resources for organizing text in a graphical way, including concept maps, Venn diagrams, flow charts, and story webs.

✔ **WordSearch Deluxe** (Nordic, $19.95): Adds artwork, color, and sound to puzzles as you create them.

Teacher-Approved Computer Resources

Each of us has a favorite publication that we turn to time and time again because we know that it contains the most up-to-date information available. One of my favorite publications is *USA Today.* I've quoted it throughout this book and read it religiously every day (well, almost). Why? I really don't have time to sift through all the pages of the *Washington Post,* the *Wall Street Journal,* the *Chicago Tribune,* or any other large newspaper, each of which is also a wonderful source for keeping up to date on the hottest topics that affect computer technology, the Internet, and so on. It really doesn't disturb me at all to hear *USA Today* referred to as *McPaper* because I like it (especially all the pretty pictures!).

How many of you have time to read all the magazines that relate to your subject area or grade level? I thought not. I don't have time to read every magazine about computers, either — and computers are my life's work. Not only that, I don't have time to look through publications out there to find out which ones I *would* like to get. There are simply too many. So what's a person to do? You got it: Ask someone else. That's exactly what I did to come up with the following list.

What's neat about this list is when the librarian comes around asking whether you'd like to see anything added to the library for the following year, you can surprise her and hand her the following:

Classroom Connect
Wentworth Worldwide Media, Inc.
P.O. Box 10488
Lancaster, PA 17605-0488
800-638-1639
http://www.classroom.net

Educational Resources
1550 Executive Drive
P.O. Box 1900
Elgin, IL 60121-1900
800-624-2926
http://www.edresources.com

Educational Software Institute
4213 S. 94th St.
Omaha, NE 68127
800-955-5570
Fax: 402-592-2017
http://www.edsoft.com

Electronic Learning Scholastic, Inc.
2931 McCarty St.
P.O. Box 3710
Jefferson City, MO 65102-3710
800-544-2917
http://scholastic.com/EL

Family PC
P.O. Box 400454
Des Moines, IA 50340-0454
800-413-9749
http://web1.zdnet.com/familypc/

Laser Learning Technologies
120 Lakeside Ave., Suite 2240
Seattle, WA 98122-6552
800-722-3505
Fax: 206-322-7421
http://www.llt.com or
http://w3.llt.com/LLT

Learning and Leading with Technology
International Society for Technology
in Education
1787 Agate St.
Eugene, OR 97403-1923
541-346-4414
Fax: 541-346-5890
http://isteonline.uoregon.edu/
istehome/PUBS/llt.html

PC Magazine
P.O. Box 54093
Boulder, CO 80322-409
800-289-0429
http://www.pcmag.com

PC World
501 Second St. #600
San Francisco, CA 94107
800-234-3498
http://www.pcworld.com

School Library Journal
(subscriptions)
P.O. Box 57559
Boulder, CO 80322-7559
800-456-9409
800-824-7476
http://www.cahners.com/
mainmag/SLJ.HTM

Smart Computing
P.O. Box 85380
Lincoln, NE 68501-5380
800-733-3809
http://www.pcnovice.com

Technology & Learning
P.O. Box 49727
Dayton, OH 45449-0727
800-607-4410
http://www.techlearning.com

T.H.E. Journal (Technological Horizons
in Education)
150 El Camino Real, Suite 12
Tustin, CA 92680-3670
714-730-4011
Fax: 714-730-3739
http://www.thejournal.com

Popular magazines (*Newsweek,* for example) also have weekly sections devoted to cyberspace or computer updates. I've found them to be great sources for Internet addresses. In addition, watch for references in your professional journals. Journals provide great subject-matter references for specific areas.

Catching a virus

Five years ago, Michelangelo restored his claim to fame. He became notorious by becoming a virus that infected hundreds of thousands of computers across the country. Michelangelo probably is the artist whose birthday is best-remembered in computer circles. His annual aging sparks fear of hard-disk failure each year. What's a virus got to do with computers?

Your computer can catch a virus, too. A sick computer is nothing to sneeze at (okay, I'm sorry for the sick joke). A computer virus isn't the same type of virus that lays you low when you get sick. Computer viruses are bits of computer-programming code that either overwrite or attach themselves to programs. Then they replicate themselves and pass from program to program, hard disk to hard disk, until everyone in the classroom or school is infected.

Some viruses are irritating; others are devastating to your computer's hard disk because they tend to wipe it clean or interfere with the work that you're trying to get done. Obviously, if you are becoming dependent upon your computer, you want to protect it from catching a virus. Think about the forms that you have in your computer now: the attendance records and grades that you keep there, and the files of all your worksheets and tests. Are you properly concerned? You should be asking me how to check for viruses.

Viruses usually invade a computer through an infected floppy disk. Any disk that has been in another computer is suspect. You can imagine the jokes that fly through the teachers' lounges when you find out that a faculty member has brought in an infected disk — a social disease of the technology age. Because of the influx of programs and material downloaded from the Internet, however, infection through the phone lines is becoming rampant.

This is going to sound like a health lecture, but prevention is the key. Check any disk before you use it in your computer, and be careful what you allow your students to download from the Internet. Your health (your mental health, that is) may be at stake!

Microsoft has joined forces with the National Computer Security Association (http://www.ncsa.com/) to battle the growing threat of viruses. For an up-to-date listing of known viruses, reach out to these organizations' joint Web site at http://www.microsoft.com/office/antivirus/.

Then make sure that you're protected by finding out more about the following antivirus software programs:

- ✔ IBM AntiVirus (http://www.av.ibm.com)

- ✔ Symantec Norton AntiVirus (http://www.symantec.com)

- ✔ McAfee VirusScan (http://www.mcafee.com)

One of these products *must* be just what the doctor ordered.

Chapter 16

The Multimedia Explosion: CD-ROM

●●

In This Chapter

▶ Identifying hardware needed for multimedia

▶ Looking at the advantages of CD-ROMs

▶ Developing activities by using encyclopedias and card catalogs

▶ Reviewing lists of recommended CD-ROMs

●●

*Y*ou've learned about all the great things that your computer can do for you, from averaging your grades to keeping information on your students. You find out in Chapter 15 that some terrific software is available, too. Now are you ready to step out into the world of CD-ROMs? Prepare yourself for an exciting adventure.

Hard Stuff for Getting Into Multimedia

Multimedia means (stay with me here) more than one medium is used at a time. Ha! You thought that it was going to be more complicated than that, didn't you? Well, relax. Multimedia doesn't mean that *you* have to wrestle with all the equipment, link it all together, and get it to work simultaneously. CD-ROMs have already done that for you.

This fact may seem to be simple (or maybe you really are beginning to get the hang of all this computer talk), but you must have a CD-ROM *drive* to use CD-ROMs. Your computer may have an internal CD-ROM drive, in which case you see a slot in the console that has an eject button near it. If you push the button, a drawer appears, and you place the CD-ROM in it, or you remove the caddy and place the CD-ROM into the slot, according to your system's directions. When you have the CD-ROM in place, close the tray or return the caddy to the CD-ROM drive, and you are ready.

2x, 4x, 6x, a dollar (or 8x or 12x)

When you start looking at CD-ROMs, one question rears its head time and time again: Do you want a 4x, 6x, 8x, or 12x? How do you answer this question?

Here's what you should know about these numbers:

✔ These numbers refer to speed, and the higher the *x* number, the faster the drive. The faster drive is usually better and, of course, more expensive.

✔ Your students will tell you that the higher the number, the more times the laser eye reads the disk before emitting sound or information. These students generally are referring to their audio CDs for their stereo systems. The more times the laser reads the sound before sending it out, the clearer the sound and the less chance that the disc will skip.

✔ The highest speed today is 16x, but you know that speeds will increase. Don't put off buying a CD-ROM drive just because you think that it will be out of date soon. (You already did that about computers, and look where it got you.)

Which CD-ROM drive should you buy? The best one that you can afford!

Most newer machines have an internal CD-ROM drive (and, incidentally, encourage your school to *always* include a CD-ROM drive as part of any new computer purchase). If your computer does not have this device, don't worry. External CD-ROM drives are just as useful, and they have the added advantage of going with you to other computer stations.

If your CD-ROM drive came as part of a multimedia kit, it is equipped with a sound system for blowing the sound from the CD-ROM out through the speakers. If your CD-ROM drive doesn't have such a system, you need to get speakers and a sound card and have your computer wizard put them into your console so that you can get the best out of this new technology. If you have a CD-ROM drive with no sound system, you were ripped off. Although the graphics are wonderful, sound pulls everything together.

Advantages of CD-ROMs

Probably the main advantage of having a CD-ROM drive is the fact that more and more programs are on CD-ROMs rather than on floppy disks. Why? As programs become more sophisticated (and you crave greater performance from your software all the time), they require more storage space. The most powerful programs often require more than 30 floppy disks of storage space, and the files usually are squished (compressed) onto them. You can spend a great deal of time installing programs from floppy disks because you continually have to change disks and monitor the progress of the installation process.

Installing large applications from CD-ROMs is much faster and requires less user interaction. Watching the installation process is neat; you see words such as *exploding* and *decompressing* as the installation program puts the software programs on your hard disk.

CD-ROM technology seems to provide the answer for quicker installation of these multi-disk programs, at least for now. (Everything changes with computers.) New versions of word processing programs and office suites are likely to be available only on CD-ROM, or you may have to pay extra to get a floppy-disk version. The inconvenience may be incentive enough to get a CD-ROM drive.

Another reason to become familiar with CD-ROM technology is the fact that you can create your own CD-ROMs. CD-ROM *burners,* which cost anywhere from $300 up, are hardware components that allow you to "burn," or digitize, your own CD-ROMs. You can save your really big files (and multimedia projects require really big storage space) on CD-ROMs rather than on several floppy disks. Students can graduate with electronic portfolios on their own CD-ROMs rather than with the paper portfolios that are currently popular. CD-ROM technology is everywhere, so take advantage of it!

Multimedia Focus of the CD-ROM

CD-ROMs provide video as well as audio; they enable you to interact with them. Some CD-ROMs allow you to import other media (graphics, video clips, and sound effects) to create stunning multimedia presentations. (Just be warned that if you want to import these media, you may once again need the assistance of your technology coordinator.)

Where have all the card files gone?

If you are currently a student (maybe you're just getting your degree in education), you're not a bit fazed by libraries these days. But for those who have been out of school for a while, libraries are not the same as Andrew Carnegie envisioned. Oh, sure, libraries are lined with tomes of knowledge bound the old-fashioned way into books. You can recognize microfiche and copiers, of course — proof that technology has advanced. But where is the card catalog? You guessed it: It's online. Absolutely everything is cataloged on computer. If you can't navigate the online services, you can't find what you're looking for.

Online reference sources

A typical high-school library these days has several online databases, all of which can be saved to disk or sent to the printer immediately. Here are some good reference sources, most of them on CD-ROMs:

- **Discovering Authors:** Complete biographical and critical commentary, searchable by author, title, and subject
- **InfoTrac:** A listing of periodicals
- **Magill's Survey of Science:** A database that allows a student to search and to create a bibliography along the way
- **NewsBank:** A listing of newspaper articles
- **SIRS Government Reports:** Complete text of major documents and speeches that you can access by alphabetical listing, chronology, and subject (By the way, SIRS stands for Social Issues Resources Series.)
- **TOM:** An index for 180 general-interest magazines, with full text for 125 of them and for newspaper articles
- **World Book Information Finder:** An online encyclopedia

Survival requirements for all students

As my classes work with online services, I have discovered three major points that they must master. These survival skills for students of the 21st Century are:

- **Students must learn how to conduct searches.** With so much information available, getting lost in these databases is easy. Practice in advanced search modes helps students capitalize on their time and eliminates the extraneous material that can come up.

- **Students need to become critical readers who can scan electronic material, select it for printing, and then print only the necessary sections.** Much paper is wasted by a trigger-happy finger. Although each program has its individual way of saving and/or printing material, directions are always on-screen.

Purchasing for the packages

After you get an idea about the programs that you need (or want), you should consider the most expedient way to purchase them and to protect yourself and your school at the same time. These definitions should help:

✔ **Single copy price.** Obviously, this is the price for one copy of the program. You are expected to use this program on only one computer and not duplicate it.

✔ **Lab pack.** Although these packs may vary from publisher to publisher, the most common packs contain five copies of the program, along with related teaching materials.

✔ **Site license.** A site license may be available from the software publisher. The price for a site license is always the highest of the four options, but buying this license gives a single building or location (site) the right to install the program on many computers. Some site licenses limit the number of computers that can use the program (30, for example — a number that accommodates most schools' computer labs). Check with the publisher or vendor of the software for the specifics.

✔ **Network version.** This version is specially created for schools that network their computers so that the computers can be run from the same server and share software.

> ✔ **Students must routinely cite their sources as they incorporate computerized material into their reports.** Plagiarism is still plagiarism. Ask your technology coordinator for current fair-use guidelines.

The following sections offer titles that educators seem to find useful. Check out the titles, but examine them for your school's needs. Do you need a lab pack, a site license, only one copy for a classroom or media center, or a network version? How important is cost? Can the reference materials be upgraded yearly for a nominal fee? Other titles may be equally good, so investigate carefully.

Reference Works

Many products identified in Chapter 15 are available on CD-ROM as well as on floppy disk. Some programs also are listed in Part III as being available online. In this section, I offer you titles grouped by subject and grade level. Overlapping may occur. Maybe duplication is a hint that a certain title is really terrific.

Oh, and by the way, all prices listed here are approximate — if you're a better shopper than I am or live in a different part of the country than I do, you may find these products listed for lower prices. And, of course, prices have a tendency to eventually come down on anything related to technology.

Encyclopedias and general reference

- ✔ **CNN Newsroom Global View** (Vicarious Entertainment, $29.95, elementary through secondary): A video atlas with a world clock, detailed maps on every country, and CNN narration of the video footage are included on this CD-ROM.

- ✔ **Compton's Interactive Encyclopedia** (The Learning Company, $45.95, all ages): This CD-ROM includes images, maps, and graphics. The 1997 edition includes more than 40,000 articles, along with photos, video, animation, and slide shows. The Monthly Updater is an online source that provides up-to-date information.

- ✔ **Encarta 97** (Microsoft, $69.95, all ages): Updated yearly, this program contains more than 30,000 articles, as well as more than 8,000 photos and illustrations. You can connect to the World Wide Web with the hundreds of links that are built into the program.

- ✔ **Encyclopaedia Britannica CD** (Encyclopaedia Britannica, $150, elementary through secondary): This CD-ROM offers students the depth of *Britannica*.

- ✔ **First Connections: The Golden Book Encyclopedia** (Hartley, $55.95, primary): Stimulating video, animation, sound clips, and speeches, along with color pictures and maps, make interactive learning easy.

- ✔ **Great Literature Plus** (Thynx, $64.95, middle and secondary): The complete text of more than 2,000 great literary works, incorporating illustrations and music.

- ✔ **1997 Grolier's Multimedia Encyclopedia** (Grolier, $49.95, all ages): A popular choice, this encyclopedia connects thousands of articles to specific Internet sites selected by a team of educational experts.

- ✔ **Guinness Multimedia Disc of Records** (Grolier, $19.95, all ages): Pictures, movies, and facts provide information about more than 15,000 of the world's records.

- ✔ **History of the World** (Thynx, $79.95, middle and secondary): Students can search for major events from prehistoric times through the present by looking up a phrase, a subject, or even a photo.

- ✔ **Microsoft Bookshelf** (Microsoft, $99.95, elementary through secondary): This CD-ROM contains several reference volumes, including *The American Heritage Dictionary, The World Almanac and Book of Facts,*

The Columbia Book of Quotations, and *The Hammond Intermediate World Atlas*. The CD-ROM also has graphics, audio clips, and video clips.

✔ **The Way Things Work 2.0** (DK Multimedia, $41.95, all ages): Based on David Macaulay's book, this CD-ROM cross-links inventions by machine types, inventors, principles, and timeline.

✔ **World Book Multimedia Encyclopedia** (World Book, $105, elementary and middle): This electronic version of the *World Book Encyclopedia* has a timeline and other tools, plus two search strategies.

Dictionaries and atlases

✔ **American Heritage Talking Dictionary** (Softkey, $25.95, elementary through secondary): More than a third of the 200,000 entries are presented by human voices. You can find definitions, parts of speech, proper use, synonyms, and sample sentences on this CD-ROM.

✔ **Cartopedia: The Ultimate World Reference Atlas** (DK Multimedia, $43.95, elementary through secondary): Billed as an "encyclopedia, gazetteer, and atlas" combined, this CD-ROM provides pop-up windows that present information about all the world's countries.

✔ **Macmillan Dictionary for Children** (Davidson, $29.95, primary and elementary): Host Zak takes young readers through the dictionary, which includes word games, 12,000 words, 1,000 illustrations, and 400 sound effects.

✔ **Merriam-Webster's Dictionary for Kids** (Mindscape, $29.95, primary through middle): This CD-ROM is not only a reference tool; it also contains games that can be played at three levels. The CD-ROM includes 400 color illustrations and 200 animated graphics, plus sound effects.

✔ **Picture Atlas of the World** (National Geographic Society, $64.95, elementary through secondary): This atlas invites students to visit every nation on earth by means of interactive maps, movies, photographs, animation, and sound clips provided by native speakers. You can clip and copy maps to create your own atlas.

✔ **Small Blue Planet: Real Picture World Atlas** (Now What Software, $49.95, elementary through secondary): Billed as being an atlas that offers a view of the earth that only the astronauts may have seen until now, this program allows students to zoom in on the Earth's surface, from cities to rain forests.

✔ **Street Atlas USA** (Delorme Mapping, $79, elementary through secondary): Find streets, roads, and highways in the United States, and even locate your own home address.

Productivity and creativity for all ages

- **Classroom Clips** (Creative Pursuits, $39.95): This CD-ROM contains a collection of more than 850 quality color graphics that cover any curriculum's needs.

- **Easy Book** (Sunburst, $69.95): This program prints students' stories in real book form. The CD-ROM includes an assortment of custom drawing tools and clip art.

- **HyperStudio** (Roger Wagner Publishing, $112.95): This program allows you to create your own multimedia program, complete with text, graphics, video, and sound clips. You can even connect to the Internet.

- **KidPix Studio CD** (Brøderbund, $49.95): An exciting opportunity awaits students: They can create multimedia productions by using video and sound effects (including animation). Try the demo on the CD-ROM that comes with this book.

- **Kids Works Deluxe** (Davidson, $89.95): Students can color existing pictures, draw new pictures, or write stories. Internet capabilities allow students to share their stories online.

- **MasterPhotos** (IMSI, $35.95): This CD-ROM gives you photos, fonts, sound effects, full-motion video, and animation, which you can publish on paper or on the World Wide Web.

- **TimeLiner 4.0** (Tom Snyder Productions, $89.95): This program creates terrific timelines and is suitable for all grades and subjects. Additional data disks complement the basic program; titles include *Dinosaurs and Other Big Stuff, Elementary Language Arts, Oceans, Native Americans, African-American History,* and *World History.*

Directed Studies

The following list is a result of the suggestions of many teachers. These titles are classroom-appropriate and successful. Again, you must assess your own needs and requirements; be sure to check out other titles as well. There's something for every curriculum in this section, but read through the entire list. Who knows what great idea you might come up with for your own class? To help you decide, I include great demos of some of the following titles on the CD-ROM that comes with this book.

Good titles for lower to middle grade levels

✔ **A.D.A.M.: The Inside Story** (Brøderbund/A.D.A.M., $49.95, elementary and middle): This CD-ROM has the same quality of illustrations and videos as the more ambitions Essentials CD-ROM (see the next section for details) but brings the material down to a simpler level.

✔ **Age of Exploration** (Entrex, $42.95, primary through middle): Students explore history by traveling on a sailing ship to the New World. Critical decisions determine the course; pirates, scurvy, wealth, and success are all possibilities.

✔ **Bailey's Book House** (Edmark, $44.95, pre-K and primary): This program allows students to build their vocabulary and communications skills while creating rhymes and stories. Each word on the screen is read aloud and highlighted so that even nonreaders can enjoy this program. Check out the demo on the *PCs For Teachers* CD-ROM.

✔ **Dr. Seuss' ABC** (Brøderbund, $36.95, pre-K and primary): Dr. Seuss' style of humor, illustration, and rhyme are evident in the 26 pages of learning activities.

✔ **Dr. T's Sing-A-Long Around the World** (Scholastic New Media, $39.95, pre-K through elementary): This CD-ROM provides a multicultural collection of authentic musical performances.

✔ **Grammar Rock** (Electronic Arts, $24.95, primary and elementary): This CD-ROM combines the ABC cartoon videos with grammar games.

✔ **Let's Go** (DynEd, $68.95 per level, primary through middle): Songs, graphics, word puzzles, and games help students learn English. The CD-ROM is especially appropriate for ESL.

✔ **Living Books** (Brøderbund, $36.95 each, pre-K and primary): This CD-ROM contains the interactive text of several stories, including *The Tortoise and the Hare, Just Grandma and Me,* and *Arthur's Teacher Trouble.*

✔ **The Magic School Bus Explores the Human Body** (Microsoft, $44.95, primary and elementary): Mrs. Frizzle leads students on a field trip into the human body. All the characters give show-and-tell presentations. This title includes science experiments and games.

✔ **The Magic School Bus Explores the Solar System** (Microsoft, $44.95, primary and elementary): This field trip goes to space, but the bus gets lost. By exploring the solar system's secrets, students find their way home. This title includes science experiments, NASA videos, and space-related games.

✔ **Reader Rabbit Interactive Reading Journey** (Learning Company, $75.95, pre-K and primary): The 40 progressively challenging storybooks on this CD-ROM teach word recognition and phonics through entertaining stories.

✔ **Sammy's Science House** (Edmark, $29.95, pre-K and primary): Students learn about plants, animals, seasons, and the weather while they develop skills in scientific problem-solving.

✔ **Science for Kids** (Science for Kids, $159, primary through middle): This bilingual (Spanish and English) program contains videos, photographs, sound clips, art, lab kits, and teaching materials. Several packages are available: *"Cell"ebration, Forces and Motion*, and *Simple Machines*.

✔ **Thinkin' Things** (Edmark, $45 to $50, pre-K through elementary): Introduces Oranga Banga, Feathered Friends, and other fun characters to help students develop critical-thinking, memory, and problem-solving skills.

✔ **Where in the World Is Carmen Sandiego? Jr.** (Brøderbund, $79.95, primary and elementary): This CD-ROM is a simpler version of the geography game.

✔ **Word Attack 3** (Davidson, $49.95, elementary through secondary): This CD-ROM teaches students the definitions and spellings of more than 3,200 words. Words are divided into categories by difficulty level or subject.

Good titles for middle and upper grade levels

✔ **A.D.A.M. Essentials** (Brøderbund, $89.95, secondary): This title introduces human anatomy and provides interactive puzzles that allow students to build various systems (such as respiratory and digestive). The teacher's guide is comprehensive.

✔ **The Cruncher** (Davidson, $74.95, elementary through secondary): Many templates teach students how to use spreadsheets. The results can be displayed with graphs and charts or with animation and sound effects.

✔ **Edustar Mathematics** (Edustar, $49.95 per title, middle and secondary): Students are challenged with problems that are similar to real-life situations. Tutorials, review lessons, and online help are included. Titles range from *Arithmetic* and *Pre-Algebra* to *Statistics and Probability* and *Trigonometry*.

✔ **Exploring Modern Art** (Attica Cybernetics, $69.95, elementary through secondary): Search this database of art collections by artist, type, or geographic location.

✔ **Her Heritage** (Cambridge Publishing, $41.75, middle and secondary): This CD-ROM features the accomplishments of more than 1,000 women through photographs, etchings, and film and newsreel clips.

✔ **In My Own Voice: Multicultural Poets on Identity** (Sunburst, $129.95, middle and secondary): Students can enter a bookstore where contemporary poets read their own work, or they can browse an art gallery. Students can also create and record their own work.

✔ **Juilliard Music Adventure** (Theatrix, $29.95, middle and secondary): Rhythm, melody, orchestration, and instrumentation are introduced as students solve musical puzzles. This program was developed with the Juilliard School.

✔ **Microsoft Multimedia Musicians** (Microsoft, $49.95 per title, middle and secondary): As students study the life of a composer (Beethoven, Mozart, Schubert) and the composer's music, the CD-ROM enriches the students' experience with sound and graphics.

✔ **The Myths and Legends of Ancient Greece** (Clearvue, $74.95, middle and secondary): This interactive CD-ROM tells ten well-known Greek myths. The package includes information on the plots, themes, and characters.

✔ **Opening Night** (MECC, $79, elementary through secondary): Students design sets, lighting, and music, and place digitized actors in their own plays.

✔ **Prehistoria** (Grolier, $49.94, elementary through secondary): This program allows students to study any animal that was alive during prehistoric times.

✔ **The Presidents: A Picture History of Our Nation** (National Geographic, $49.95, middle and secondary): This CD-ROM includes more than 1,000 color photos, a trivia game, narrated photo essays on the presidency and the political process, video clips, and famous speeches, all of which bring the American presidency to life.

✔ **RedShift** (Maris Multimedia, $49.95, middle and secondary): This space-simulation program turns the computer into a planetarium.

✔ **Research Paper Writer** (Tom Snyder Productions, $99.95, middle and secondary): This program has won awards for its step-by-step guide to writing a research paper. Students learn how to select a topic, take notes, create a bibliography, write a rough draft, and then perfect the final copy as they work with a fictitious hijacking of Flight 102.

✔ **The Rosetta Stone** (Fairfield Language Technologies, $395 per language, middle and secondary): Learn English, Spanish, French, German, or Russian in a self-paced program that includes both written and oral language in carefully sequenced lessons.

✔ **Where in the USA Is Carmen Sandiego?** (Brøderbund, $79.95, elementary through secondary): Students follow clues and *Fodor's USA Travel Guide* to track down Carmen. Other titles include *Where in Europe*, *Where in Space*, *Where in Time*, *Where in the World*, and *Where in America's Past*.

Getting Material off the CD-ROM

One interesting possibility for computer users is never having to take notes with pen and paper again. Most reference CD-ROMs provide instructions for selecting material and then saving it to a printer or a floppy disk. Once captured, the material is yours to use at will (with a reminder, of course, to use it responsibly).

Using floppy disks saves paper. (One of our school librarian's chief complaints is that students indiscriminately print everything on their subject. As a result of this lack of evaluation of material, reams of paper pass through the printers daily.) Carrying around a disk is also much easier than carrying the pieces of scrap paper used in conducting research. Disks also allow you to capture images, which can be transferred to documents. Think of the photos, graphs, and charts that you can import!

Don't forget to check your disks for viruses before using them to store your information. Viruses are contagious. Refer to the tips in Chapter 15 if you need a basic course on deleting viruses.

Chapter 17

Multimedia Fun in Windows 95

· ·

In This Chapter

▶ Playing audio CDs on your computer

▶ Recording sounds

▶ Viewing videos

▶ Recording videos

▶ Discovering fun multimedia things to do with your students

· ·

*J*ust about the time your students learn to sit in their assigned seats and listen quietly to what you have to say (okay, I'm stretching it here, but you get the idea), you may start looking for innovative ways to keep the students awake. Now, you may think I'm literally nuts to suggest that you introduce more noise into your classroom, but keep in mind that most students have come to expect some type of background noise or sound effects — and if you don't provide the sound, they learn to make up their own (like the *pffffft* that comes from squeezing your hand beneath your armpit). The "noise" that *you* create, you can control.

Some of the most fascinating features for introducing new ideas and entertaining your students as they learn are right there in your computer; all you need are Windows 95, a sound card, and speakers.

Sounding Off with Music, Noise, and Narration

If you've already explored some of the fantastic CD-ROMs that come with sights and sounds that your students love, suggest to your students that it's time to create some multimedia of their own. Regardless of students' ages and the subject that you're teaching, students will learn as they complete their projects. They can gather information about their topic from surfing the Net (see Chapter 14 for great resource spots on the Internet), and add music and narration for multimedia fun.

Before you can create these multimedia masterpieces, however, you need to know some facts about getting sound into your computer — and getting sounds back out of the computer.

Playing music softly

I once had a student who wore a T-shirt with "If it's too loud, you're too old" emblazoned across the back. It doesn't take a genius to figure out that this student bought the T-shirt at a rock concert. My student wore the T-shirt so often, I decided that he was trying to make a point. I'm the first to admit that, yes, rock-concert music is definitely too loud!

Imagine for a moment, though, tasteful music playing softly in the background as your students do their classwork. Sound inviting? It is. And there's no better way to enjoy sounds coming from your computer than by choosing *your* favorite audio CD, popping it into the CD-ROM drive, and turning down the volume. Some of the nature CDs offer soothing background sounds, such as oceans or the ripple of a canoe on a loon-filled lake. It's time to learn how to turn on the music.

To get your CD up and running, follow these easy steps:

1. **Choose Start⇨Programs⇨Accessories⇨Multimedia.**

   The multimedia program list displayed in Figure 17-1 appears. You may not have all the programs I have — and that's okay. I simply have different stuff on my computer than you do (and the menus on my computer are different, too).

2. **Choose CD Player.**

   The CD Player window, displayed in Figure 17-2, opens.

   If you are accustomed to working with the buttons on a CD player or cassette recorder, you'll recognize most of the buttons on the computer CD player. I placed the Gettysburg CD-ROM in the CD-ROM drive, rather than a CD by a vocalist, so the artist displayed in the Artist box is New Artist rather than Elvis, Pat Boone, the Beatles, or Barry Manilow. If you choose a CD by a vocalist, chances are good that you see the singer's name in the Artist box.

3. **Click the Play button.**

Assuming that you have a sound card installed properly in your computer and speakers plugged into the computer, you should hear sound almost immediately. Feel free to turn down the volume (you'll find Volume Control in the View menu). Click the Stop button to stop the music.

Sound Recorder program   Multimedia menu

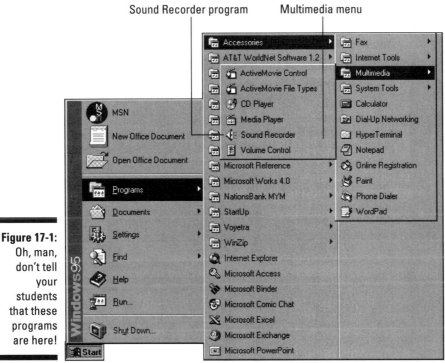

Figure 17-1:
Oh, man,
don't tell
your
students
that these
programs
are here!

Pause

Disk artist   Play   Stop

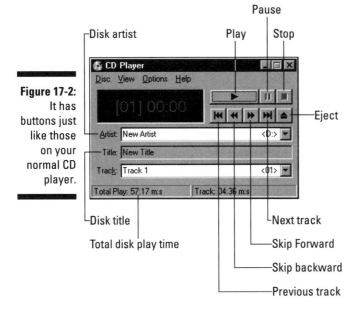

Figure 17-2:
It has
buttons just
like those
on your
normal CD
player.

Eject

Next track

Disk title

Skip Forward

Total disk play time

Skip backward

Previous track

Recording your voice: music for your students

If you thought that hearing your favorite music echo throughout your classroom was refreshing, you may want to wake your students with the sweet music of your gentle voice. You can record your lesson and then take a break or leave it for your substitute teacher to use when your class becomes unruly in your absence. (For this use, simply saying "Class!" usually is sufficient; the substitute can use the recording over and over again.) All you need is the same sound card that you used to play your CD and a microphone specially designed to plug into the computer's sound card. What you say is up to you.

To record narration, you must have Sound Recorder installed on your computer (it's in the Accessories Multimedia group with CD Player). It comes with Windows 95 and is installed automatically when you install Windows 95 if you have a sound card on your machine.

To use the Sound Recorder, follow these steps:

1. **Choose Start⇨Programs⇨Accessories⇨Multimedia.**

   The multimedia program list appears (refer to Figure 17-1).

2. **Choose Sound Recorder.**

   The Sound Recorder window, displayed in Figure 17-3, opens.

3. **Click the Record button and speak into the microphone to record your voice.**

Sound wave

Figure 17-3:
More
buttons, just
like those
on your
cassette
recorder.

Seek to end ⌐ Play Stop Record
⌐ Seek to start

I love to test everything before going for a final take on what I want to record. Then I always write it down or at least develop an outline so that I don't get off on a tangent. Yup, even without students, it's easy to get distracted while you are presenting a lesson.

Try recording a quick "Testing, one, two, three, testing" just so you can see how easy it is to record. When you're finished with your test, you can save the recording and play it just to see how you sound. Sounds that you record and save are stored as .wav files so that you can open them later to play for the class. You can also add the recordings to presentations and Web pages to add the "live and in person" touch. (For more information about presentations and Web pages, check out Chapter 11.)

To save, play, and open sound files, follow these steps:

1. **Choose File⇨Save to open the Save dialog box.**

2. **Enter a filename.**

3. **Select a folder in which to store your sounds.**

4. **Click the Seek to Start button to rewind your sound.**

5. **Click the Play button to hear your recording.**

6. **Choose File⇨Open to display the Open dialog box.**

7. **Open the folder that holds the sound file.**

8. **Double-click the file to open it.**

Make sure that everything is running right and tight before you turn your students loose with the microphone. And then be sure that you know where the microphone is at all times, to prevent hidden-microphone blues (and embarrassment).

Viewing Vibrant Videos

Sound recording and mellow music are all well and good, but videos provide action, drama, and punch to your lessons. Remember the days when you walked into a high-school classroom and saw the movie projector all set up? The graduation from movie film to videotape was remarkable — and video CD-ROM is even better.

Whether you choose to download video files from the Internet (see Chapter 14 for more information) or decide to create your own videos by using a special video camera designed just for your computer, you find that viewing them on the computer is easy. Shooting them yourself . . . well, that depends on your production expertise!

Looking at videos — simply looking

Whether you view your first computer video on the Internet, the World Wide Web, or multimedia CD-ROMs that you happened to come across, you may be amazed by the quality of the video. The equipment that you need to view these videos comes as part of your Windows 95 program, just as CD Player and Sound Recorder do.

Here's how to use the Video viewer:

1. **Choose Start⇨Programs⇨Accessories⇨Multimedia.**

   The multimedia program list appears.

2. **Choose Media Player.**

   The Media Player program window opens. If you happen to have ActiveMovie Control on your Multimedia list, you can open it instead of the Media Player. The Media Player program works a bit differently from the CD Player and Sound Recorder programs. Because it's a viewer of different types of media (sound and video), you first have to open a movie to view.

3. **Choose File⇨Open.**

   The Open dialog box appears. If you have floppy disks or CD-ROM disk that contains videos (videos have .avi extensions), choose the disk drive and folder from the Look In list. If you have downloaded a file from the Internet and stored it in a folder on your hard drive, open the folder. If you don't have a video to view, place your Windows 95 CD-ROM in the CD-ROM drive and open the Funstuff folder. You'll find a stash of videos in the Videos folder. I chose the Weezer.avi file, which is a clip from "Happy Days."

4. **Open the folder that contains the video that you want to view and double-click the video file.**

   The title of the video appears in the title bar of the Media Player window (or the ActiveMovie Control window, if you're using that viewer) and in the separate viewing screen, as shown in Figure 17-4.

5. **Click the Run button.**

You not only see video, but you hear sound as well (if you have a sound card). Amazing little tool, isn't it? To stop the video, click the Stop button. Then rewind it by clicking the Rewind button (ToolTips helps identify the right button) to get the video ready to run again. If you're using the ActiveMovie Control program, the video automatically rewinds.

Viewing screen

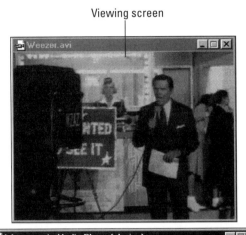

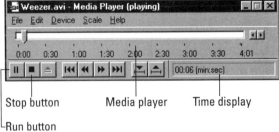

Figure 17-4:
Live-action
video!

Stop button   Media player   Time display

Run button

Capturing videos on-site

When you catch a glimpse of the wonders that others have captured on video and recorded on floppy disks or CD-ROM, you'll be itching to try this phenomenon yourself. Here's the hitch: You need a video-recording device. If you use a standard video camera, you must have a device that changes the video to a digital format that your computer can understand. Most PCs come equipped to handle VCR connections, so all that you need is the correct cable (more wires!) to connect the VCR to your computer. Check with your technology coordinator or school computer expert to find out which cable is right for you.

You'll also find handy-dandy pieces of equipment called *digital video cameras* that record action in a format that computers understand. If you use a digital video camera, you can record directly from the computer and save the file in a format that you can use to show your students, and you don't need the VCR to show the videos. Digital video cameras provide a *great* way to capture classroom action for those Back-to-School nights that we all love. (Check out Chapter 20 for the scoop on digital video cameras.)

Showing Off

You'll find a couple of neat multimedia programs on the CD-ROM that comes with this book. Take a look at these and then use them to test your creative multimedia talents:

- HyperStudio
- HyperCam

Use these programs to add flavor to your curriculum. Then invent ways to use multimedia to do the following:

- Teach students or faculty members how to use the multimedia programs and hardware.
- Introduce faculty and staff members to new teachers.
- Highlight students for special projects or "students of the month".
- Create a classroom scrapbook or celebrations of special events in sports, academics, school in general, senior night, and so on.
- Have students chart their own family histories and add timelines of their ancestors' journeys to and through America.
- Identify endangered species (and remember the spotted owl — it's not endangered as most people believe; it's just threatened).
- Prepare for a field trip.
- Create a journal (chronicle) for a field trip.
- Send students on an Internet treasure hunt and have them record the places that they visit.
- Have students create résumés that they can *burn* onto a CD-ROM (see Chapter 16 for information about this technique) and take with them to use for job-seeking or college admittance. Multimedia résumés allow students to introduce themselves through voice and video — a step up from the standard one-page, two-dimensional format.

Be sure to include graphics, movies, photos, animation, and clip art in your multimedia presentations. Showing off is *so* much fun, and it convinces your parents, school board, and administration that their support and fund-raising efforts are paying off.

Part V
Lagniappe (Lan-Yap) — Something Extra for Nothing

The 5th Wave By Rich Tennant

"OH, I'LL GET US IN — I USED TO BE A TEACHER IN CHARGE OF A HIGH-SCHOOL COMPUTER LAB."

In this part . . .

When all is said and done, there's still so much we want to tell you. *Lagniappe* is a Cajun word that dictionaries say means an incentive or gift designed to induce the shopper to buy; a tip or gratuity; something thrown into the bargain; or an extra.

Lagniappe describes the chapters in this part very well. Each one lists things that I believe are important for you to know. These lists are designed to inform without overwhelming you with a great deal of detail. Like summing up your teaching experiences in 15 words or less or asking your grandmother to describe life when she was a young girl . . . and giving her ten minutes to tell you about it. You can find something from each of the definitions for lagniappe in this part . . . just a little bit extra . . . a bargain, indeed.

Chapter 18

Teaching with Any Number of Computers (Including None)

. . . .

In This Chapter

▶ Ten tips for teaching computers without a computer

▶ Ten tips for the one-computer classroom

▶ Ten tips for getting the most from going to the lab

. . . .

*B*ack in the '80s, when I started teaching computer classes, it was not unusual to teach computers without a computer. Today, I like to think that we've come far enough in implementing school technology that teachers have at least one computer with which to teach computer basics.

One of the most rewarding computer-teaching experiences that you can have is introducing students to the wonderful and fascinating world that they can reach by using computers. Unfortunately, this opportunity presents itself less frequently today than it did back in the '80s, because so many students have computers at home or have seen their parents use computers. As a result, the tips that you find in this chapter can be intermixed — tips from the following section are valuable for the one-computer classroom as well as for going to the lab. So take a look at all the ideas and choose the approach that you like best.

Ten Tips for Nada Computer

The object of this lesson is to make learning about computers fun and to convince students that it's good to share things; sharing makes the wait for lab time even more exciting. Just don't forget to sign up for that time in the lab so that your students will actually get to put their knowledge to work. You'll all have something to look forward to.

Why try to teach computers without a computer? If you wait until you go to the lab to introduce all concepts, you spend valuable lab time on things that really can be taught without a computer. (Also, you'll never have your students' undivided attention once they have the real thing in front of them!) You'll be surprised by how much they learn this way.

The ideas presented in the following list — nothing that you haven't seen before — are methods that I've seen used effectively. Don't hesitate to add your own ideas to extend this list.

✔ **Use audiovisuals.** Going from the Internet and the World Wide Web back to the mundane world of transparencies, videotapes, 8mm films, or even filmstrips can be difficult. You have to search far and wide to find filmstrips or 8mm films about computers, I'm afraid. But you can find full-color transparencies of hardware, screen shots, and magazine graphics if you search hard enough.

- Contact your local high school's computer or business department, district administrative offices, the state Department of Education, or the local or university library for the most up-to-date videos of computer products and how to use them.

- Download information from the Internet or World Wide Web where you can find out about visuals that you can order, and then add them to your annual list of library requests. Download sample action files and other multimedia files from online. Use your classroom television as the monitor to display information from the computer.

- Record computer programs from television to the VCR, and then use the classroom VCR to show the programs in class the next day — or plan even farther ahead.

✔ **Make a filmstrip with your 35mm camera.** Ask that the negatives not be clipped, and then go looking for a filmstrip projector. Good luck!

✔ **Pick up some props.** Contact the local computer fix-it person and ask for any bum parts that he has lying around. The parts don't have to work, because you don't have a computer! Computer shops are often glad to get rid of old motherboards, RAM chips, expansion boards, dead mice (the plastic kind), and all types and sizes of disks.

- Hang props around the classroom a day or two before you are going to introduce a new term or concept, to pique students' interest.

- Put up a picture of a ram a few days before you discuss RAM, for example.

✔ **Post lots of signs and posters around the room to hold students' interest.** Use different programs to create your displays, so that students see things that were created on the computer in programs that they will use. Post common acronyms that you want your students to remember, your school's rules for using computers, the agreement that students (and/or their parents) signed, samples of newsletters, notes to parents, graphics, student pictures generated by a computer, log of time accumulated, and anything else that you can think of.

✔ **Allow students to do your work.** Students, you will find, often know a great deal about computers; never let them see you sweat. Use their questions as opportunities for them to research the answers and share them with the class. You'll be amazed by how much you'll learn! They might even work for extra computer time when they do get their hands on a keyboard.

✔ **Initiate a "Bring an Expert to School" program.** Students enjoy introducing a friend (or parent) who is knowledgeable about computers as a guest speaker. (Maybe the guest can even bring a computer for the presentation.)

✔ **Take a field trip to a company or organization that uses computers extensively.**

✔ **Encourage students (and allow them time) to share their experiences with home computers.** Many students have already gone online and can share their discoveries, as well as the abuses that they've seen. If they have hardware that they want to tell you about, ask them to find a picture so that you can see it while they talk about it; then make a transparency of the picture.

✔ **Have each student find out what hardware and software people use.** A few years ago, this idea would have left some students out in the cold; now, relatively few organizations are computerless.

Tips for the Classroom Lone Ranger

Congratulations! You now have a computer in your classroom. When you think about having a whole classroom of computers to use when you need them, having only computer may be depressing — but compared to having none, getting only one is marvelous. As they say, "Everything is relative!"

Now that you have a computer, you'd better use it or lose it. I've heard that concept mentioned often, such as, "Well, Mrs. Smith has a computer, and all it does is sit there. If I had it I'd . . ." You'd what? Why, you'd put it where it could be used the most and then let everyone take turns using it, right?

(That would happen in a perfect world!) You have some decisions to make regarding this Lone Ranger computer . . . and then you have to put the computer to use. Here are some things to consider:

✔ **Put it on wheels or plant it.** Putting your computer on a cart that has wheels makes it more versatile. The cart swings the computer toward you when you want to use it and gets it out of the way when you don't. Consider these points when you place your computer:

- The computer needs to be plugged in, so it should be positioned close to an electrical outlet.

- If you have a modem, it needs to be close to the phone outlet. (Ideally, the electrical and phone outlets will be close together.)

- If your school is networked, the computer must be close enough to the network hookup.

- The cords need to be out of the way so that students won't trip over them.

- The monitor should be positioned so that you can see what's on it at all times.

- Never forget that a computer on wheels can walk — sometimes, after hours into someone else's room.

✔ **Create a wish list.** Develop a list of computer needs, and keep it handy so that you're prepared the first time someone asks, "Need any supplies or equipment?" Start your list with the following items, and check them off when you get them. You'll find plenty of others to add on your own.

- *Extension cord* — to make it easier to move the computer ($3 and up)

- *Power strip* — to plug all computer components into so that you can turn them all on by using the master switch (less than $10)

- *Speakers* — for that full-bodied flavor of multimedia ($20 and up)

- *Headphones* — to eliminate the interference between sounds from the computer and what you're telling the other students ($1 up)

- *Floppy disks* — for students to use to store their work (50 disks for $12 to $18, formatted and in color)

- *Dust cover* — to protect the computer — especially if you have a chalkboard ($5 to $15)

- *Printer* (not required) — to enable students to print their own work ($150 and up)

- *CD-ROM drive* — to open the volumes of multimedia CD-ROMs that are out there ($100 and up)

- *Software* — you name it . . . and list each software item separately ($5 specials and up)

- *Modem* — for staying in touch ($29 and up)

✔ **Project the computer screen through the TV set.** I won't insult your intelligence by trying to explain how a projection device can help. The cable that you need to connect your computer to the TV set costs about $20.

✔ **Get an LCD panel to project your computer screen.** LCD (liquid crystal display) panels attach to your computer, sit on your overhead projector (yes, the same one that you use for transparencies), and project the images on your computer onto a screen or the wall. One advantage to using an LCD panel is that it comes with all the cords, cables, and attachments that you need and costs less than other projection devices. The quality of the projected images has improved over the past couple of years, so they make a good alternative to a full-blown projection device.

✔ **Schedule student time.** When you have as many as 25 to 30 students vying for computer time, you need to try innovative approaches to scheduling use time. You can schedule and monitor students' time on the computer in several ways:

- *Assign a set base time,* requiring each student to log a basic amount of time.

- *Set up a voucher system* that enables students to earn computer time rather than a "when you finish your work" system. Award points (not just grades) for students' work, and allow students to use the points that they accumulate by spending time on their favorite school-related activities. Allow them to use the points for computer time only after all students have completed their assigned computer tasks.

- *Assign timed tasks* to ensure that all students have completed their assigned work (and have done it themselves).

The Lone Ranger computer revisited

Need additional help getting the most from your lone computer? You may want to check out *The One Computer Classroom and More,* created by Tom Snyder Productions. You'll find a number of different materials designed for use in one-computer classrooms, because they encourage cooperative learning and problem-solving, and the materials are free! Tom Snyder Productions provides a free video for loan to schools. For more information, call 800-342-0236.

- *Allow students to devise a fair system for setting online (or on-system) time.* They often come up with innovative rewards that you and I don't think of. Assign them the responsibility for monitoring the time.

✔ **Set up accounts.** Setting up accounts is a good way to teach students accountability. Then make sure that they log their time accurately. You might use a spreadsheet to do this (aha!).

✔ **Create group tasks that require several students to work together on the system at the same time.** The group may create a newsletter, develop a template, research a topic, or whatever. (Do you envision more computer-related assignments?)

✔ **Group students, and assign each of them a specific day on which each group can use the computer.** (I know — yuck! But it works as a last resort, and it's easy!)

✔ **Give instruction on new computer topics to the class as a whole.** This is especially important when the instruction involves new hardware and how to use it.

✔ **Display students' computer work, classroom logs, and time charts in the classroom,** and allow students to take printouts home. This shows parents, teachers, and administrators that students are using the computer.

Using the services of the technology coordinator

Many schools use the term "technology coordinator" to refer to their lab teacher. Other school systems hire technology coordinators to oversee the use of technology within an entire district. No longer do technology coordinators just teach students how to use the computer, they also do the following:

✔ Help staff members learn how to use computer hardware and software

✔ Locate and develop ways to integrate computers into standard curricula

✔ Monitor student computer use and provide instruction

✔ Identify new software and hardware that can benefit teachers and students

✔ Attend technology conferences and workshops

✔ Maintain lab equipment, as well as computer equipment in classrooms

✔ Act as a liaison between the staff and administration about technology advancements and needs

✔ Keep lists of technology needs and wants, and set goals for obtaining them

✔ Purchase technology equipment

✔ Recruit, train, and schedule volunteers who can help in computer labs

✔ **Make sure that you know what students are doing on the computer.** Keep the screen visible. This prevents students from inadvertently wandering into the "X" zone.

✔ **Review all software (even games) that you buy before allowing students to use it.** You may find that what appears to be innocent and fun really isn't.

✔ **Observe the copyright laws.** Keep your software yours and students' software theirs; software usage is not a mix-and-match environment.

Of course, there's no substitute for using the computer yourself, so use it — often. Your computer activity presents a positive view for students, impresses parents and administrators, and keeps students from fighting over whose turn it is when it's yours.

Ten Tips for Going to the Lab

Okay, you get to take your class to the computer lab this Friday! Yippee! Hooray! Say *what?* Oh, no, don't panic. You've used your own computer and know at least as much as your students do about the programs that you're going to be using, right? Well, if you don't, you need to bone up before Friday. Here are some tips to help you get the most out of your lab time:

✔ **Visit the lab ahead of time.** Use the extra time to discuss with the technology coordinator what you'd like to accomplish. The technology coordinator can ensure that the programs you want to use are set up and running properly.

✔ **Schedule lab time early.** The lab schedule at most schools fills up quickly. Get your days scheduled early so that you get the days that best fit your curriculum. (Remember that fitting computers into the curriculum is the top priority.) To stay on friendly terms with your fellow faculty members, don't hog the lab. Also, if your plans change, release the lab for the dates when you don't need it. Everyone wants a piece of this action!

✔ **Become the lab assistant.** If you're feeling a bit insecure about your computer prowess, never fear; technology coordinators still enjoy working with students. When teachers who are unfamiliar with certain programs require help, the technology coordinator is available while the class is in the lab. Seeing teachers work with their students also assures the technology coordinator that the teacher can be counted on to supervise students while they are in the lab — something that's important to lab coordinators.

Ten essential computer lab items

If you have the enviable task of setting up a lab in your school, consider the following to be a no-nonsense list of computer lab must-haves:

✓ Computers — a minimum of one for every three or four students, with mice

✓ CD-ROM drives in all computers

✓ Software (Windows 95 and Microsoft Works).

✓ Most new computers come with extra programs, and sometimes, you can pick out the programs that you want, so choose wisely.

✓ A modem for at least one computer unless you have a direct connection to the Internet; then request such a connection for *every* computer

✓ Ergonomically appropriate computer desks or tables for your students, and chairs that fit them, too

✓ Overhead projector with an LCD panel or a video projector

✓ Outlets — lots and lots of electrical outlets

✓ At least one printer for every four computers and one color printer for the lab and nice, if possible

✓ Dry-erase marker board (no chalk, please)

✓ Supplies, including floppy disks, paper, dry-erase pens, an eraser, and transparency film

There they are — the bare-bones requirements for your lab

✓ **Make sure that students understand the lab's code of conduct.** Have students sign a computer-use agreement, if desired, and send the form home so that parents are aware of lab rules.

✓ **Consider lab time to be a privilege rather than a break.** And, stay with the students while they're in the lab — you may just learn something.

✓ **Assign students to groups early.** Then they will know where they should go and who will be working together before they get there. Believe me, this procedure reduces the amount of confusion immensely.

✓ **Provide instruction about computer equipment.** Turning on the system, using mouse techniques, the specifics of entering text, and inserting and removing disks from disk drives can be reviewed before the first visit. Check out the hints for no-computer and one-computer classrooms in the earlier sections of this chapter to provide this instruction.

✓ **Review students' assignments and even demonstrate the programs that they will use to complete the assignments.** Have your students do the preliminary work (such as creating a letter or outlining a report) so that content questions surface in the classroom rather than in the lab.

Ergonomics and the well-designed computer lab

Have you ever wondered what the term *ergonomics* means? The word sounds as if it is the study of something. (I always think of finances when I see *omics*.) Well, according to *World Book Dictionary*, ergonomics is "the study of the relationship between individuals and their work or working environment, especially with regard to fitting jobs to the needs and abilities of workers."

How does ergonomics affect you? You've probably read about carpal-tunnel syndrome and other effects that computer use has on the human body. As you design your lab, keeping ergonomics in mind is important. The chairs that you choose, for example, should fit your students and be adjustable for various shapes and sizes of people. The desks that you choose should be computer desks or tables made specifically to house computers. Please, please, please don't assume that regular fold-up tables or normal-height tabletops will do just as well.

Look carefully at the workstations in other labs to help determine what to order. If you still have questions, check with OSHA (the U.S. Occupational Safety and Health Administration) to see if they have a guide to help you identify other areas and considerations to make.

✔ **Remember that students need the same time to close up shop in the lab that they need at the end of every school day to get ready to go home.** Waiting until the next class arrives is not the time to tell your students to wrap up.

✔ **Always — and I mean always — have a backup plan ready to go.** This amazing computer technology occasionally has a mind of its own. All it takes to blow your day is for a program to lock up or the network to be down, and your students suddenly have 45 minutes of "free time." Obviously, your backup plan should not involve using a computer. Do you have a crossword puzzle handy? A creative-writing assignment? A few extra minutes of math practice?

Chapter 19

Foolproof Ways to Finance Your Computer Needs

••

In This Chapter

▶ Find out what's worked before

▶ Advertise, advertise, advertise

▶ Solicit grants

▶ Sell your computer time

••

*O*kay, you're hooked. You know how valuable computers and other technology can be to you and your students. Will your enthusiasm alone be enough to influence others and persuade your administration to spring the big bucks that you'll need to finance your new habits? That's like asking your students how far they think they will go toward supporting themselves on a smile!

You know basically what equipment and supplies you want; you've done your homework and know how much it will cost. In this chapter, I give you some ideas about how to get what you want.

Here's the plan. What? You don't have a plan for raising money to buy computer equipment and supplies? Well, it's time to get one! Don't do anything until your plan is well thought out and a schedule has been set up. Then follow these guidelines for making sure that your fund-raiser will raise interest as well as money.

Research Past Fund-Raising Successes

Find out from others in the school, community, and area what fund-raising schemes have generated the greatest profit. Identify those ideas that other organizations lay claim to (such as the spaghetti supper sponsored by the Lions Club every year), and cross them off the list.

Advertise to the Masses

Advertise often — everywhere, anywhere. Unless the community knows what you are trying to do, you will get nowhere. Tell everyone, every chance you get and every way you can possibly think of; just get the word out there. Give it to them piecemeal (a little bit at a time), put your talents to work, and get your schedule out there. Be sure that your students are involved in whatever idea you decide on; they have a stake in this, too, so give them computer points for their help.

With your schedule in hand, plan an aggressive advertising campaign. Use other events as opportunities to tout your ideas, and paper the town with tidbits of information to pique interest.

Throw a Party

If you have one computer, a few pieces of software, and some other equipment (borrow them, if necessary), you can invite parents, friends, and neighbors to school, and ask them only to bring one of their toys (software) to share with others during the party (you don't want to break any copyright laws). Getting people to bring in the software they like and use frequently is a good way to preview the software that people are using at home and at work and to give you an idea of software that you may want to buy. You might leave a can for donations by the doorway, just in case someone has a few extra pennies (or dollars) to contribute.

Solicit Grants

Funds are out there for the asking — if you put together a formal request for them. Write a proposal for a grant or some other award that is designed strictly to obtain funds for classroom technology. The sources of some of these grants are posted on the Internet. (Check out Chapter 12 for more information about going online.)

Scholastic Network (http://www.scholastic.com) is a good place to start. Then get together with the person in your school system who has the most grant-writing savvy (and skill). People who have written successful proposals in the past can show you ways to get special attention for your proposal.

All roads lead to school

I don't know the extent of technological advancement in Rome, but I do know that somehow, either directly or roundabout, all roads in town eventually can be directed to end at the school. So paper the roads with flyers, crepe paper, and paper flags; TP the trees (yes, you know what I mean). Get everyone's attention by making sure that they know something is up. When interest is at its peak, start feeding bits of information about your computer objectives to the public that will eventually lead the news media to you and your class or school.

Then promise the generous public and media anything — and take their money and all the free publicity you can get. Whether you're planning actual fund-raising activities for the week following the advertisements or simply going the old "please contribute" route, broadcasting information free through all types of media is an excellent way to remind the community daily of how important computers are and how much community support is needed.

Keeping the public informed of your progress toward reaching your goal is also important. Record contribution totals on a thermometer or some other measurement device, and display it in a prominent place, such as the front of the school. Anyone passing the school gets a gentle reminder of the need to support the project, and all you have to do is sit back and rake in the donations.

When all your computers are happily in place, follow up the fund-raising effort with a party or open house to give contributors an opportunity to see the spoils of your efforts (and to give yourself a chance to show off your computer prowess!).

P.S.: Make sure that students get people's permission before papering their trees. Students won't need to tell their neighbors exactly what their total plan is, but students do need to assure them that they (the students) will clean up any mess they make; make sure that they do.

My school goes after every grant it can get its hands on. The grant doesn't have to offer really big bucks; even $1,000 (which is small for grants) will help get you started. So try, try, and try again.

Take in Strays

Taking advantage of free press seems to make equipment pop out of the woodwork. Tell your students' parents that donating their unused computers, desks, and supplies (especially disks) is *tax-deductible,* and you may find that you have more equipment than you can possibly fix up to meet your needs. The advantage is that you can often combine pieces from different units to create something close to what you need. Then all you need is a couple of more-sophisticated systems, and you're off and running.

If you can't use something, pass it along to another teacher. Don't forget to acknowledge every gift, no matter how small. Maybe your students can work out a thank-you template!

Hold a Tag Day

Tag day — don't know why they call it *tag day* because no one actually gets tagged — is a popular event in my area of the country. On tag day, students from the local high-school band canvass the neighborhood, asking for donations; it's as simple as that. Before you choose this fund-raising possibility, here are key things to check out:

- ✔ What are the restrictions for collecting donations in your area? Do you have to be a not-for-profit agency?

- ✔ Be sure that your school administration knows what you are doing. Administrators may want to coordinate this effort with other school fund-raisers, and they need to be well equipped to handle phone calls and donations that are sent directly to the school.

- ✔ Make sure that students have identification that introduces them to the people they approach, so that potential donors know that the students are collecting for a worthy cause.

- ✔ Set up tables outside area businesses on tag day so that people who aren't home will have a chance to donate.

- ✔ Leave self-addressed envelopes with notes, telling those who aren't home that you stopped by and asking them to mail in their donation. In fact, organizations sometimes find that leaving envelopes to mail to the school is more profitable than asking people to give cash to kids. (Imagine that!)

Start Adoption Procedures

Some companies adopt entire schools, and others adopt only a division, department, or class. If you can't get your school's administration to allow a company to adopt the school, see whether it's okay to find a corporate "parent" for your class. You'll reap not only the possible cash donations, but some other benefits as well (maybe a "career day" or mentoring programs).

Sell Computer Time

After you get your lab up and running, you'll need money to support the lab — to buy disks, printer paper, and so on. Here are some tried-and-true ideas that have proven to be quite successful:

- ✔ Sponsor computer workshops to teach others in the school or community how to use these marvelous pieces of equipment. Depending on the size of your community, you may or may not find many local businesses equipped with complete computer labs to train their employees. In towns where computer labs are scarce, your lab becomes a prized commodity.

- ✔ Sell computer time to clubs, the school newspaper or yearbook, or community organizations that need a room with more than a few computers to provide instruction to their employees.

- ✔ Create a summer camp for students, with classes taught by other students and monitored by you, the teacher.

- ✔ Create a computer club.

- ✔ Take in work and charge for it; then have students type stuff for other teachers and students. But remember to keep all teacher stuff confidential.

Pick a Plan Your Students Can Handle

The ages of your students will control, to some extent, the fund-raiser you choose. Biting off more than you can chew is a sure bet for disaster — or lots of extra work on your part.

Work with a Practical Schedule

Choose a time (say, October) when the fund-raising project can run straight through its course — times when there are no holidays or other events to interfere with your plan. Although football games, school carnivals, and other regularly scheduled events may at first appear to be conflict with your ideas, you can actually use those events to your advantage and help build interest in your activity — use your imagination to come up with ideas that fit your school and community.

Keep Up with Current Legislation

Keep in touch with legislation that affects education, particularly technology use and purchases. One state has dedicated a tax on video rentals to be spent on technology in public schools; the money goes to the county in which the video is rented.

Your state department of education should be helpful to you, along with your local legislators. Get them on your side! The goal ought to be to get teachers out of the fund-raising business and squarely in front of the classroom, right?

Selling the football field

Another neat thing — and one that immediately grabs community attention if it's never been done in your area — is to sell plots of your school's football field for four hours on Saturday morning. Figure out how many plots (at, say, $10 each) you need to parcel out to earn the money that you need for your venture. Then figure out how big the plots of the field need to be. Use your desktop-publishing skills to develop deeds for the plots, and sell them to the community for four hours. Promise them anything — just get their money.

Actually, you can use your imagination to determine what to permit "owners" to do with their land. I've seen schools throw a homecoming tailgate party and allow plot buyers to "settle" on their property. I've also seen students hold a "beach" party and sun themselves on their own plots. Probably the funniest thing that I've seen done with a plot was awarding a prize (again, use your imagination) to the owner of the plot upon which a well-fed cow dropped her patty.

There must be some inducement to encourage people to buy the plots! Let me know what you come up with. By the way, if the football coach doesn't go along with this idea, consider selling parts of the school parking lot.

Chapter 20

Stuff You Can "Hardly" Live Without

In This Chapter

▶ Ten pieces of hardware to make your life easier

▶ Ten ways to upgrade hand-me-down computers

▶ Ten computer supplies to always have in stock

*H*ave you ever considered how difficult it would be to identify everything in lists of ten? Just think what it would be like if you had to do the following?

- ✔ Tell someone your ten favorite lessons to teach.

- ✔ Limit (or expand) your lecture to ten major points.

- ✔ Speak for only ten minutes about anything, anywhere, anytime.

- ✔ Tell someone your ten favorite exercises.

- ✔ Imagine your ten favorite foods.

- ✔ Think about the ten most important events in your life.

- ✔ Invite only ten people to a birthday party — without leaving anyone out!

Sometimes, identifying ten of anything is difficult. At other times, limiting yourself to ten things is hard. In this chapter, you'll find that I've probably left things out in one list and scraped the bottom of the barrel trying to come up with ten things in other lists. Everyone has an opinion!

Add your own personal touch to the information that I've started. Make notes. Add to those lists in which I've been too limited; strike through the bottom-of-the-barrel items that you believe are really stretching it!

Ten Pieces of Hardware to Make Life Easier

You've finally got everything set up and have mastered the basics of using the equipment that you have. Feeling restless? Then investigate these pieces of equipment and figure out how you can use them to make your life easier.

Now, if you're a great shopper, you may find better deals on this equipment than I found browsing through the stores and catalogs I have available (and the way technology changes, these prices will be out of date almost as soon as they're published). As a result, all of the prices given in this chapter are approximate and are subject to change. Look for the best price you can find.

LCD panels

An *LCD (liquid crystal display) panel* is a hardware unit that connects to your computer, sits on your overhead projector, and projects whatever you have on your computer screen. In my opinion, in the list of "must-haves," an LCD panel is second only to the computer itself. But remember how long it took you to convince the administration that every classroom needed an overhead projector? You may find it almost as difficult to convince the administration that an LCD panel is necessary.

If you plan to use your computer to enhance your instruction or to help teach students about the computer, you must have an LCD panel. Without it, you will end up trying to squish all your students around your computer so that they can see what you're trying to teach. The LCD panel magnifies an image and throws it onto a screen (or the wall) and allows you to stand up straight while you show your students what you want them to see.

Unfortunately, LCD panels are relatively expensive; a grayscale model costs more than $1,000, and one that projects color images costs around $1,800. There's always another hitch, of course: You need a high-quality overhead projector to make your LCD panel work well. It's likely that the one you use now isn't good enough for your images.

Scanners

A *scanner* takes a picture from a piece of paper and stores it on a disk so that you can insert the picture into newsletters and other documents. After you get the picture on your computer, you can change the size, take out some of the picture (crop it), flip it, turn it sideways, and basically manipulate it any way you want. I once took a picture of the principal of a high school and put the picture in the center of play money for students to use at a carnival. This money went over quite well (and I didn't see any of it used for target practice).

Scanners look like magic wands (hand-held) or desktop copy machines (flatbed), as shown in Figure 20-1, and are connected to your computer by cables. Scanners come equipped with the software that you'll need to run them, and the instructions for installing the software are easy to follow.

Figure 20-1:
Scanners
are great
for getting
pictures on
disks.

Scan Man hand-held scanner (© 1995 Logitech, Inc. used by permission)

Apple flatbed scanner (photo courtesy of Apple Computer, Inc.)

Some scanners scan images by using black and white or shades of gray; others capture all the colors of the rainbow. Scanners cost anywhere from roughly $100 for hand-held scanners to $300 and up for flatbed color scanners. Buy the best one that you can afford, but don't forget that if you want to scan anything larger than a snapshot, a flatbed scanner is better — and life without color is rather drab.

Touch screens

You've probably seen touch screens at museums and welcome centers when you cross the border into a new state. *Touch screens* usually present a map or a list of items; touching an area of the map or one of the listed items accesses information about the topic. In my area, an outlet mall has a touch screen that accesses local job opportunities.

Touch screens can be used to enable students who are physically challenged to use the computer. These screens also provide a way for students to become interactive with the system. A touch screen usually costs less than $500.

OCR devices

OCR (*optical character recognition*) devices read text and other strange characters by using specialized techniques — similar to those that your eyes use — to try to figure out what your students write. OCR has been used for years by the U.S. Postal Service to read zip codes. You can use an OCR device (an optical character reader) to copy text-based documents into your computer so that you can edit them later. Simply scanning a document with a scanner turns it into a graphic picture that won't allow you to edit the text; OCR devices, however, do.

OCR devices cost between $200 and $1,000, depending on the level of text sophistication that you want to read. Lower-end devices read basic typed styles (fonts), whereas the most sophisticated read handwritten text as well.

Zip drives and all that Jazz

Zip, Jazz, QUICKDrive, and Ditto drives provide an excellent way to store large volumes of data outside the computer on a single disk. These drives are great for storing large multimedia presentations so that they don't clutter your hard drive. I finally bit the bullet and purchased a Zip drive. (Well, actually, my son had to have a Zip or Jazz drive for a multimedia class he is taking in college, so it becomes mine after he finishes the course.)

Zip, Jazz, and Ditto drives connect to your computer through cables attached to your printer outlet on the back of your computer, which means that you need no special equipment to get these drives up and running. All you need is the software that tells your computer that there's a new piece of equipment attached, and that software comes with the drive. Installation is semiautomatic and quite easy.

Each drive type has certain characteristics that distinguish it from the others:

- **Zip drives** store up to 10MB of information on one Zip disk. The drives cost about $200, and the disks average $15 each.

- **Jazz drives** store up to 1GB of information on one Jazz disk. The drives cost $400 (for an internal Jazz drive) to over $500 (for an external Jazz drive), and the disks average almost $100 each — whew! Jazz drives resemble Zip drives.

- **Ditto drives** store from 2GB to 3.2GB of information on one Ditto Dash Card. The drives cost from about $200 to over $250 and come in an internal style and an external style. Ditto Dash Cards cost roughly $60 each. Ditto drives look like Zip drives.

> ✔ **QUICKDrive units** store up to 1.6GB in a single unit and connect to other computers via a printer port or a PCMCIA card. The units cost just less than $200 and essentially are external hard drives that don't require expensive floppy disks.

Laptops

Laptops are wonderful, marvelous . . . you know the rest. You've probably seen them in the malls (the man who dutifully took his wife shopping and is still getting some work done), on airplanes, in airports, and on television. Because laptops hold a battery, they don't have to be plugged in. Some people even think that *PC* stands for *portable* computer rather than *personal* computer!

I've seen the portable-computer arena go from computers that I called luggable to computers that really are portable and pack the power of a desktop model in a small case. I have one system that transmits data so quickly that I miss the transmission if I blink.

Before you buy a laptop, be sure to use the same techniques that you used before buying the desktop computers for your class. Define your objectives, do your homework, and then enjoy your investment. I use my laptop to show presentations while I'm on the road and to stay in touch with my online service by using my laptop modem. But be prepared to pay more for your laptop than you paid for your desktop computer. The luxury of port-ability is costly.

Laptops range from slightly less than $2,000 to more than $10,000, depending, of course, on what you want on them. Noncolor monitors cost less than color monitors do, and you can get the same types of hardware for your laptop that you have on your desktop.

There are now CD-ROM drives for laptops, portable printers for use on the road (even *color* printers!), and laptops with LCD panels that break away from the monitor to make projecting your presentations even easier. Be sure to get a special carrying case to protect your equipment, as well as an extra battery. If you know that you will want to use your laptop in special situa-tions, you also should buy adapters to make your laptop work with the other equipment.

Video paraphernalia

Want to really get the most from your computer? Try adding video extras: a video camera to take movies, a microphone to record sound, and high-powered speakers to get it all out in the air. Video paraphernalia is a *great* way to turn your classroom into a motion-picture studio — and it's fairly easy to do (but expensive).

You can buy a digital camera (such as the one shown in Figure 20-2) that captures images and stores them until you connect to your computer and dump the file onto a disk. The cost of these cameras ranges from about $200 on up.

You also can record video by using a standard video camera and then show the video on the computer by sending it through a VCR. All it takes is the right cable to link the pieces of equipment; and although it may be slow, you can send video over the Internet. The cables that you need vary according to the type of equipment that you have.

Digital video cameras, such as the Connectix camera shown in Figure 20-3, are great little ditties to add to your computer so that you can tape your class in action. The cameras run from about $100 for grayscale video to about $200 for color video.

Figure 20-2:
This Kodak
Digital 40
takes great
pictures
you can use
on the
computer.

Kodak Digital Camera 40 (Photo courtesy of Eastman Kodak Co.)

Figure 20-3:
Record your classroom activities using a video camera that connects directly to your computer.

Microphones and speakers

To record sound on your system, you need a standard sound board that comes with most new systems. Then you can buy a microphone, which costs anywhere from $10 to a more-sensitive microphone that costs more than $100.

Perhaps the most surprising thing that I've run across in years is the price of speakers. Of course, I'm not sure that I ever priced speakers alone before; they always came with my stereo or other type of system. I found them for as low as $20 (my son says, "Mom!") to more than $600 (I say, "No way!"). Determine the quality of the sound that you want, look at your budget, and then buy the best speakers you can afford.

PCMCIA cards

PCMCIA (*Personal Computer Memory Card Interface Adapter* — wow, is that a mouthful!) has devised a neat way to make different units compatible with your computer system without having to open the system unit and install circuit boards. (No, PCMCIA is not a new division of the Central Intelligence Agency.) Although PCMCIA cards are popular for use in laptops, they can also be installed on desktop models.

A PCMCIA slot built into the computer holds PCMCIA cards that serve as modems, store extra memory, or connect an external unit to a system. Each PCMCIA card is about the size of a credit card. I have two cards for my laptop; one is for my fax/modem, and the other allows me to connect an external CD-ROM. The cost varies according to the type of unit that the card represents.

Projection systems

The LitePro by InFocus projection system is only one of a variety of special projectors that you can attach to your computer to project images onto a screen or the wall. Although these projectors are more expensive (they can run from about $3,000 to $8,000) than LCD panels are, they reduce the number of separate pieces of equipment and cables that you need to connect. Check out these units to see which one is the most expedient for your school. By sharing the projector among the teachers who may want to use it, you increase your chances of getting one.

Is your wish list growing?

Ten Tips for Upgrading Hand-Me-Downs

"Never look a gift horse in the mouth" is an old saying that most teachers believe. When someone offers you free computer equipment, say yes! Although this equipment may not live up to your dream expectations, you can use your ingenuity and a few bucks to upgrade a system. And if you can't use the system, you may be able to use its parts (or sell the system or parts for supply cash).

Keep in mind that computers are out of date almost as soon as you buy them, but that doesn't mean that they aren't useful or that you need to upgrade yours. Worry about upgrading only when your system can no longer do what you want it to do.

Add memory

As computer systems age, their memory seems to go, too (sound familiar?). Actually, the memory that your system has doesn't change, unlike human memory; it just becomes insufficient (as you've found in some of your students). Computer memory is relatively cheap; the cost varies sort of like the stock market these days. The cost goes up and down according to supply and demand. (You learned that in economics, remember?)

Increasing memory (RAM) in older systems helps you use the systems to run more powerful (the latest) software. Read about RAM in Chapter 1.

Install a bigger hard drive

If a hand-me-down computer doesn't have a hard disk, get one; if it does, get a bigger one. I recommend at least 720MB as a good starting size for a new hard disk. The sizes available tend to grow by leaps and bounds (as do the computer programs), so bigger is better. The cost is less than $150 for a 720MB drive to about $400 for a 4GB (4 billion bytes) drive.

Add a CD-ROM drive

Most systems have space where you can install a CD-ROM drive and enter the multimedia generation. Check to see whether the system that you inherited can support a CD-ROM drive before you run out and get one. (The computer that I handed down to my son was a 386 processor with a top speed of 33MHz, so his thinking about getting a CD-ROM drive was pretty useless.) Look at Chapter 16 for the scoop on CD-ROM drives.

Change floppy-disk drives

If the hand-me-down that you have has a $5^1/_4$-inch floppy-disk drive, pull it out and get a new one that holds $3^1/_2$-inch disks. I believe it's safe to say that you won't find much software on the larger disks today, and the software that comes with the system will probably be out of date. Floppy drives cost less than $100.

Get a color printer

Regardless of what your system looks like, what programs you use, and how fast your system works, the bottom line is what the printed page looks like. Putting the page in color makes even the most unlikely systems smile. Color ink-jet printers will cost you less than $300, but color laser printers run over $3,000.

Change the motherboard

The *motherboard* of your computer controls a number of things, and as a result, it is the most costly upgrade. The motherboard is the whole inside of the computer; it connects the disk drives, holds the memory chips (RAM), contains the processor, holds the power unit, houses expansion slots, and (most important) controls the speed.

When you have a *really* old system (such as the 33MHz machine that I dumped on my son), you may find that you can change the motherboard and reach the power of a brand-new system for less money than buying a new system. A case is a case is a case; the housing usually makes no difference. Think of upgrading as redecorating your kitchen — pulling out your cabinets, scraping up the tile flooring, trashing the stove and refrigerator . . . and putting in new cabinets, new flooring, and new appliances. (Sigh!)

Add a modem

If the system that you inherit isn't *that* old, you may simply need to add a modem. If the system already has one, consider getting a faster one — and make it a fax/modem, please. A fax/modem can get you talking with everyone else! To find out more about modems, see Chapter 12.

Get a new monitor

So the system arrived with a monochrome (green on black, amber on black, or gray on black) monitor, eh? Well, send that monitor to the high-school electronics lab, and get a new color one. (Make sure that you get the new video adapter that you'll need to attach the monitor to your system.) You'll find that working with a color screen makes you feel happier.

Update to Windows 95

Go for extra credit: Install additional RAM (you need at least 8MB), and get Windows 95 so that you can take advantage of all the stuff that you've been reading about.

Sound things out with a new sound card

If the sounds in your classroom are more than you bargained for, try installing a new sound board in your computer, pick up some speakers, add a CD-ROM drive, and play some music. The sounds coming from your computer will quiet your students, and peace will reign.

If you aren't sure that you can replace the parts alone, bribe your school's technology coordinator to guide you through the process, or contact the technology or electronics teacher at the nearest high school or college to see whether upgrading is the right step to take. As a last resort, send your machine to the computer graveyard, and be sure to dispose of it properly.

Feeding Your Computer Supplies Habit

Even though your room is stuffed to the brim, you're going to need a new supply cabinet when you get a computer. Get the cabinet and set it up before sauntering down to the office-supply store, because when you see what's in store for you there, you won't come home empty-handed. Here are some supplies to look for.

Computer paper

If you're fortunate to have a cut-sheet printer (a printer that uses regular paper instead of paper that comes on a roll), stock up on paper that fits your machine. I buy my paper from a wholesale club because I find that it's cheaper there. You may find that you can order paper from your school's central supply place for less than you can buy it at a wholesale club. Buy the cheapest paper you can for the type of printer you have. Any 20-pound paper works well, and if you have a laser printer, you can often get by with 16-pound paper. If you're working with an ink-jet printer, however, avoid paper that's less than 20 pounds, because ink has a tendency to bleed through.

Colored paper

Whether you choose pretty in pink, goldenrod yellow, or fluorescent chartreuse, colored paper brings graphics, flyers, and art to life. You can change text that's simply "happy" (such as WordArt) to laugh-out-loud exuberant by using colored paper.

Designer transparencies

You've heard of designer clothes, designer shoes, and designer fingernails, but have you heard of designer transparencies? If you haven't, you'll turn them up during your trip to the supply store. Designer transparencies come with special designs on them. If you have a black and white (or grayscale) printer rather than a color printer, you can use these designer transparencies to add color to an otherwise dull presentation.

CD-ROMs with clip art and photo images

Inexpensive CD-ROMs stocked with plenty of clip-art images and photographs will help you enhance documents, notes, letters, tests, and anything else that you and your students produce by using the computer. Order the CD-ROMs that contain images that you find useful, and make a wish list of those that you think the school can use. Then, when the librarian asks for your library order, hand the list of clip art right over. Check out the CD-ROM that comes with this book for a couple of my favorite clip-art collections.

Disks

You'll need lots and lots of floppy disks of the type that fit into the disk drives of your computers. Use these disks to store students' work, as well as your tests — and take your test disks home so that your students don't "accidentally" find them.

Storage cases for all the CD-ROMs and disks you use will be sure to accumulate from day to day and semester to semester. Consider a method for organizing these cases (by teacher? by class period? by subject matter?) before you purchase so that you're sure to buy enough!

Printer cartridges

Murphy (the guy who wrote the set of laws) once said that the first time you run out of printer ink, printer toner, or whatever medium your printer uses will be right in the middle of the most important document that you've printed all year. Never fear — if you have a good supply of printer cartridges on hand, you'll be prepared (and your students will get to take that final exam tomorrow after all).

Erasable ink markers

The pens that you use on erasable marker boards will eventually dry up; you know that. If you're careful and make sure that your students don't use them, of course, they'll last longer than you think. The same Murphy's Law that applies to printer ink applies to erasable markers as well — just when you need them most, they run dry, and your students won't know what their homework assignment for tomorrow is supposed to be.

Marker-board erasers

These little fluffy fellows you use to erase marker-board ink seem to wear out more frequently than the chalkboard erasers do. And if you're excited about going home with no chalk dust on your clothing, calm down. Chalk dust is much easier to get out of your clothing and off your hands than dry-erase marker scrapings are.

Miscellaneous paper supplies

Make sure you're stocked up with supplies such as envelopes, labels, certificates, banner paper — all the varieties that might come in handy for any and all print possibilities. Sure, tape works to connect sheets but using banner paper is so much easier. You can create certificates handily with your word processing program, but special certificate papers look classy. We're into the field of luxuries here, but why not?

Cleaning kits

Don't forget mouse-cleaning kits, computer vacuums, premoistened screen-cleaning wipes, disk-drive cleaners — well, anything that can get dirty on the computer has a kit to clean it up. You know that a lab of computers used by many hands every a day is sure to get a few smudge marks!

Are you worried about affording all these things? Think about the fund-raising ideas earlier in this chapter; even if the school corporation provides the hardware, tell your public that these extras are important for getting the full range of talents out of your kids and your technology.

Now go shopping!

Chapter 21

Help and Helpful Resources

. . . .

In This Chapter

▶ Ten troubleshooting tips

▶ Ten tips that are just plain good to know

. . . .

Something always has to be first . . . and something always has to be last. The same rule applies to topics in a book. As I begin this chapter, I feel somewhat lost, because there's still so much I want to tell you. When time and space are running out (I have to keep those deadlines, you see), it's time to cut to the chase and give teachers things that they can use without having to think, create, or worry.

This chapter gives you some tips to keep (or get) you out of trouble and provides a great list of resources where you can learn lots more about computers, programs, and all things educational. (Why reinvent the wheel, right?)

Enjoy.

Ten Troubleshooting Tips

I've narrowed this section down to the most common problem situations that I've seen in the classroom recently. This is my disclaimer: Each time I think that I won't see something I haven't seen before, some student proves me wrong. So what you see in your classroom (or what you cause), you won't necessarily find here. Make notes, and send me your problem situations; I enjoy good reading. Then contact your computer expert for help.

The computer doesn't work

Although this advice may sound elementary, check to see whether your computer is plugged in. Those meaningful people who cleaned last night may actually have moved the desks and tables just a smidgen too far and caused the cord to come unplugged. Then check to see that all units are plugged in correctly. Finally, plug the computer into a different outlet to see whether there's a blown circuit, or plug it directly into an outlet without going through a power strip.

The monitor is blank

Some monitors have a power saver feature that will cause the monitor to go black after the screen saver has been on for a while. Check to see whether the monitor is on; then make sure that it's plugged into the back of the system unit. If doing that fails to work, turn the monitor off and then back on. If that doesn't work, check the knobs that control the brightness and contrast. Sometimes, other people's eyes see things differently and the monitor controls may have been adjusted for that.

I have a Nonsystem Disk or Disk error

This message often appears when you start your computer — and it will happen more than once. After the first time, you'll just be aggravated at yourself. You can relax; you most likely have *not* blown your hard disk (relief). You probably have a floppy disk in your A drive. Remove the floppy disk, and press any key on the keyboard to continue the boot process.

If you don't have a disk in the floppy drive, however, and you hear some clunking going on inside the computer that sounds like ca-thunk, wr-wr-wr-wr, ca-thunk, turn it off and run for cover (or help). It's possible, just possible, that something has gone wrong with your hard disk.

The keyboard froze up

Keyboard freezing just *happens* — and it's usually not something that you did wrong. Usually, your system tried to do too many things at the same time and got lost, so it's just wandering around inside itself, trying to remember what it was supposed to be doing (you know, like the times you walk into a room and forget why?). If you're using Windows 95, simply press Ctrl+Alt+Del (all three keys at the same time) to bring up the Task List. Select the program that you were using when the keyboard froze (or the program with (not responding) beside it), and click the End Task button.

If that fails, press the Reset button on the system console. As a last resort, turn the power off and wait a couple of minutes before turning it back on.

Be aware that you may lose any unsaved changes to your documents if you restart your system by powering off and turning the system back on.

I have an Out of Memory error

Sometimes, you see a message right in the middle of your screen that tells you the system is out of memory. I know how it feels; I sometimes need more RAM myself! A couple of things could be happening: You could have too many applications running or too many documents with lots of graphics open. Short of adding more RAM right now, you need to finish your job.

First, acknowledge the error message and then check the taskbar to see what applications are running. Close applications that you aren't using. If you don't have extra applications running, check the window menu of the application that is running to see what documents you have open. Close those documents that you aren't using (be sure to save changes as you close them) and then try completing your task. If you still get the message, save your work, exit everything, and reboot your system. Sometimes, things get stuck in memory (like the song that you keep humming all day long). Rebooting allows you to start fresh.

If, after restarting the system, you still can't accomplish the task because of memory problems, go get more RAM!

I lost my document — it just disappeared!

Well, maybe — but then, maybe not. One thing that I often see is that instead of losing the work, you've told your computer that you want to start some-thing new and have created a new document. As you already know, new documents are plain blank pages. Getting a new document on-screen suddenly gives you the impression that the work that you *had* on your screen is gone — like the Cookie Monster ate it.

Look at the title bar of your screen to determine what document you are working with; then display the Window menu to see whether your document really is there. Whew! It's there. But if not, maybe you accidentally selected text and then pressed another key on the keyboard while the text was highlighted. If you did, you told the computer that you wanted to replace all the text that you had selected with the character that you pressed. If you can keep from panicking, you usually can reverse the action by using the program's undo feature.

I deleted my file from the disk

Thought you were just cleaning things up, did you? Then you found out that the test you spent hours creating is now a thing of the past? Well, thank goodness you upgraded to Windows 95! Remember Mr. Recycle Bin? Well, he's holding your work as long as you haven't emptied the trash. All you have to do is display the Windows 95 desktop and double-click the Recycle Bin icon to locate your file. Now do you understand why I recommend that you allow your trash to fill up until you *have* to empty it? If you have your Recycle Bin set to empty each time you turn off your computer, your file won't be there when you go looking for it.

What if you're still using Windows 3.*x* or DOS? Here are a couple of ideas that may help you get a deleted file back. Whatever you do, don't turn off your machine until you exhaust all alternatives.

Windows 3.*x* makes getting your file back a bit easier than DOS does (though not quite so easy as Windows 95 does). Windows 3.*x* comes with an Undelete application that is stored in the Applications group in the Program Manager. Double-click the Undelete icon in the Applications group window to start the Undelete program and display the list of files recently deleted. If you exit Windows and turn your machine off before getting your file back, you may be out of luck; the undelete bucket on some machines is set to dump out when you shut down the system. If this happens, you can try using DOS and the procedures described in the next paragraph to get your files back — but no one offers any guarantees.

Okay, now for the DOS systems. If you're running a version of DOS earlier than DOS 5.0, you are most likely out of luck. If you're running DOS 5.0 or later, you should find the Undelete.exe command and instructions for using the command in your DOS manual; pull it out to get all the nitty-gritty details.

Good luck!

Access to my file is denied

Unfortunately, your students won't see this message when they try to open a test that you stored on the hard disk. But when you try to copy or do something else with a file while it is open, your system tells you that access is denied. In general, only one copy of a document can be open at a time; thus, you will get this message. Check your taskbar and Window menu to see what you have open.

My printer gives me squiggles

Is it your printer, your computer, your software, or the way that they are communicating that puts those funny looking characters on the paper when you print? They probably look something like the Greek alphabet (such as this: φε) My guess would be that those cute little characters (by the way, you won't be able to get them when you really want them), are the result of a communication problem. Although you know that you don't need a phone line to connect your printer to the computer, you do have to tell your system what printer you have attached. Then the computer and the printer can speak the same language, and you'll get more than gibberish on the paper.

Check with your printer manual to see what steps you should take to make sure that your printer settings include the printer that you have. Then make sure that the printer you are trying to use is the one listed in the Printer text box of the Print dialog box. If it isn't, click choose your printer from the Printer drop-down list.

My mouse is dead

In his book *All I Really Need to Know, I Learned in Kindergarten,* Robert Fulghum reminds us that "goldfish and hamsters and white mice and little seeds — they all die." And so will your mice. The average life expectancy of classroom mice is roughly two years (watch your students use them and you'll know why!) If the mouse is really dead, replace it; then restart your computer.

If, on the other hand, your mouse is *pretending* to be dead, there's a good chance that you have a another communication gap. The solution that I find most effective for restoring a pretender is to exit the program, turn off the computer, and then boot up again. If the mouse still doesn't work, get your technology coordinator (sounds better than guru, huh?) to take a look.

Again, try these troubleshooting tips before panicking and before turning off the computer (unless shutting off the computer is a possible solution to the problem). You'll know that you've done the right thing when you have to go to the computer guru, and the first thing the guru says is, "You didn't turn off the computer, did you?" (This will be accompanied, of course, by a panic-stricken look that you've seen on the face of your best student who discovers, upon entering your class, that there's a test today.)

Ten Tips That Are Just Plain Good to Know

Even in a lagniappe chapter, there are pieces of information that don't quite fit anywhere else. Of course, this is my way around it. Trying to limit this to ten tips was a challenge, but if nothing else, maybe these will bolster your confidence by just knowing them.

You are in charge

This advice applies to your computer as well as to your classroom. One reason why computers are so popular with children (young and old) is that even the most timid feel a sense of power when they use a computer, just as they do when they have possession of the remote control.

Insert one disk at a time

When you are installing a new program and the message says to insert a different disk, be sure to take out the one that's in there first.

Restart using a "warm" boot

You can restart (reboot) your computer by briefly holding down three keys together: Ctrl+Alt+Del. This method is called a "warm" boot. In Windows 95, the Task List comes up, and you can choose Shut Down right from the Task List. In Windows 3.*x,* you'll be advised about how to proceed.

Use your escape hatch

The Esc key (abbreviation for Escape) is often the escape hatch for getting you out of a command that you accidentally gave the computer. If you accidentally click the Open button in a toolbar, for example, you can press Esc to close the dialog box (you also can click the Cancel button). When you aren't certain what to do to stop a function, press Esc first; you'll be amazed at what it will get you out of.

Clean the keyboard with a damp cloth

Don't put your keyboard in the bathtub to clean it. The keyboard contains lots of little electronic circuits that need to stay dry; otherwise, they short-circuit. Even spray polish is liquid, so a damp cloth (not a wet one) can be used to clean the dirt off the keys. Clean the keys only when the computer is off; doing the cleaning while it's on sends mixed signals to the computer.

You don't have to upgrade your software

When you get a computer, you will become aware (if you aren't already) of the constant stream of software releases for the products that you already have. You may think that these upgrades will continually drain your monetary resources — but have faith. Do you upgrade your car every time a new version or model comes out? Of course not. Do you buy a new set of desks for your students each time a new design comes out? You wish! Do you buy a new dress or suit just because the styles have changed? Well, maybe.

You don't *have* to upgrade your software. In fact, the only reason why you may want to upgrade is because the software version that you are currently using doesn't do everything that you want it to do. And if you do decide to upgrade, the cost of an upgrade is usually not nearly so much as the cost of purchasing the program for the first time.

Saving and backing up your files is important

I've already told you how important it is to save your work — often. I've also identified several types of disk units that you can use to store large files outside the computer. You can use Zip-type drives as backup units to store all your hard-disk data in case one of your students gets adventuresome and does some hard-disk housecleaning for you.

Backing up individual documents in case of . . . well, just in case, is also important. I often tell my students that when I was working on my master's thesis, I had copies of the tabulated data files in four locations: at school, at the university, at home, and with me always. I wasn't taking any chances.

Unless you have unusually unwieldy documents (really large ones), you usually can store many files on one standard floppy disk and avoid the cost of buying a Zip, Jazz, or some other fancy drive. Storing your documents in more than one place means that you lose only work that you've done since the last backup.

Floppy disks are sensitive

Floppy disks are as sensitive to natural and unnatural phenomena as your skin is. Treat them gently — but don't use lotion. Avoid extremes of temperature; heat warps them, and cold freezes them. Disks also don't like magnetic fields; such fields scramble the data and give you as much gibberish on-screen as you got when you identified the wrong printer. Avoid exposing your disks to scanning devices, X-ray machines, telephones, TVs, stereos, and other areas where magnetic fields may interfere.

Floppy disks also break, and even though they are fairly resilient when sat upon, avoid doing so whenever possible. Remember that floppy disks contain files, data, and whatever that represent *hours* of work. So please don't roll them into a typewriter to label them!

You don't have to know everything

Everyone has a specialty. Yours may be third grade, chemistry, or physical education. Telling you that you need to know *everything* about computers before you get your first one is like telling your students that they need to know and understand all the words associated with your subject or grade level on the first day of school.

What you *do* need to know is where to find the information. Whether you ask a student or another teacher for help or look up information in a resource manual or on the Internet, being able to find the information is more important than trying to memorize all the information you need in the first place.

What's scarier is that the more you learn about computers, the more you realize how little you really know. That's okay. As long as one person in the class can program that VCR, the job will get done! So if one person in class knows how to use the computer, that person can share the knowledge with others.

If your computer's sick, leave the kitchen sink at home

If you're lucky enough to have a technology coordinator in your facility, you may not have to solve this issue yourself; you'll just call the tech coordinator and report the problem. Still, when breakdowns occur, you might get your computer back faster if you can transport it to the repair shop yourself.

The good news is that you don't need to take everything you have into the computer shop. Believe it or not, repair shops have plenty of cords and cables available for connecting your system. Taking in your cables and everything else is no guarantee that you'll get them back. You'll also want to check with the computer doctor to find out whether he or she wants you to carry in the monitor with the system. Repair shops usually have an extra monitor lying around, and because the monitor generally is the heaviest part of the system, leaving it at home is nice.

Oh, and be sure to ask for an estimate. That way, you'll find out whether the computer's worth fixing or whether it's time to buy a new one.

Appendix A
Techno Terms Translation

active window — the top window or the window with the colored title bar.

application — a computer program.

application menu — the menu just below the title bar.

application menu button — in Windows 95, the application icon that appears in the upper-left corner of the window and can be used to control the window; you can change the size of the window or close the window using commands on the control menu.

ASCII — American Standard Code for Information Interchange — makes it possible for computers to identify text characters.

backup copy — an extra copy in case you mess up the first one.

baud rate — how fast your modem works.

bit — abbreviation for _binary digit_.

bitmap — a type of image created by putting lots of little dots very close together.

bookmark — Web page address that you save so that you can go back to it quickly. (Pretty self-explanatory, huh?)

boot — start the computer.

bps — bits per second — usually the speed of something.

browser — a program that lets you read HTML documents and move around the Internet.

bug — computer programming error that causes all types of commotion.

button — a switch on your mouse or a square in a dialog box that accesses commands.

byte — 8 bits — or one character.

cache — a place in which the browser stores the Web pages you've called up in any given online session.

CD-ROM — compact disks for the computer that contain programs, videos, music, games, and more.

check box — a square beside dialog box options; when an *x* is in the box, the option is active.

click — pressing and releasing the primary (usually the left) mouse button.

clip art — a collection of pictures that comes with computer programs.

Clipboard — a temporary, invisible holding place for things you cut or copy. It can hold only one piece of information, graphic, or other object at a time.

command — an instruction you give your computer without saying "please."

copy — tell the computer that you like something you see so you want to leave it where it is and put it somewhere else as well.

CPU — central processing unit — the brains of the computer that performs the processing (adding, subtracting, printing, typing, and so on).

crash — big blowout of your system — sort of like an airplane that travels to earth when least expected.

Ctrl key — the key on the keyboard that you hold down while pressing another key to move around the screen, to issue a command, or to carry out some other activity.

cursor — the active location on the screen; the position where the characters you type appear; a blinking light in the shape of a square or an underscore on the screen.

cut — what to tell the computer when you like something but would rather see it somewhere else.

cyberspace — the place all information goes when you send it over the Internet.

database — a collection of related information such as electronic card files.

default — the automatic settings — the commands or formats that appear if you don't tell it something else.

deselect — click a neutral area of the screen to remove the highlighting.

desktop — the screen and everything on it.

dialog box — a window-like rectangle containing options for performing actions but no main menu.

disk — the physical medium that holds software.

disk drive — the piece of hardware, connected to the computer, that holds the disk.

DOS — stands for *disk operating system;* a system program that contains housekeeping commands so that you can make your computer do something; it interfaces with other programs so that everyone can get along.

dot-matrix — a printer that puts characters on paper by forming a series of dots.

double-click — pressing and releasing the primary mouse button quickly in rapid succession (not to be confused with clicking twice).

download — transfer from the Internet (or some other place in cyberspace) to your computer.

drag — press and hold the primary mouse button while rolling the mouse across the mousepad.

Enter key — the key you press when you want to start a new paragraph.

expansion slot — a slot in the back of your system unit covered by a silver tab (not for money!) where you can expand your system by adding more hardware.

extension — the three characters that follow the period in a filename; for example, .doc, .wps, .dbv.

favorites — a place to store the Web pages or program areas you like to visit most often — a fancy bookmark system.

fax — a copy of a document transmitted by sending digital signals from one machine to another and getting a printout all at the same time.

field — one itty-bitty piece of information in a database or on a form — or a place to grow corn.

file — a document or anything else you save on the computer.

folder — a place on the computer where you can save or store documents and other types of files.

font — a typeface.

frozen — when your insertion point, mouse pointer, and keyboard get stuck and you can't seem to get your computer to do anything.

FTP — File Transfer Protocol — a tool that makes transferring files between computers using the Internet or another online service possible.

gig — short for gigabyte — a billion bytes — which is a lot of bytes.

Gopher — a system for locating items or topics on the Internet from a series of menus. Each time you select from a menu, the system will "go for" (get it?) another menu.

grayscale — images and other objects printed in different shades of gray rather than in black and white or color (sigh!).

GUI — Graphical User Interface — a program that links icons (pictures) to programs and commands.

hard copy — something printed by using a printer.

hard disk — the disk inside your computer that stores most programs — it's hard, so it's called the hard disk.

hardware — equipment connected to your computer (no, not the koala bear you stuck on the side of the monitor).

highlight — to select text or other objects so that they appear in reverse print (white characters on a black background, for example).

home page — the first page of a document stored on the World Wide Web.

host — a computer, connected directly to the Internet, that serves files to other computers.

HTML — HyperText Markup Language — the markup language used to create Web pages.

HTTP — hypertext transfer protocol — the language used for data transmission of Web pages across the Internet.

icon — a picture that stands for a program, a folder, or a document.

insertion point — the location on-screen where the next character appears.

install — to get a program all set up and ready to go on your computer. Usually refers to getting the program form a series of floppy disks or a CD onto the hard disk so that all program features work.

Internet — an international system of computers that are all connected together.

K — the acronym for kilobyte — roughly 1,000 bytes (okay, exactly 1,024 bytes).

landscape — printing on a piece of paper sideways so it's wider and shorter. Sometimes followed by the word *orientation*.

laser printer — a high-quality printer that seals toner onto a page to form images and characters.

launch — to start a program running.

link — an invisible connection between two documents, a document and a picture, or a document and some other medium that allows the latest version of the linked object to be accessed.

macro — a set of instructions typed into the computer and saved so that you can use them again.

maximize button — in Windows 95, the button to the immediate left of the close button in the top-right corner of the window; it makes the window fill the screen.

megabyte — approximately one million bytes or 1024K.

megahertz — your computer's speed — how fast it crunches that data.

memory — the size of the storage area inside the computer that controls how much it can remember.

menu — a list of commands for accomplishing tasks or accessing dialog boxes.

merge — to take data and other information from different sources and use them to create something else; for example, you can use a database list of names to create envelopes in a word-processing program.

MHz — short for megahertz.

minimize button — in Windows 95, the button with the short heavy line on the bottom, which appears in the top-right corner of a window; it gets the window out of the way but doesn't close it.

modem — <u>mo</u>dulation/<u>dem</u>odulation — a machine for converting characters to signals and signals to characters so that they can be sent from one computer to another.

monitor — the TV-like screen connected to your computer — it may even *be* a telecision screen.

Mosaic — the first graphical browser on the Internet.

motherboard — the main circuit board inside the computer that holds the memory, connects everything together, and holds the processor.

mouse — the little helper than sits beside your computer, points for you, and rolls around on your desk to provide entertainment.

multimedia — a disk, program, or file that contains several forms of information — audio, video, graphic, text, and so on.

Netscape Navigator — currently the most popular browser on the Web — used by many online services.

network — two or more computers connected to each other in some way.

nibble — half a byte.

OCR — optical character recognition or optical character reader — software used with a scanner for getting information into the computer, or the equipment used by the postal service to read ZIP codes.

online — connected to another computer, a service provider, or the Internet.

paste — tell the computer to put something you've copied or cut at the active insertion point.

PCMCIA — stands for *Personal Computer Memory Card Interface Adapter* — it's the little credit-card size unit that fits into a special slot and makes connecting peripherals much easier.

peripheral — a piece of hardware connected to your computer but located outside the system unit.

pixel — one dot on the screen. Each character you type is made up of hundreds of pixels.

port — a built-in connection socket on your computer; used to connect the electrical cord, a printer, the monitor, or other peripheral devices such as modem, joystick, and so on.

portrait — picture-perfect shape of paper — right-side up — a page that is taller than it is wide — long and lean.

primary button — the button on the mouse that you press with your index finger or the button that gets the mouse to do something; usually the left mouse button, but can be the larger button.

program — a set of instructions, stored in the computer, that tells the computer how to do things: word processing, spreadsheets, add, subtract, and so on.

protocol — a set of rules that control how computers transmit information so that different types of hardware and software can "talk" to each other.

QWERTY — the standard typewriter keyboard; it's the six alpha characters on the left of the top row.

radio button — a small circle to the side of an option in a dialog box — when it's active, it looks like the little knobs on an old-fashioned radio. Only one radio option button in a group can be active at a time.

RAM — random access memory — the working brain capacity of your computer.

reboot — to start up your computer all over again.

record — a card in your database card file.

restore button — in Windows 95, the button that appears to the left of the close button when the window is maximized; when the window is minimized, the restore button appears on the taskbar.

ROM — short for *read only memory* and represents the instructions that enable your computer to "turn on" and work — built in at the factory so that your students can't destroy it.

sans serif — typeface with no little curlicues or "legs" on the characters.

scanner — a hardware unit that takes pictures of anything on paper so that you can use it in computer files.

screen saver — a program that causes flying toasters, fish, windows, and other objects to appear on your screen when you don't do something for several minutes; it prevents images from permanently burning into the screen.

scroll bar — the narrow areas on the right and bottom sides of a document that contain an arrow at both ends.

scroll — to get another part of a document on the screen.

SCSI — stands for *Small Computer System Interface* — pronounced "scuzzy" — and it's a type of port on your computer that makes sending and receiving data quicker — sort of "turbo charges" the system.

secondary button — the mouse button you press to access shortcut menus and perform special tasks; usually the right mouse button and sometimes the smaller button; the "other" button.

select — to highlight.

serif — typeface with curlicues or "legs" on the characters.

server — computer running a special program that can store and send out documents when they are called for (sort of like the librarian who can somehow find that book you've been searching for for ten hours!).

service provider — a company that provides an Internet connection.

shareware — programs distributed free but with a request for a small contribution if you keep them after your trial period is up.

soft copy — what you see on your screen that could be gone in an instant if Johnny bumps the switch or electrical cord.

software — programs, applications, and disks.

spreadsheet — a program that lets you enter data in rows and columns so that you can keep track of it; sort of an electronic worksheet.

submenu — a menu that appears when you choose a menu command that has a greater-than arrow at the right edge of the menu.

telecommunication — using the telephone wires to send or receive something with your computer.

TIFF — stands for *Tagged Image File Format;* one of any number of graphic file formats.

title bar — the band at the top of any window that tells you the window's name.

ToolTips — the pop-up box containing the name of a toolbar icon.

upload — to send from your computer to someone else's by using a network or modem.

video card — the circuit board that connects your monitor to your computer system unit.

window — an outlined space on your monitor that has a title bar and a border.

Windows — a DOS enhancer that makes the "big black screen" picture pretty and a whole lot easier to use.

Windows 95 — a new operating system that combines DOS and Windows into one slick program.

word wrap — a feature of word-processing programs that causes text to go to the next line when you bump into a margin.

WWW — World Wide Web — a software system running on the Internet. It consists of pages (documents), servers (computers storing pages), and browsers (programs that show you the pages).

WYSIWYG — stands for *what you see is what you get* — but usually means, well "almost."

Yahoo! — a well-known search engine on the Web and the end — Yahoo! — of the book.

Appendix B

About the CD

*H*ere's the "Free Inside" that everyone likes to see printed on the front of books and boxes. Look for delightful demos, super shareware, awesome tools for going online, and artful art guaranteed to bring a smile. Here's what you'll find tucked away on your CD-ROM:

- Grade level shareware arranged by discipline
- Fun things to explore when you have plenty of time
- Online programs to have you powered up and on your way to locating information along the superhighway
- Tools to make your teaching day easier

System Requirements

PC users need the following system requirements for using this CD:

- Windows 95 installed on your computer

  If you're running Windows 3.*x,* you will not be able to use some of the programs on the CD.

- A 486 or faster processor with *at least* 8MB of total RAM if you're running Windows 95
- At least 103MB of hard drive space available to install all the software from this CD.

  You'll need less space if you don't install every program.

- A CD-ROM drive — double-speed (2x) or faster
- A sound card with speakers
- A monitor capable of displaying at least 256 colors or grayscale
- A modem with a speed of at least 14,400 bps.

If you need more information on PC or Windows basics, check out *PCs For Dummies,* 4th Edition, by Dan Gookin; *Windows 95 For Dummies* by Andy Rathbone; or *Windows 3.11 For Dummies,* 3rd Edition, by Andy Rathbone (all published by IDG Books Worldwide, Inc.).

Installing Software

You'll find installation of all (or some) of the programs on the CD is easy and relatively painless whether you're using a PC with Windows 95 or Windows 3.1.

For Windows users, I've included the "CD Assistant." It's a master program on the CD that lets you install or run any software on the CD just by clicking selections from the CD Assistant's window.

Windows 95 users can jump right into "Getting started in Windows 95 with AutoPlay CD-ROMs." Windows 3.1 users can begin with "Getting started with Windows 3.1, or Windows 95 without AutoPlay."

Getting started in Windows 95 with AutoPlay

If you're running Windows 95, just remove the CD from the plastic inside the back cover of your book and place it in your computer's CD-ROM drive with the label up. Close the CD-ROM drive.

If you have a CD-ROM drive that uses AutoPlay, the CD Assistant starts up and takes control — and you'll see a License Agreement message in the middle of your screen. If nothing happens after a minute or so, you probably have a CD-ROM drive that can't run the CD Assistant without some help from you. Skip to the section "Getting started in Windows 3.1, or Windows 95 without AutoPlay."

If the CD Assistant has already displayed your License Agreement, read the agreement carefully and then click the Accept button to get to the CD. (If you click the Do Not Accept button, the message window closes and nothing else happens.)

The License Agreement appears only the first time you use the CD on a computer — you don't have to read the rules again unless you use the CD on a different computer.

After you click the Accept button, the CD Launcher message window opens and tells you that the interactive CD will launch after you click OK. This message appears each time you insert the CD into the CD-ROM drive to let you know the disk and drive are working properly. Go ahead and click OK — the fun is just starting!

In a few moments, your screen fills with a stack of books that list the major categories of programs contained on the CD. Simply point to a category and click. The list you see next depends on which category you select.

Getting started in Windows 3.1, or Windows 95 without AutoPlay

All Windows 3.1 users (and some Windows 95 users) need to install an icon in their Program Manager (or the Windows 95 Start menu) to run the CD Assistant. To install the icon, follow these steps:

1. **Insert the CD into your computer's CD-ROM drive.**

2. **For Windows 3.1, choose File⇨Run from the Program Manager window; for Windows 95, choose Start⇨Run.**

3. **In the Run dialog box, type** D:\SETICON.EXE

   Substitute your actual CD-ROM drive letter if it's something other than D.

4. **Click OK.**

   An icon for the CD Assistant appears in a separate program group named For Teachers in the Program Manager window of Windows 3.1 and on the Start⇨Programs menu of Windows 95.

To start the CD Assistant, open the For Teachers program group and click (or double-click) the icon.

The first time you run the program, a License Agreement appears on-screen. Read the agreement carefully and then click the Accept button to get to the CD. (If you click the Do Not Accept button, the message window closes and nothing else happens.)

The License Agreement appears only the first time you use the CD on a computer — you don't have to read the rules again unless you use the CD on a different computer.

After you click the Accept button, the CD Launcher message window opens and tells you that the interactive CD will launch after you click OK. This message appears each time you insert the CD into the CD-ROM drive to let you know the disk and drive are working properly. Go ahead and click OK!

In a few moments, your screen fills with a stack of books that list the major categories of programs contained on the CD. Simply point to a category and click. The list you see next depends on which category you select.

Restarting the CD Assistant in Windows

If you're using Windows 95 and were able to start the CD Assistant just by popping the CD into your CD-ROM drive, restart the CD by double-clicking the My Computer icon and then double-clicking the CD-ROM icon. This method works only if your CD-ROM drive automatically started the CD Assistant when you first popped the CD in your CD-ROM drive.

If you had to follow the steps in "Getting started Windows 3.1, or Windows 95 without AutoPlay," you can restart the CD Assistant by opening the For Teachers program group (Windows 95 users can find it on their Start⇨Programs menu) and double-clicking the CD Assistant icon named after this book.

Remember that you have to keep the CD in the CD-ROM drive to use the CD Assistant.

Programs for Every Kind of Instruction

Here's an overview of what you'll find in each category on the *PCs For Teachers,* Second Edition CD:

- ✔ **Elementary** contains programs designed to help you with your elementary age students.

- ✔ **English/Language Arts** includes programs to use in the middle school and high school English classroom.

- ✔ **Science & Mathematics** has programs to help math and science students in middle schools and high schools develop their skills.

- ✔ **Social Studies** includes programs to help you and your middle and high school students create timelines and maps and explore ancient civilizations.

- ✔ **Fun** comes in all types and sizes, and individual programs are listed for the Fun category.

- ✔ **Bonus Software** is sort of a *lagniappe* (something extra for nothing — like the part of this book by the same name. It's a selection of programs that we didn't have room to place in another category. You'll find programs to help you go online, more clip art, neat shareware programs, and additional demos in this category (and tools to help you get some work done, too).

Choosing a category from the main menu leads to a list of the programs contained in the category. When you click on a program name, you'll see a description of the program, special requirements for installing the program, and the program author's name and/or the name of the company that developed the program. After you read the description, you can install the software by clicking the Continue button. If you don't want to install the program, click the Cancel button to return to the previous list. From any category menu, you can get to the previous menu by clicking the Go Back arrow in the bottom-left corner of the window.

 Remember, installing the program on your hard disk takes up disk space — if your hard disk is almost full, you may want to be more selective in choosing programs to install. Check out the next section to see what's available, or click the Cancel button to return to the previous menu.

What You'll Find

This section gives you a summary of the software on this CD. Installation of each program is easy, thanks to the CD Assistant. Select the program you want to install from the list of programs available. Read the information that appears automatically — it describes how you may use the program and how to get additional information about the program. In some cases, you'll also find URLs you can use to access an individual's or a company's Web site (where you'll usually find additional programs to download). Then click the Continue button. The Assistant does the rest.

I've supplied an overview of some of the software you'll find in each category on the CD. Because we often get permission to include stuff on the CD at the last minute, be sure to check for additional gems buried within each category.

Incidentally, I encourage you to explore programs that may, at first, appear out of your subject area. While programs technically may fit into one category, you can adapt them to use in your subject area as well. For example, a vocabulary builder program that appears in the English/Language Arts category can be used to drill students on vocabulary in science or mathematics.

Elementary

In the Elementary category, look for these fascinating programs:

Program	Description
Where in the World Is Carmen Sandiego?	This demo introduces you to products from Brøderbund that invite students to become detectives as they unravel clues and trace the whereabouts of a character named Carmen who is hiding somewhere in the world.
Thinkin' Things 3 Demo	Thinkin' Things is a series of educational programs that help young children master a variety of concepts. This demo of Thinkin' Things 3 is a movie-like presentation that introduces you to some of the interactive games and characters in the Thinkin' Things series.
A Musical Tutorial	A shareware program that encourages musical study using a graphically oriented environment. Includes chords and a chord dictionary, musical games, scales, and more.
Roxie's Reading Fish	Multimedia game designed to help you teach students to read. It comes in different formats for Windows 3.1 and Windows 95.
Trudy's Time and Place House	Another demo from Edmark that introduces you to a program that helps students learn time and geography.
Children's Writing & Publishing Center	This Learning Company program provides writing activities and allows desktop publishing of documents.

English/Language Arts

If you're a secondary or middle school English teacher, you'll enjoy using these products. If you teach a different subject, why not find new ways to incorporate the programs into your subject-specific vocabulary drills and other classroom activities?

Program	Description
Adverb Practice	If you want your students to feel more comfortable identifying adverbs, try this shareware program. It gives users sentences and asks them to type in the adverbs.
Grammar Slammer	A great utility to enhance word processing programs — this program actually helps students check their grammar.

Program	Description
Spelling Frenzy	A shareware program, Spelling Frenzy conducts a spelling lesson right on the computer. The program shows a word on-screen, and the student must indicate whether the spelling is correct or incorrect.
TipTap Lite	This multimedia shareware program is designed to teach phonics and grammar, typing, and handwriting skills to students of all ages.
Vocabulary Builder English 1	This shareware program is set up to resemble a space-invasion-type game. It tests knowledge of words by ordering you to shoot at a specific object. If you defy its orders, you risk being annihilated by an assortment of high-flying, sharp-shooting objects!

Science & Mathematics

A search of the Web yields any number of math and science programs for you to use. Be sure to check out these and then go searching for more.

Program	Description
Biology Review	Like Chemistry Review, this shareware program is a basic review of high school biology. It's nothing fancy, but provides a great review sheet for students to use as they prepare for a final exam.
Chempen+	Using the Chempen shareware program, you can create chemistry diagrams to add to word processing documents and graphics applications. Special libraries enable you to do chemical calculations.
MathMedia demo 1.1	MathMedia Educational Software, Inc. (3100 Dundee Road, Suite 703, Northbrook, IL 60062; phone: 847-564-1441; fax: 847-509-1464) offers curriculum-based interactive programs with instructions so that students can learn geometry and algebra. Check their Web site at `http://www.mathmedia.com`
Unios	Unios 1.6 is a shareware program for Windows 95 designed to convert units (such as inches) to another format (such as centimeters).

(continued)

Program	Description
Virtual Reality Labs Demo	Students enter a virtual reality simulation using some of the most popular software from Virtual Reality Labs.
WINKS	A statistical data analysis and graphs program based on the award-winning SWIKSTAT program from TexaSoft. Use it to analyze business or scientific data.

Social Studies

A long list of Social Studies demos are included on the CD. You'll probably find several that you'll want to order.

Program	Description
Africa Trail	This MECC demo puts students of all ages in charge of a bike trek across Africa. It's based on a real-life 1992 trip!
Decisions, Decisions: Overview	This Tom Snyder Productions demo presents a series of group role-playing simulations, in which students take decision-making roles in dealing with complex historical situations and current issues, such as colonialism and the environment. This demo also includes information about how to use these programs in the classroom.
MayaQuest	MECC created this demo to show students how they can become high-tech explorers on a trip to the Mayan ruins.
TimeLiner 4.0	Tom Snyder Productions developed this program that students of all ages can use to print a time line for any data entered.
Label this Diagram ... USA #1	Don't know where Indiana is located? No problem! Open up this shareware program and try placing state labels next to the appropriate dots on the map.

Fun

The Fun category was a challenge to set up because so many of the programs contained in the other sections of this CD are also so much fun to use. Here you'll find loads of programs to please the young and the young at heart.

Program	Description
Earshot SFX	A sampler of 47 sounds for Windows 95 from among the 1,500 available from New Media Productions.
HyperCam	A preview edition of a program for Windows 95 from Hyperionics that captures actions on-screen and saves them to show again.
HyperStudio	Design multimedia interfaces and presentations and create links between documents. This demo version limits the size of your presentation, but is otherwise fully functional.
More than Words v. 3.0	When you want to send an online greeting card, open up this shareware program and jazz up your card by adding sound to grab the reader's attention.
Paint Shop Pro	Create, edit, draw, and manage images using this fascinating program — and you don't have to be an artist to use it!
Screen Beans ClipArt	This collection of clip art from A Bit Better Corporation (`http://www.bitbetter.com`) includes images of energetic characters engaged in all types of activities from lifting weights to thinking about life.

Bonus Software

This collection of software products contains lots of extra goodies that we didn't have room to list in the other categories.

Program	Description
Exercise & Data Files	Here's where you can find your practice files I talk about in Chapters 9 and 10 as well as some of the samples of documents you see throughout the book.
EFS Animal ClipArt v 2.0	Elfring Soft Fonts, Inc., developed this sample collection of animal clip art to introduce you to their full stash of animal images. They formatted the images for you to review and put them into .pcx format so you can easily add them to your documents and presentations.
AT&T WorldNet Service	AT&T WorldNet Service offers you offers you a direct connection to the Internet, complete with an e-mail address and a Web browser. We have three versions here so you can install AT&T WorldNet Service with Internet Explorer for Windows, Netscape Navigator for Windows 95, or Netscape Navigator for Windows 3.*x*.

(continued)

Program	Description
Bitstream Fonts	A couple of fun typestyles you can use to dress up your documents.
Chemistry Review	This shareware program for high school students provides a basic chemistry review, in a test format, of chemistry. You can open the review questions in any word processor that can open a WordPerfect document.
CleanSweep 95 demo	Quarterdeck CleanSweep 95 can save you megabytes of disk space by easily and safely removing unusued or unwanted Windows programs, system components, and duplicate files easily and safely. This demo is fully functional, but stops working after 30 days unless you register it.
Internet Coach Lite for Internet Explorer	An abbreviated try-out version of Apte's Internet Explorer teaching software that's interactive. It lets you learn more about surfing the Net, shows you what the Net looks like before you go online, and answers some common questions about surfing the Net.
Internet Coach Lite for Netscape Navigator	An abbreviated try-out version of Apte's Netscape Navigator teaching software that's interactive and lets you learn more about surfing the Net, shows you what the Net looks like before you go online, and answers some common questions about surfing the Net.
Eudora Light	An e-mail program for Windows that can be used to send and receive e-mail.
FoolProof Security for Windows 95	A security program demo from SmartStuff Software that prevents users from moving, renaming, or deleting files. Perfect for the school environment!
Grade Manager for Windows	A special shareware program designed to eliminate grade-recording nightmares. Designed for teachers by teachers to store grades for multiple classes with 50 students in each class.
HTML Assistant Pro 97	A fully functional 30-day demo version of the latest Web page authoring tool from Brooklyn North Software Works, Inc.
MicroChart for Win 95	Music teachers and band instructors will find using this program makes designing marching band drills a snap.
EFS People ClipArt	A sample of the people clip art images from Elfring Soft Fonts, Inc., formatted as .pcx files to make adding them to your documents quick and easy.

Program	Description
Roxie's ABC Fish	Multimedia game designed to help teach students their ABCs. It comes in separate formats for Windows 3.1 and Windows 95.
Roxie's Math Fish	Multimedia game designed to help teach students their numbers. It comes in separate formats for Windows 3.1 and Windows 95.
Snag It	A great product from TechSmith Corporation that lets you capture what appears on-screen (or any part of what's on the screen) and save the capture as a graphics file. A great program for helping you develop informative material about computers and computer programs as well as for storing samples of Web pages you find online.
WinZip 95	A very popular shareware file-compression utility that uses familiar Windows features. Updates and versions for Windows 3.*x* are available for registered users at `http://www.winzip.com/`.

If You've Got Problems (Of the CD Kind)

I tried my best to compile programs that work on most computers with the minimum system requirements. Alas, your computer may differ, and some programs may not work properly for some reason.

The two likeliest problems are that you don't have enough memory (RAM) for the programs you want to use, or you have other programs running that are affecting the installation or running of the program. If you get error messages such as `Not enough memory` or `Setup cannot continue`, or `Not enough hard disk space to install the program`, try one or more of these methods and then try using the software again:

✔ Turn off any anti-virus software that you have on your computer. Installers sometimes mimic virus activity and may make your computer incorrectly believe that it is being infected by a virus.

✔ Close all running programs. The more programs you're running, the less memory is available to other programs. Installers also typically update files and programs. So if you keep other programs running, installation may not work properly.

✔ Have your local computer store add more RAM to your computer. If you're a Windows 95 user, adding more memory can really help the speed of your computer and allow more programs to run at the same time.

> ✔ Check to make sure you are running the required version of Windows — some of the programs require Windows 95 while others will run on Windows 3.*x* family of products, too.

> ✔ Empty the Recycle Bin or delete programs you no longer use from your hard disk to free up some space so that you can install some of the programs on the CD.

If you get errors that stop the demos from running, you may want to try running the demos without the CD-ROM *interface*. To bypass the interface, follow these easy steps:

1. **Reboot your computer.**

2. **If you have AutoPlay, you'll need to close your CD-ROM window before proceeding.**

3. **In Windows 95, choose Start⇨Run and then type D:\ and click the Browse button; in Windows 3.1, double-click the Main group in the Program Manager, then double-click the File Manager, and click the drive name for the CD-ROM drive.**

4. **Double-click the folder for the category that contains the program you want to view.**

5. **Double-click the folder that represents the program you want to view (in some cases the folder is the company name, such as Edmark).**

6. **Double-click the filename for the program that you want to run (if there are multiple filenames, choose the filename that has an extension .exe or .com).**

If you still have trouble with installing the items from the CD, please call the IDG Books Worldwide Customer Service phone number: 800-762-2974 (outside the U.S.: 317-596-5261).

Index

• Symbols •

* (asterisk), 50, 67, 217
@ (at sign), 223, 229
^ (caret), 67
: (colon), 12, 147, 169, 229
© (copyright symbol), 187, 207
... (ellipsis), 30, 37
= (equal sign), 68
. (period), 229
+ (plus sign), 59
® (registered trademark symbol), 187, 207
/ (slash), 67, 229
~ (tilde), 44, 229

• A •

ABC News Web site, 235
acceptable-use agreements, 210
access control software, 210, 233–235, 237
"access is denied" error message, 306
accessories, 55–74, 77
  arranging, on-screen, 63–65
  locating, 71
Accessories submenu, 39–40, 60–61, 62
accounting information, 215–216
A.D.A.M. Essentials, 260
A.D.A.M.: The Inside Story, 259
Add to Favorites button, 231
Adobe Acrobat, 184
Adobe PageMaker, 182, 244
Adobe PageMill, 184
Adobe Persuasion, 181
Adobe Systems, 182, 184, 244
Advanced Automated Accounting, 243
Africa Trail, 246
Age of Exploration, 259
Alignment command, 156
alignment of text, 128–130

All Star Drill, 243
alphanumeric data, 146
Alt+F4 (Close command), 69, 85
AltaVista search engine, 236
American Heritage Talking Dictionary, 257
AntiVirus, 250
AOL (America Online), 206, 228, 242
  e-mail, 218, 222
  parental controls, 233
Appearance tab, 45
applications
  basic description of, 14
  closing, 69–70, 85–86
  creating shortcut icons for, 72–73
  launching, by clicking an icon, 26, 44, 81
  locating, 71–72
Apply button, 47
Arial font, 92
ARPAnet, 228
ASCII (American Standard Code for Information Interchange), 207, 311
Astound WebMotion, 184
AT&T WorldNet Service, 206
atlases, 257–258
audio, 263–268
  cards, 298–299
  CDs, playing, 264–265
  clips, 193
  recording, 266–268
Auto Hide option, 48
Average button, 148

• B •

Back button, 135
background color, of your desktop, 44–45
Backspace key, 122
backup systems, 309, 311
Bailey's Book House, 259

baud rates, 202
billing information, 215–216
bit, 14, 311
bits per second (bps), 202, 311
Bold button, 110
boldface font, 110, 124–125
boot (startup) procedure, 16, 304, 308, 311
Border command, 156
borders, 139, 153, 156
Borland IntraBuilder, 184
branching, 180
Bravo (Alpha), 181
Browse button, 176
browsers, 206–207, 311. *See also* Internet
    Explorer; Netscape Navigator
bulletin boards, 232
bullets, 139
bytes, definition of, 14, 311

• *C* •

Calc.exe, 72–73
Calculator, 69, 84–85
  basic description of, 60–62
  creating a shortcut icon for, 72–73
  icon, positioning, 63–64
calendars, creating, 182–183
cameras, digital, 13, 269, 294–295
Cancel button, 116, 308
capitalization, 207
*Cartopedia: The Ultimate Reference
    Atlas,* 257
cartridges, 90, 300
CD Player, 264–266
CD-ROM(s), 14, 300
  basic description of, 10, 12, 251–262, 312
  drives, 251–253, 276, 280, 297
  playing audio CDs in, 264–265
  reference sources, 254
  saving material from, 262
cell(s)
  active, 143
  addresses, 142, 143, 147
  aligning, 153
  aligning text in, 156

basic description of, 142
  entering data into, 145–148
Center align button, 110
Charting module, 106
chat rooms, 207
check boxes, 31–32
check marks, 30, 47
Children's Writing and Publishing
    Center, 244
Choices, Choices: On the Playground, 246
Cinderella, 245
citations, 234, 255
CIX (Commercial Internet Exchange), 228
Claris Home Page, 184
Classroom Clips, 258
Classroom Connect, 248
cleaning kits, 301
*Click*book, 184
clip art, 139, 185, 258, 300, 312
Clip Gallery, 185
Clipboard, 65–68, 77, 85, 124, 312
Clipboard Viewer, 65
clock, 24, 47, 60–62, 84
Close button, 27–28, 41, 69, 76, 119–120,
    131, 173
Close command, 29, 131
CNN Newsroom Global View, 256
CNN Newsroom Web site, 235
Coach's Assistant, 247
color(s)
  paper, 299
  printers, 90–91, 297
  schemes, for your desktop, 44–45
  in spreadsheets, 153, 156
  of words in the Help feature, 52
Column Width command, 152
columns, 139, 142, 151–152
command buttons, 31–32
commands (listed by name)
  Alignment command, 156
  Border command, 156
  Close command, 29, 131
  Column Width command, 152
  Copy command, 67
  Create Directory command, 83

Database Field command, 172
Delete Column command, 152
Delete Row command, 152
Empty Recycle Bin command, 71
Exit command, 29, 69, 85
Field command, 169
Hide Help command, 120, 143
Insert Column command, 152
Insert Page Break command, 153, 176
Insert Row command, 152
New command, 60, 107, 190
Object command, 176
Open command, 111, 132, 267, 268
Paste command, 68
Print command, 97–98
Row Height command, 152
Ruler command, 126
Save As command, 197
Save command, 112, 131, 137, 267
Show command, 171
Toolbar command, 56
Common Tasks button, 133
Communications module, 106, 109
Compton's Interactive Encyclopedia,
    245, 256
Compton's Web site, 235
CompuServe, 206, 228, 242
    e-mail, 218–219, 222
    parental controls, 233
computer(s)
    donated, 285–286, 296–299
    equipment, financing, 283–288
    host computers, 205, 228, 314
    labs, 106, 279–281, 287
    one-computer classrooms, 275–279
    selling, 287
    startup (boot) procedure, 16, 304,
        308, 311
    supplies, 299–301
    teaching, without a computer, 273–275
    troubleshooting, 302–307
    turning on/off, 15–18
    upgrading, 296–299
Congress, 136, 233
console, 12. *See also* system unit
Control Panel, 42–46, 77

control-menu buttons, 78–79, 80,
    82, 85, 131
copy and paste, 124
Copy button, 110
Copy command, 67
copying
    to the Clipboard, 65–68, 77, 85, 124, 312
    files, to floppy disks, 44, 113, 131, 262
    formulas, 150–151, 156
    software products, 106
copyright law, 106, 279
Corel Ventura, 7, 182
CorelWEB Data, 184
C prompt, 76, 86
Create Database dialog box, 161–162
Create Directory command, 83
Create Directory dialog box, 84
Creative Pursuits, 258
Cruncher, The, 260
C-SPAN Web site, 235
Ctrl+Alt+Del, 304, 308
Ctrl+F4 (Close command), 132
Ctrl+O (Open command), 111, 132
Ctrl+S (Save command), 131
Ctrl+V (Paste command), 68
Ctrl+W (Close command), 132
Ctrl+Z (Undo command), 68, 125
cut and paste, 65–68, 85, 124
Cut button, 68, 110
Cyber Patrol, 210, 233
CYBERsitter, 210
cyberspace, 201. *See also* Internet

database(s). *See also* Database module
    basic description of, 160–178, 312
    ground rules, 160–161
    master, 175
    saving, 162–163
Database Field command, 172
Database module, 106, 109. *See also*
        databases
    basic description of, 160–178
    entering data with, 164–166
    file extensions used in, 111

Database module button, 160
Date format, 164
Date of Birth field, 170
Decisions, Decisions, 246
default, 98
Delete Column command, 152
Delete key, 123
Delete Row command, 152
deleting. *See also* Recycle Bin
  columns, 152
  fields, 169–170
  rows, 152
  text, 123–124
DeltaPoint QuickSite, 184
Department of Defense, 228
desktop, 16–17, 19–22, 45, 71–73,
    78–79, 312
desktop publishing software, 182–183
Details button, 72
dialog boxes
  accessing tabbed pages in, 118
  basic description of, 31–32, 312
dictionaries, 257–258
dimmed
  commands, in menus, 30
  options, in dialog boxes, 31–32
directed studies, 258–261
Discovering Authors, 254
Discovery Channel School Web site, 235
disk drive(s). *See also* floppy disks;
    hard disks
  basic description of, 313
  displaying the contents of, 57
  errors, 304
  external, 292–293, 309
  icons, 82
  names of, 12
  searching for files on, 49
disk tree, 83
Display icon, 44
Display Properties dialog box, 44–46
Ditto drives, 292
document(s). *See also* files
  creating, 107, 117–118
  headers, 119–120
  lost, 305

opening, 41–42, 107, 132
opening recently used, 107, 132
setting up, 126–130
templates, 107, 114–116, 118, 133–138,
    154–158, 192–193
Documents submenu, 41–42, 44
donated computers, 285–286, 296–299
DOS (Disk Operating System), 16, 306
  basic description of, 13, 313
  enhancer, 76
dot-matrix printers, 88–89, 91
downloading files, 89, 232–233, 267, 313
drill and practice software, 243–244
drives. *See* disk drives
drop-down arrows, 31–32
Dr. Seuss' ABC, 259
Dr. T's Sing-A-Long Around the World, 259

• E •

Easy Book, 258
Easy Calc button, 148
Easy Calc dialog box, 150
Easy Calc feature, 148–150
Easy Format feature, 139
Easy Text feature, 139
Edit menu
  Copy command, 67
  Find command, 171
  Paste command, 68
Educational Resources, 248
Educational Software Institute, 248
Edustar Mathematics, 260
Electronic Bookshelf, 243
e-mail, 213, 218
  addresses, 5, 215, 222–225
  via Microsoft Network, 211–213, 218–225
  netiquette for, 207
  reading, 219–221
  writing/sending, 221–225
Empty Recycle Bin command, 71
Encarta 97, 245, 256
Encarta Schoolhouse Web site, 235
Encyclopedia Britannica CD, 256
encyclopedias, 245, 256–257

End Task button, 304
Enter key, 121
erasers, marker-board, 301
ergonomics, 281
ERR message, 151
errors, 151, 304–306
  "access is denied" message, 306
  "out of memory" message, 305
  typing, 121, 122–124
Escape key, 308
Existing Documents page tab, 107, 110, 132
Exit command, 29, 69, 85
Explorer, 39–40, 58–60, 72, 77
Exploring Modern Art, 260

• *F* •

Family PC, 249
favorites, 231, 313
fax
  drivers, 98, 99
  modems, 98–99, 202–204, 296, 298
field(s)
  basic description of, 160
  adding, 169–170
  defining, 161–162
  entering data into, 164–166
  formats, 164
  moving, 166–168
  removing, 169–170
  renaming, 169
  sizing, 168
Field command, 169
file(s). *See also* documents; filenames
  definition of, 313
  downloading, 89, 232–233, 267, 313
  saving, general importance of, 309
  types, identifying/displaying, 72
File Manager, 77, 81–84
File menu
  Close command, 29, 131
  Create Directory command, 83
  Empty Recycle Bin command, 71
  Exit command, 29, 69, 85
  New command, 60, 107, 190
  Open command, 111, 132, 267, 268

  Print command, 97–98
  Save As command, 197
  Save command, 112, 131, 137, 267
filename(s)
  extensions, 44, 71, 77, 111, 197, 313
  rules for, 44, 76
Find command, 48–50, 171
Find dialog box, 49, 171
Find Now button, 49
finding
  files/folders, with the Find feature, 48–50
  information, with Microsoft Network, 48, 50
  program files, 71–72
  Web pages using search engines, 236
Finish button, 116
First Connections: The Golden Book Encyclopedia, 256
floppy disk(s), 14, 276, 300
  drives, 10, 12, 297
  errors, 304
  protecting, 309
  saving files on, 44, 113, 131, 262
folders
  active, 59
  creating, 59–60, 83–84, 112
  definition of, 313
  displaying the contents of, 57, 83
  master, 105
  opening, 57, 83
  student, 113
fonts, 91–94, 98, 124–126, 136
  scalable, 122
  size, 93–94, 110, 125–126
  in spreadsheets, 153
Fonts folder, 94
Footnotes feature, 139
foreign-language study, 157, 243
Form View, 163–164, 164–170
Form Design View, 163–164, 166, 169, 170, 176
Format Cells dialog box, 156
Format menu
  Alignment command, 156
  Border command, 156
  Column Width command, 152

Format menu *(continued)*
  Field command, 169
  Insert Page Break command, 176
  Number command, 153
  Row Height command, 152
FormBuster, 247
forms, 166–168
formula bar, 143, 145
formulas, 146, 148–151, 156
forums, 230–232
Fractions format, 164
frames, spreadsheet, 142
FreeHand, 181
FTP (File Transfer Protocol), 229, 313
functions, 146, 150–151
fund-raising, 283–288

• G •

General format, 164
gigabyte, 15, 314
Global Schoolhouse Web site, 235
Grade Book TaskWizard, 154–155
Grade Busters: Making the Grade, 247
Grade Machine, 247
Grammar Computerized, 243
grammar practice, 157, 243, 259
Grammar Rock, 259
grant proposals, 284–285
graphics
  clip art, 140, 185, 258, 300, 312
  photographs, 193, 258, 300
  in presentations, 193
  scanning, 13, 290–291, 317
  software, 106, 258
  wallpaper, 44–45
  Works and, 184–187
Great Literature Plus, 256
Grolier's Multimedia Encyclopedia, 245, 256
GUI (Graphical User Interface), 20, 77, 314
Guinness Multimedia Disc of Records, 256

• H •

handouts, 180
hard disks
  available space on, 70, 113, 131
  basic description of, 11, 314
  installing bigger, 297
hardware
  basic description of, 10–13, 314
  recommended, 290–296
Harvard Graphics, 181
headers, 119–120, 140
help, 119–120, 143, 160, 302–310
  basic description of, 50–52
  hiding, 120, 143
  for installing new fonts, 94
Help dialog box, 51–52
Help menu, 120, 143
Helvetica font, 92
Her Heritage, 260
hiding
  Help command, 120, 143
  the taskbar, 48
highlighting text, 66–67, 124, 314
History of the World, 256
HomePage Publisher, 184
HomePage Wizard, 184
homework assignments, typing, 136
host computers, 205, 228, 314
Hot Bot search engine, 236
hot keys, 30, 31, 37. *See also* keyboard
  shortcuts
HotTopics Web site, 235
HTML (HyperText Markup Language),
  197, 314
HTTP (Hypertext Transfer Protocol),
  229, 314
HyerCam, 270
HyperStudio, 245, 258, 270

• *I* •

I-beam pointer, 62–63, 66, 119, 122, 123, 126
IBM
  clones, 9–10
  Web site, 250
icons, 77, 78–79, 80–81
  basic description of, 21, 314
  creating, 72–73
  group, in Windows 3.*x,* 41
  launching programs by clicking, 26, 44, 81
  used in this book, 4–5
IDG Books Worldwide
  e-mail address, 5
  Web site, 5
IEP Writer Supreme, 247
images
  clip art, 140, 185, 258, 300, 312
  photographs, 193, 258, 300
  in presentations, 193
  scanning, 13, 290–291, 317
  software, 106, 258
  wallpaper, 44–45
  Works and, 184–187
In My Own Voice: Multicultural Poets on Identity, 261
indents, 126–128
InFocus, 296
InfoTrac, 254
ink markers, 300
inkjet printers, 88–92
input devices, 10, 12
Insert Column command, 152
Insert Field dialog box, 169, 172–173
Insert menu
  Database Field command, 172
  Delete Column command, 152
  Delete Row command, 152
  Insert Column command, 152
  Insert Page Break command, 153
  Insert Row command, 152
  Object command, 176

Insert Object dialog box, 176
Insert Page Break command, 153, 176
Insert Row command, 152
Insert Symbol button, 187
insertion point, 62, 66, 119, 314
installing
  fonts, 94
  hard drives, 297
  Microsoft Network software, 212–216
  printers, 89, 95–97
  software, with the Run feature, 52–53
  use of the term, 314
integrated programs, 105
interactive software, 246
International Society for Technology, 249
Internet, 21, 22, 314. *See also* World Wide Web
  access control software for, 210, 233–235, 237
  bulletin boards, 232
  connecting to, 201–210
  history of, 227–228
  netiquette, 207
  newsgroups, 232
  surfing, 227–238
  time spent on, organizing, 208–210, 277–278
Internet Explorer, 207, 210, 230
Internet Protocol (IP), 228
Internet Society, 228
InterNIC, 228
invitations, 136
IP. *See* Internet Protocol
ISPs (Internet Service Providers), 228. *See also* online services
italic font, 110, 124–125

• *J* •

Jazz drives, 292, 309
Julliard Music Adventure, 261
justification, of text, 129

• K •

keyboard(s). *See also* keyboard shortcuts
  basic description of, 11
  cleaning, 308
  freezing up, 304
  numeric keypad, 11
keyboard shortcuts. *See also* hot keys
  basic description of, 32–33
  Alt+F4 (Close command), 69, 85
  Ctrl+Alt+Del (Reboot command), 304, 308
  Ctrl+F4 (Close command), 132
  Ctrl+O (Open command), 111, 132
  Ctrl+S (Save command), 131
  Ctrl+V (Paste command), 68
  Ctrl+W (Close command), 132
  Ctrl+Z (Undo command), 68, 125
  listing of, in menus, 30
  in Windows 3.x, 77
keyboarding software, 243
KidPix Studio, 258
Kids Works Deluxe, 258
kilobytes, 14, 314
koala pads, 13

• L •

Labels feature, 140
languages, foreign, 157, 243
Laser Learning Technologies, 249
laser printers, 88, 90–92, 297, 315
launching programs
  by clicking an icon, 26–27, 44, 81
  with the Programs submenu, 38–41
  with the Run feature, 52
  in Windows 3.x, 81
LCD (liquid crystal display) panels, 277, 280, 290, 296
Learning and Leading with Technology, 249
Learning Company, 243, 245, 256, 259
Left align button, 110
Let's Go, 259
Letterhead TaskWizard, 133–137
letterwriting, 133–137, 172–175
Library of Congress Web site, 235

licenses, 106, 255
List View, 163–166, 169–171
LitePro, 296
Living Books, 259
Lookup Reference feature, 139
Lotus, 184, 244
  Freelance, 181

• M •

Macintosh, 233
Macmillan Dictionary for Children, 257
Magic School Bus Explores the Human Body, The, 259
Magic School Bus Explores the Solar System, The, 259
Magill's Survey of Science, 254
MailCity Web site, 224
Main group icon, 80, 81
management software, 246–248
margin settings, 62
Maris Multimedia, 261
marker boards, 300–301
MasterPhotos, 258
Mavis Beacon Teaches Typing, 243
Maximize button, 76, 78–79, 80, 82, 119, 315
MayaQuest, 246
McAfee Web site, 250
MECC, 243–244, 246, 261
Media Player, 268–269
megabytes, 15, 315
megahertz, 15, 315
memory. *See also* RAM (random-access memory)
  adding, 296–297
  basic description of, 315
  housing of, in the system unit, 11
  out of memory errors, 305
  ROM (read-only memory), 14, 15, 317
menu(s)
  bar, 27, 58, 77–79, 82, 109, 119
  basic description of, 29–31, 315
  shortcut, displaying, 25–26
  submenus (cascading menus), 30, 37, 39–41

merging data, 172–174
Merriam-Webster's Dictionary for Kids, 257
MetaCrawler search engine, 236
Micromedia, 247
microphones, 13, 295
microprocessors, 10–12
Microsoft Bookshelf, 256
Microsoft Draw, 106
Microsoft Exchange, 219–220
Microsoft FrontPage, 97, 184
Microsoft Multimedia Musicians, 261
Microsoft Publisher, 182–183, 194–196
Microsoft Web site, 235
Microsoft Works, 3, 72
  basic description of, 103–116
  Charting module, 106
  Communications module, 106, 109
  Database module, 106, 109, 111, 160–178
  graphics and, 184–187
  publications and, 194–197
  Spreadsheet module, 106, 109, 111, 141–158
  Word Processor module, 105, 111, 117–140, 172–175
Microsystems Software, 210
Mindscape, 257
Minimize button, 26–28, 76, 78–79, 80, 82, 119, 315
Misty City Software, 247
mnemonic characters, 31. *See also* hot keys
modems, 21, 276–277, 280
  basic description of, 201–205, 315
  fax, 98–99, 202–204, 296, 298
  speeds, 202–203
monitors, 10, 12, 15–16, 298, 304, 315. *See also* screens
motherboard, 298, 315
mouse, 143, 307, 316
  basic description of, 11–12
  I-beam pointer, 62–63, 66, 119, 122, 123, 126
  tips for using, 22–26
MSN (Microsoft Network), 21, 36–37, 206, 242

basic description of, 211–226
forums, 230–232
locating information on, 48, 50
signing on to, 216–218
software, installing, 212–216
MSWorks.exe, 72
multimedia, 245, 263–270, 316. *See also* graphics; sound; video
music, 263–267. *See also* sound
My Briefcase, 21
My Computer, 21, 24–25, 55–60, 72
Myths and Legends of Ancient Greece, The, 261

• N •

narration, 263–267
National Computer Security Association Web site, 250
National Geographic Society, 235, 257, 261
National Geographic Web site, 235
National Science Foundation, 228
navigation buttons, 109, 110, 119
NBC News Web site, 235
Net Nanny, 210
NETCOMplete, 184
netiquette, 207
NetLauncher browser, 207
NetObjects Fusion, 184
Netscape Navigator, 207, 230, 316
Network Neighborhood, 21–22
networks, 21–22, 48, 316
New command, 60, 107, 190
New Entry dialog box, 223
NewsBank, 254
newsgroups, 232
newsletters, 136, 194–196
Next button, 116, 134
NLQ (near letter quality) mode, 88
"nonsystem disk" error, 304
Nordic, 248
Norton AntiVirus, 250
Notepad, 84
Notes Pages view, 180
Now What Software, 257
nudge buttons, 32. *See also* spin buttons

Number Munchers, 243
numeric data, 11, 146, 164
numeric keypad, 11

• *O* •

Object command, 176
OCR (optical character recognition), 292, 316
Office 97 (Microsoft), 36–37, 219
OmniForm, 184
on/off button, 15
online services, 205–207. *See also* MSN (Microsoft Network)
  America Online (AOL), 206, 218, 222, 228, 233, 242
  CompuServe, 206, 218–219, 222, 228, 233, 242
  Prodigy, 206, 242
Open a Document Not Listed Here button, 132
Open command, 111, 132, 267, 268
Open dialog box, 110–111, 132, 267
Open text box, 52
Opening Night, 261
oral presentations, 157
Organizer (Lotus), 244
OSHA (Occupational Safety and Health Administration), 281
"out of memory" errors, 305
Outline view, 180–181
output devices, 10, 12
overhead transparencies, 92

• *P* •

page breaks, 153
PageWizard Assistants, 194–196
paper, computer, 88, 90–91, 299, 301
paragraphs, 121, 127–130
parents
  acceptable-use agreements and, 210
  access control software for, 210, 233–235, 237
  notes to, regarding use of online services, 236

passwords, 113, 210, 213–214, 216–217
Paste button, 110
Paste command, 68
pasting, 65–68
PC. *See* personal computer
PC Magazine, 234, 249
PC World, 249
PCMCIA cards, 201–203, 295–296, 316
Pentium processors, 12. *See also* processors
personal computer (PC), 1–2
phone lines, 204–205
photographs, 193, 258, 300
Picture Atlas of the World, 257
piracy, 106
plagiarism, 234, 255
Play It by Ear, 243
Plug-and-Play, 96, 204
Plus! for Kids (Microsoft), 210
Portfolio Assessment Kit, 247
portfolios, 175–177, 247
Postal Service (United States), 211, 292
PosterWorks, 183
power strips, 16, 276
powering down, 15–18. *See also* shutting down
powering up, 15–18
PowerPoint, 180–182, 190–193
Prehistoria, 261
presentation software, 179–182, 185, 188–193, 244
Presidents: A Picture History of Our Nation, The, 261
Print button, 110
Print command, 97–98
Print dialog box, 97, 98–99, 109
Print Preview button, 110, 174
Print Shop, 183, 244
printers, 42, 276. *See also* printing
  basic description of, 11–12, 87–100
  color, 90–91, 297
  dot-matrix printers, 88–89, 91
  drivers, 89, 96–97, 98
  inkjet printers, 88–92
  installing, 89, 95–97
  laser printers, 88, 90–92, 297, 315

problems with, 306–307
toner cartridges, 90, 300
using fax machines as, 98–99
printing. *See also* printers
basic description of, 87–100
merged documents, 174
on overhead transparencies, 92
spreadsheets, 153
processors, 10–12
Prodigy, 206, 242
productivity software, 244–245, 258
Program Manager, 17, 41, 76, 80–81, 86
programs
closing, 69–70, 85–86
creating shortcut icons for, 72–73
definition of, 316
launching, by clicking an icon, 26, 44, 81
locating, 71–72
Programs submenu, 38–39, 41–42, 58
progress charts, 157
Pronunciation Tutor, 243
proofreading, 139
publishing, with Microsoft Publisher, 194–195

• Q •

Quark Xpress, 183
QUICKDrive, 292–293
Quicken, 244

• R •

radio buttons, 31–32, 317
RAM (random-access memory), 130, 180, 274, 298, 305. *See also* memory
basic description of, 14–15, 317
freeing up, 43
launching programs and, 41, 43
ranges, 147
Rated-PG, 210
Reader Rabbit Interactive Reading Journey, 243, 259
rebooting, 304, 308, 317
records, 160, 163, 165–166, 170–171, 317

Recycle Bin, 21, 70–71, 76, 305–306
RedShift, 261
Reference Dictionaries Web site, 235
reference sources, 235, 245, 254, 256–257
replace mode, 67
reports, typing, 136
Research Paper Writer, 261
Reset button, 304
Restore button, 28, 29, 71, 119, 317
résumés, 136
Right align button, 110
ROM (read-only memory), 14, 15, 317
Rosetta Stone, The, 261
Row Height command, 152
rows, 142, 151–152
Ruler command, 126
rulers, 62–63, 126–138
Run dialog box, 52–53
Run feature, 37, 52–53

• S •

Sammy's Science House, 260
San Diego State University, 236
Save As command, 197
Save As dialog box, 112–113, 131, 197
Save As Template dialog box, 137, 156
Save button, 131, 137, 156, 162
Save command, 112, 131, 137, 267
Save dialog box, 109, 267
saving
changes, when exiting an application, 70
documents in HTML format, 197
documents in Microsoft Works, 112–113, 130–132, 137–138
files, general importance of, 309
files on floppy disks, 44, 113, 131, 262
letterhead, 137–138
material from CD-ROMs, 262
publications, 195
sound files, 267
spreadsheets, 148
templates, 137–138, 156
scanners, 13, 290–291, 317
Schedule Wizard, 114

schedules, 208–210, 277–278
Scholastic Network Web site, 284
Scholastic New Media, 244, 259
School Library Journal, 249
Schools Online Web site, 235
Science for Kids, 260
screen(s). *See also* monitors
  LCD (liquid crystal display) panels,
     277, 280, 290, 296
  savers, 44–46, 317
  touch screens, 291
Screen Saver tab, 45
ScreenTips, 83
scripts, 136
scroll bars, 58, 82, 83, 119, 317
search engines, 236
seating charts, 157
security, 113. *See also* passwords
Send button, 224
Serialized format, 164
servers, 228, 317
Settings submenu, 37–38, 42–48
setup programs, running, 53
shading, 139, 153
Shakespeare on Disk, 245
shortcut menus, displaying, 25–26
shortcuts. *See* keyboard shortcuts
Show command, 171
shutting down, 17–18, 37, 53, 308
Sign Up button, 214
SimAnt, 246
SimCity 2000, 246
SimFarm, 246
SimLife, 246
simulation software, 246
SIRS Government Reports, 254
site licenses, 255
size handles, 168
Slide Shop, 244
Slide Sorter view, 180–181
Slide view, 180–181
*Small Blue Planet: Real Picture World
    Atlas,* 257
Smart Computing, 249
Softkey, 257

software
  application, 14
  basic description of, 13–15, 318
  buying tips, 241–242
  interactive, 246
  licenses, 106, 255
  management programs, 246–247
  multimedia, 245
  operating system, 13
  productivity, 244–245
  recommended, 241–250
  registering, 106
  skill-building, 243–244
  suites, 105
  upgrades, 298, 308–309
Solid Oak Software, 210
sound, 263–268
  cards, 298–299
  clips, 193
  playing audio CDs, 264–265
  recording, 266–268
Sound Recorder, 265–267
speakers, 13, 276, 295
special effects, 193
Speed Reader, 244
spell checkers, 125
spin buttons, 31–32, 45
SportsPro, 247
spreadsheet(s). *See also*
    Spreadsheet module
  definition of, 318
  grade book, 145–148
  navigating, 144
  printing, 153
Spreadsheet button, 142
Spreadsheet module, 106, 109. *See also*
    spreadsheets
  basic description of, 141–158
  extensions used in, 111
Spyglass, 210
Start button, 21, 35, 36
Start menu
  basic description of, 35–38
  features, 38–54
startup (boot) procedure, 16, 304, 308

status bar, 58–59, 82, 83, 163
  basic description of, 27
  disk capacity display on, 57
storage devices, 10, 12
Street Atlas USA, 257
study guides, 157
submenus, 30, 37, 39–41
Suite Manager, 105
suites, 105
Sunburst, 258, 261
Super Munchers, 244
Super School Software, 247
SurfWatch, 210
Symantec Web site, 250
system unit
  basic description of, 11–13
  turning on, 15–16

• T •

Tab key, 36
Table feature, 139
tabs, 126–127
tag days, 286
Task Launcher, 103, 114–118, 132–133,
    137, 197
  Existing Documents page tab,
    107, 110, 132
  TaskWizards page tab, 107–108,
    114–116, 118, 133, 137–138
  Works Tools page tab, 107, 118, 142, 160
Task Launcher dialog box, 115–116
Task List, 304, 308
taskbar, 24–26, 76
  basic description of, 21
  hiding, 48
  options, 42, 46–48, 64
Taskbar Properties dialog box, 47–48
TaskWizards page tab, 107–108, 114–116,
    118, 133, 137–138
Teacher's Helper Plus, 247
Technological Horizons in Education, 249
Technology & Learning, 249
technology coordinators, 278

telephone lines, 204–205
templates, 107, 114–116, 118, 133–138,
    154–158, 192–193
text. *See also* fonts
  aligning, 128–130, 156
  deleting, 123–124
  inserting, 122–123
  selecting, 66–67, 124, 314
text boxes, 31–32
text format, 164
T.H.E. Journal, 249
Thesaurus feature, 139
Thinkin Things, 245, 260
tiling windows, 64–65
time displays, 24. *See also* clock
Time format, 164
TimeLiner, 244, 258
Times font, 92, 93
title bar, 26–28, 58–59, 76, 78–80,
    82, 119, 318
toggling, 47, 125
toner cartridges, 90, 300
Toolbar command, 56
toolbars, 29, 52, 58, 143, 163
  basic description of, 27
  displaying, 56
  in Microsoft Works, 105, 109–110,
    119, 124
  in Windows 3.*x,* 77, 82–83
  in WordPad, 62–63
Tools menu, 139
ToolTips, 57, 83, 110, 137, 318
touch screens, 291
tower unit, 12–13
trackballs, 13
transparencies, 92, 399–300
treasure hunts, 48
troubleshooting, 302–307
Trudy's Time and Place House, 245
TurboTax, 245
turning off the system, 17–18
turning on the system, 15–16
typing, 121

• U •

underlining, 30, 37, 124–125
Undo command, 68–69, 77, 125
Up One Level button, 112
USA Today, 207, 224, 248
Use Database dialog box, 172
User Defined Templates button, 137–138

• V •

versions
  of Microsoft Windows, 77
  of Microsoft Works, 103–104
video(s)
  cards, 318
  clips, 193, 260
  hardware, 293–295
  recording, 269
  viewing, 267–269
View menu, 27, 83
  Ruler command, 126
  Toolbar command, 56
Virtual Reality, 247
viruses, 113, 250, 262
VirusScan, 250
Visions, 247
Visual Planner, 247
voucher systems, 209, 277

• W •

wallpaper, 44–45
warm boots, 308
Way Things Work, The, 257
Web-authoring software, 183–184
Web browsers. *See* browsers
Web sites. *See also* Web sites (listed by
    name); World Wide Web
  creating your own, 183–184
  downloading printer drivers from, 89
  HTML (HyperText Markup Language)
    and, 197, 314
  locating useful, 236
  top educational, 235

Web sites (listed by name)
  ABC News Web site, 235
  CNN Newsroom Web site, 235
  Compton's Web site, 235
  C-SPAN Web site, 235
  Discovery Channel School Web site, 235
  Encarta Schoolhouse Web site, 235
  Global Schoolhouse Web site, 235
  HotTopics Web site, 235
  Library of Congress Web site, 235
  MailCity Web site, 224
  McAfee Web site, 250
  Microsoft Web site, 235
  National Computer Security Association
      Web site, 250
  National Geographic Web site, 235
  NBC News Web site, 235
  Reference Dictionaries Web site, 235
  Scholastic Network Web site, 284
  Schools Online Web site, 235
  Symantec Web site, 250
  White House Web site, 235
WebBase, 184
WebPrinter, 184
WebQuest, 236
WebSeeker, 184
WebSite Professional, 184
WebWhacker, 184, 233
Wentworth Worldwide Media, 248
Where in the USA Is Carmen Sandiego?, 261
*Where in the World Is Carmen
    Sandiego?,* 246
*Where in the World Is Carmen
    Sandiego? Jr.,* 260
White House Web site, 235
wildcards, 50
window(s)
  borders, 27–29, 78–79
  closing, 26, 27–29, 69–70
  definition of, 318
  manipulating, 28
  maximizing, 28–29
  minimizing, 28
  moving, 28
  opening, 26–27

restoring, 28
sizing, 28
tiling, 64–65
viewing multiple, 63–64
Windows 3.0, 77
Windows 3.1, 77
Windows 3.11, 77
Windows 3.*x*
  accessories, 84–85
  basic description of, 75–86
  classification of, as an operating
    system, 13
  exiting, 86
  group icons in, 41
  opening screen, 78–79
  retrieving deleted files in, 306
  ten distinctive features of, 76
Windows 95
  basic description of, 19–34, 318
  classification of, as an operating
    system, 13
  exiting, 17–18, 53
  launching, 16–17
  Microsoft Works and, 103–104
  multimedia and, 263–270
  Plug-and-Play, 96, 204
  upgrading to, 298
  Windows 3.*x* features that are integrated
    with, 76–77
Windows NT, 77
wizards, 142, 183
  basic description of, 107, 115–116
  Grade Book TaskWizard, 154–155
  HomePage Wizard, 184
  for installing printers, 97
  Letterhead TaskWizard, 133–137

Schedule Wizard, 114
  Tests TaskWizard, 138–139
WordArt, 106, 139, 187–188
Word Attack, 244, 260
Word for Windows (Microsoft), 184
WordPad, 62–64, 66, 68–70, 84, 98–99
WordPerfect, 184
Word Processor module, 105, 172–175
  basic description of, 117–140
  document setup with, 126–130
  file extensions used in, 111
WordSearch Deluxe, 248
word wrap, 121, 156, 318
Works (Microsoft). *See* Microsoft Works
Works Tools page tab, 107, 118, 142, 160
World Book Encyclopedia, 257
World Book Information Finder, 254
World Book Multimedia Encyclopedia, 245
World Wide Web. *See also* Internet; Web
  browsers; Web sites
  access control software for, 210,
    233–235, 237
  basic description of, 318
  citations to information resources on,
    234, 255
  posting documents to, 196–197
  using search engines to locate material
    on, 236
WYSIWYG (what you see is what you get),
  130, 319

• Z •

Zip drives, 292, 309
zoom control button, 119, 163

AT&T WorldNet℠ Service

A World of Possibilities...

Thank you for selecting AT&T WorldNet Service — it's the Internet as only AT&T can bring it to you. With AT&T WorldNet Service, a world of infinite possibilities is now within your reach. Research virtually any subject. Stay abreast of current events. Participate in online newsgroups. Purchase merchandise from leading retailers. Send and receive electronic mail.

AT&T WorldNet Service is rapidly becoming the preferred way of accessing the Internet. It was recently awarded one of the most highly coveted awards in the computer industry, *PC Computing*'s 1996 MVP Award for Best Internet Service Provider. Now, more than ever, it's the best way to stay in touch with the people, ideas, and information that are important to you.

You need a computer with a mouse, a modem, a phone line, and the enclosed software. That's all. We've taken care of the rest.

If You Can Point and Click, You're There

With AT&T WorldNet Service, finding the information you want on the Internet is easier than you ever imagined it could be. You can surf the Net within minutes. And find almost anything you want to know — from the weather in Paris, Texas — to the cost of a ticket to Paris, France. You're just a point and click away. It's that easy.

AT&T WorldNet Service features specially customized industry-leading browsers integrated with advanced Internet directories and search engines. The result is an Internet service that sets a new standard for ease of use — virtually everywhere you want to go is a point and click away, making it a snap to navigate the Internet.

When you go online with AT&T WorldNet Service, you'll benefit from being connected to the Internet by the world leader in networking. We offer you fast access of up to 28.8 Kbps in more than 215 cities throughout the U.S. that will make going online as easy as picking up your phone.

Online Help and Advice
24 Hours a Day, 7 Days a Week

Before you begin exploring the Internet, you may want to take a moment to check two useful sources of information.

If you're new to the Internet, from the AT&T WorldNet Service home page at www.worldnet.att.net, click on the Net Tutorial hyperlink for a quick explanation of unfamiliar terms and useful advice about exploring the Internet.

Another useful source of information is the HELP icon. The area contains pertinent, time saving, information-intensive reference tips, and topics such as Accounts & Billing, Trouble Reporting, Downloads & Upgrades, Security Tips, Network Hot Spots, Newsgroups, Special Announcements, etc.

Whether online or off-line, 24 hours a day, seven days a week, we will provide World Class technical expertise and fast, reliable responses to your questions. To reach AT&T WorldNet Customer Care, call **1-800-400-1447**.

Nothing is more important to us than making sure that your Internet experience is a truly enriching and satisfying one.

Safeguard Your Online Purchases

AT&T WorldNet Service is committed to making the Internet a safe and convenient way to transact business. By registering and continuing to charge your AT&T WorldNet Service to your AT&T Universal Card, you'll enjoy peace of mind whenever you shop the Internet. Should your account number be compromised on the Net, you won't be liable for any online transactions charged to your AT&T Universal Card by a person who is not an authorized user.*

*Today, cardmembers may be liable for the first $50 of charges made by a person who is not an authorized user, which will not be imposed under this program as long as the cardmember notifies AT&T Universal Card of the loss within 24 hours and otherwise complies with the Cardmember Agreement. Refer to Cardmember Agreement for definition of authorized user.

Minimum System Requirements

IBM-Compatible Personal Computer Users:
- IBM-compatible personal computer with 486SX or higher processor
- 8MB of RAM (or more for better performance)
- 15–36MB of available hard disk space to install software, depending on platform
  (14–21MB to use service after installation, depending on platform)
- Graphics system capable of displaying 256 colors
- 14,400 bps modem connected to an outside phone line and not a LAN or ISDN line
- Microsoft Windows 3.1x or Windows 95

Macintosh Users:
- Macintosh 68030 or higher (including 68LC0X0 models and all Power Macintosh models)
- System 7.5.3 Revision 2 or higher for PCI Power Macintosh models: System 7.1 or higher for all 680X0 and non-PCI Power Macintosh models
- Mac TCP 2.0.6 or Open Transport 1.1 or higher

- 8MB of RAM (minimum) with Virtual Memory turned on or RAM Doubler; 16MB recommended for Power Macintosh users
- 12MB of available hard disk space (15MB recommended)
- 14,400 bps modem connected to an outside phone line and not a LAN or ISDN line
- Color or 256 gray-scale monitor
- Apple Guide 1.2 or higher (if you want to view online help)

If you are uncertain of the configuration of your Macintosh computer, consult your Macintosh User's guide or call Apple at 1-800-767-2775.

Installation Tips and Instructions

- If you have other Web browsers or online software, please consider uninstalling them according to the vendor's instructions.
- If you are installing AT&T WorldNet Service on a computer with Local Area Networking, please contact your LAN administrator for setup instructions.
- At the end of installation, you may be asked to restart your computer. Don't attempt the registration process until you have done so.

IBM-compatible PC users:
- Insert the CD-ROM into the CD-ROM drive on your computer.
- Select *File/Run* (for Windows 3.1x) or *Start/Run* (for Windows 95 if setup did not start automatically).
- Type *D:\setup.exe* (or change the "D" if your CD-ROM is another drive).
- Click *OK*.
- Follow the onscreen instructions to install and register.

Macintosh users:
- Disable all extensions except Apple CD-ROM and Foreign Files Access extensions.
- Restart Computer.
- Insert the CD-ROM into the CD-ROM drive on your computer.
- Double-click the *Install AT&T WorldNet Service* icon.
- Follow the onscreen instructions to install. (Upon restarting your Macintosh, AT&T WorldNet Service Account Setup automatically starts.)
- Follow the onscreen instructions to register.

Registering with AT&T WorldNet Service

After you have connected with AT&T WorldNet online registration service, you will be presented with a series of screens that confirm billing information and prompt you for additional account set-up data.

The following is a list of registration tips and comments that will help you during the registration process.

I. Use one of the following registration codes, which can also be found in Appendix B of *PCs For Teachers,* 2nd Edition. Use L5SQIM631 if you are an AT&T long-distance residential customer or L5SQIM632 if you use another long-distance phone company.
II. During registration, you will need to supply your name, address, and valid credit card number, and choose an account information security word, e-mail name, and e-mail password. You will also be requested to select your preferred price plan at this time. (We advise that you use all lowercase letters when assigning an e-mail ID and security code, since they are easier to remember.)
III. If you make a mistake and exit or get disconnected during the registration process prematurely, simply click on "Create New Account." Do not click on "Edit Existing Account."
IV. When choosing your local access telephone number, you will be given several options. Please choose the one nearest to you. Please note that calling a number within your area does not guarantee that the call is free.

Connecting to AT&T WorldNet Service

When you have finished installing and registering with AT&T WorldNet Service, you are ready to access the Internet. Make sure your modem and phone line are available before attempting to connect to the service.

For Windows 95 users:
- Double-click on the **Connect to AT&T WorldNet Service** icon on your desktop.
  OR
- Select **Start, Programs, AT&T WorldNet Software, Connect to AT&T WorldNet Service.**

For Windows 3.x users:
- Double-click on the **Connect to AT&T WorldNet Service** icon located in the AT&T WorldNet Service group.

For Macintosh users:
- Double-click on the **AT&T WorldNet Service** icon in the AT&T WorldNet Service folder.

Choose the Plan That's Right for You

The Internet is for everyone, whether at home or at work. In addition to making the time you spend online productive and fun, we're also committed to making it affordable. Choose one of two price plans: unlimited usage access or hourly usage access. The latest pricing information can be obtained during online registration. No matter which plan you use, we're confident that after you take advantage of everything AT&T WorldNet Service has to offer, you'll wonder how you got along without it.

Explore our AT&T WorldNet Service site at http://www.att.com/worldnet.

Order Center: **(800) 762-2974** *(8 a.m.–6 p.m., EST, weekdays)*

7/29/96

Quantity	ISBN	Title	Price	Total

Shipping & Handling Charges

	Description	First book	Each additional book	Total
Domestic	Normal	$4.50	$1.50	$
	Two Day Air	$8.50	$2.50	$
	Overnight	$18.00	$3.00	$
International	Surface	$8.00	$8.00	$
	Airmail	$16.00	$16.00	$
	DHL Air	$17.00	$17.00	$

*For large quantities call for shipping & handling charges.
**Prices are subject to change without notice.

Ship to:

Name _____

Company _____

Address _____

City/State/Zip _____

Daytime Phone _____

Payment: □ Check to IDG Books Worldwide (US Funds Only)

       □ VISA   □ MasterCard   □ American Express

Card # _____ Expires _____

Signature _____

Subtotal _____

CA residents add
applicable sales tax _____

IN, MA, and MD
residents add
5% sales tax _____

IL residents add
6.25% sales tax _____

RI residents add
7% sales tax _____

TX residents add
8.25% sales tax _____

Shipping _____

Total _____

Please send this order form to:

**IDG Books Worldwide, Inc.
Attn: Order Entry Dept.
7260 Shadeland Station, Suite 100
Indianapolis, IN 46256**

*Allow up to 3 weeks for delivery.
Thank you!*

IDG Books Worldwide, Inc. End-User License Agreement

4. **Restrictions on Use of Individual Programs.** You must follow the individual requirements and restrictions detailed for each individual program in Appendix B, entitled "About the CD," in this Book. These limitations are also contained in the individual license agreements recorded on the Software Media. These limitations may include a requirement that after using the program for a specified period of time, the user must pay a registration fee or discontinue use. By opening the Software packet(s), you will be agreeing to abide by the licenses and restrictions for these individual programs that are detailed in the "About the CD" appendix and on the Software Media. None of the material on this Software Media or listed in this Book may ever be redistributed, in original or modified form, for commercial purposes.

5. **Limited Warranty.**

   (a) IDGB warrants that the Software and Software Media are free from defects in materials and workmanship under normal use for a period of sixty (60) days from the date of purchase of this Book. If IDGB receives notification within the warranty period of defects in materials or workmanship, IDGB will replace the defective Software Media.

   (b) IDGB AND THE AUTHORS OF THE BOOK DISCLAIM ALL OTHER WARRANTIES, EXPRESS OR IMPLIED, INCLUDING WITHOUT LIMITATION IMPLIED WARRANTIES OF MERCHANTABILITY AND FITNESS FOR A PARTICULAR PURPOSE, WITH RESPECT TO THE SOFTWARE, THE PROGRAMS, THE SOURCE CODE CONTAINED THEREIN, AND/OR THE TECHNIQUES DESCRIBED IN THIS BOOK. IDGB DOES NOT WARRANT THAT THE FUNCTIONS CONTAINED IN THE SOFTWARE WILL MEET YOUR REQUIREMENTS OR THAT THE OPERATION OF THE SOFTWARE WILL BE ERROR FREE.

   (c) This limited warranty gives you specific legal rights, and you may have other rights that vary from jurisdiction to jurisdiction.

6. **Remedies.**

   (a) IDGB's entire liability and your exclusive remedy for defects in materials and workmanship shall be limited to replacement of the Software Media, which may be returned to IDGB with a copy of your receipt at the following address: Software Media Fulfillment Department, Attn.: *PCs For Teachers,* Second Edition, IDG Books Worldwide, Inc., 7260 Shadeland Station, Ste. 100, Indianapolis, IN 46256, or call 800-762-2974. Please allow three to four weeks for delivery. This Limited Warranty is void if failure of the Software Media has resulted from accident, abuse, or misapplication. Any replacement Software Media will be warranted for the remainder of the original warranty period or thirty (30) days, whichever is longer.

(b) In no event shall IDGB or the authors be liable for any damages whatsoever (including without limitation damages for loss of business profits, business interruption, loss of business information, or any other pecuniary loss) arising from the use of or inability to use the Book or the Software, even if IDGB has been advised of the possibility of such damages.

(c) Because some jurisdictions do not allow the exclusion or limitation of liability for consequential or incidental damages, the above limitation or exclusion may not apply to you.

7. U.S. Government Restricted Rights. Use, duplication, or disclosure of the Software by the U.S. Government is subject to restrictions stated in paragraph (c)(1)(ii) of the Rights in Technical Data and Computer Software clause of DFARS 252.227-7013, and in subparagraphs (a) through (d) of the Commercial Computer–Restricted Rights clause at FAR 52.227-19, and in similar clauses in the NASA FAR supplement, when applicable.

8. General. This Agreement constitutes the entire understanding of the parties and revokes and supersedes all prior agreements, oral or written, between them and may not be modified or amended except in a writing signed by both parties hereto that specifically refers to this Agreement. This Agreement shall take precedence over any other documents that may be in conflict herewith. If any one or more provisions contained in this Agreement are held by any court or tribunal to be invalid, illegal, or otherwise unenforceable, each and every other provision shall remain in full force and effect.

Installation Instructions

● ●

*Y*ou'll find installation of all (or some) of the programs on the CD is easy and relatively painless whether you're using a PC with Windows 95 or Windows 3.1.

For Windows users, I've included the "CD Assistant." It's a master program on the CD that lets you install or run any software on the CD just by clicking selections from the CD Assistant's window.

Windows 95 users can jump right into "Getting started in Windows 95 with AutoPlay." Windows 3.1 users can begin with "Getting Started in Windows 3.1, or Windows 95 without AutoPlay."

Getting Started in Windows 95 with AutoPlay

If you're running Windows 95, just remove the CD from the plastic inside the back cover of your book and place it in your computer's CD-ROM drive with the label up. Close the CD-ROM drive.

If you have a CD-ROM drive that uses AutoPlay, the CD Assistant starts up and takes control — and you'll see a License Agreement message in the middle of your screen. If nothing happens after a minute or so, you probably have a CD-ROM drive that can't run the CD Assistant without some help from you. Skip to the section "Getting Started in Windows 3.1, or Windows 95 without AutoPlay."

If the CD Assistant has already displayed your License Agreement, read the agreement carefully and then click the Accept button to get to the CD. (If you click the Do Not Accept button, the message window closes and nothing else happens.)

The License Agreement appears only the first time you use the CD on a computer; you don't have to read the rules again unless you use the CD on a different computer.

After you click the Accept button, the CD Launcher message window opens and tells you that the interactive CD will launch after you click OK. This message appears each time you insert the CD into the CD-ROM drive to let you know the disk and drive are working properly. Go ahead and click OK — the fun is just starting!

In a few moments, your screen fills with a stack of books that list the major categories of programs contained on the CD. Simply point to a category and click. The list you see next depends on which category you select.

Getting Started in Windows 3.1, or Windows 95 without AutoPlay

All Windows 3.1 users (and some Windows 95 users) need to install an icon in their Program Manager (or the Windows 95 Start menu) to run the CD Assistant. To install the icon, follow these steps:

1. **Insert the CD into your computer's CD-ROM drive.**

2. **For Windows 3.1, choose File⇨Run from the Program Manager window; for Windows 95, choose Start⇨Run.**

3. **In the Run dialog box, type** D:\SETICON.EXE.

   Substitute your actual CD-ROM drive letter if it's something other than D.

4. **Click OK.**

   An icon for the CD Assistant appears in a separate program group named For Teachers in the Program Manager window of Windows 3.1 and on the Start⇨Programs menu of Windows 95.

To start the CD Assistant, open the For Teachers program group and click (or double-click) the icon.

The first time you run the program, a License Agreement appears on-screen. Read the agreement carefully and then click the Accept button to get to the CD. (If you click the Do Not Accept button, the message window closes and nothing else happens.)

The License Agreement appears only the first time you use the CD on a computer; you don't have to read the rules again unless you use the CD on a different computer.

After you click the Accept button, the CD Launcher message window opens and tells you that the interactive CD will launch after you click OK. This message appears each time you insert the CD into the CD-ROM drive to let you know the disk and drive are working properly. Go ahead and click OK!

In a few moments, your screen fills with a stack of books that list the major categories of programs contained on the CD. Simply point to a category and click. The list you see next depends on which category you select.

IDG BOOKS WORLDWIDE REGISTRATION CARD

RETURN THIS REGISTRATION CARD FOR FREE CATALOG

Title of this book: **PCs For Teachers™, 2E**

My overall rating of this book: ❏ Very good [1]   ❏ Good [2]   ❏ Satisfactory [3]   ❏ Fair [4]   ❏ Poor [5]

How I first heard about this book:

❏ Found in bookstore; name: [6]   ❏ Book review: [7]

❏ Advertisement: [8]   ❏ Catalog: [9]

❏ Word of mouth; heard about book from friend, co-worker, etc.: [10]   ❏ Other: [11]

What I liked most about this book:

What I would change, add, delete, etc., in future editions of this book:

Other comments:

Number of computer books I purchase in a year: ❏ 1 [12]   ❏ 2-5 [13]   ❏ 6-10 [14]   ❏ More than 10 [15]

I would characterize my computer skills as: ❏ Beginner [16] ❏ Intermediate [17] ❏ Advanced [18] ❏ Professional [19]

I use ❏ DOS [20]   ❏ Windows [21]   ❏ OS/2 [22]   ❏ Unix [23]   ❏ Macintosh [24]   ❏ Other: [25]_____
                                                                                                    (please specify)

I would be interested in new books on the following subjects:
(please check all that apply, and use the spaces provided to identify specific software)

❏ Word processing: [26]   ❏ Spreadsheets: [27]

❏ Data bases: [28]   ❏ Desktop publishing: [29]

❏ File Utilities: [30]   ❏ Money management: [31]

❏ Networking: [32]   ❏ Programming languages: [33]

❏ Other: [34]

I use a PC at (please check all that apply): ❏ home [35]   ❏ work [36]   ❏ school [37]   ❏ other: [38] _____

The disks I prefer to use are ❏ 5.25 [39]   ❏ 3.5 [40]   ❏ other: [41]_____

I have a CD ROM: ❏ yes [42]   ❏ no [43]

I plan to buy or upgrade computer hardware this year: ❏ yes [44]   ❏ no [45]

I plan to buy or upgrade computer software this year: ❏ yes [46]   ❏ no [47]

Name: _____ Business title: [48] _____ Type of Business: [49] _____

Address (❏ home [50] ❏ work [51] /Company name: _____)

Street/Suite# _____

City [52]/State [53]/Zipcode [54]: _____ Country [55] _____

❏ **I liked this book!** You may quote me by name in future
IDG Books Worldwide promotional materials.

My daytime phone number is _____

IDG BOOKS

THE WORLD OF
COMPUTER
KNOWLEDGE

❏ **YES!**
Please keep me informed about IDG's World of Computer Knowledge.
Send me the latest IDG Books catalog.

COMPUTER
BOOK SERIES
FROM IDG

BUSINESS REPLY MAIL
FIRST CLASS MAIL   PERMIT NO. 2605   FOSTER CITY, CALIFORNIA

IDG Books Worldwide
919 E Hillsdale Blvd, STE 400
Foster City, CA 94404-9691